George

With my compliments

Strafer
Desert General

Tank Nash

May 2022

Strafer
Desert General

The Life and Killing of
Lieutenant General WHE Gott
CB CBE DSO* MC

NS Nash

All that is best in the profession of arms
(Carver)

Pen & Sword
MILITARY

First published in Great Britain by
PEN AND SWORD MILITARY
an imprint of
Pen and Sword Books Ltd
47 Church Street
Barnsley
South Yorkshire S70 2AS

ISBN 978 1 78159 090 4

A CIP record for this book is available from the British Library.

Printed and bound in England by
CPI Group (UK) Ltd, Croydon, CR0 4YY

Typeset in Times by CHIC GRAPHICS

Pen & Sword Books Ltd incorporates the imprints of
Pen & Sword Aviation, Pen & Sword Family History, Pen & Sword Maritime,
Pen & Sword Military, Pen & Sword Discovery, Wharncliffe Local History,
Wharncliffe True Crime, Wharncliffe Transport, Pen & Sword Select,
Pen & Sword Military Classics, Leo Cooper, Remember When,
The Praetorian Press, Seaforth Publishing and Frontline Publishing

For a complete list of Pen and Sword titles please contact
Pen and Sword Books Limited
47 Church Street, Barnsley, South Yorkshire, S70 2AS, England
E-mail: enquiries@pen-and-sword.co.uk
Website: www.pen-and-sword.co.uk

Contents

List of Illustrations

Photographs

Acknowledgements

I had heard of Strafer Gott but taken no interest in him until Gordon Brown, a fellow member of the Honourable Artillery Company, commented to me that he would be an ideal subject for my next book. I was vastly unenthused, but Gordon persisted and he introduced me to Brigadier Dick Vernon's tribute to Gott, which had been published privately by the King's Royal Rifle Corps (KRRC). This book, which had a limited and mainly 'in house' circulation, lit my fire as, belatedly, it became apparent to me that here was an exceptional man and one whose story was aching to be told.

I am accordingly vastly indebted to Gordon Brown, whose vision and persistence encouraged me, as well as to Major Peter Williamson MBE, who worked tirelessly to research the Gott family and whose work will be evident in the text.

Field Marshal, The Lord Bramall KG GCB OBE MC, the Senior Rifleman, not only agreed to write the foreword to this book, but before the text was finalised he engaged me in searching appraisals of my work. I am vastly indebted to him for his enthusiasm, interest and very practical support. We had the shared aim of ensuring that there was a definitive record of Strafer's life and, for me, our discussions were instructive – and fun.

Squadron Leader Jimmy James DFM AFC gave me a lengthy interview and the facts on Strafer Gott's death. It was he who produced the photograph of the aeroplane that he flew and in which Gott died.

Peter Gallagher and Jeff Birch collaborated with me on my three previous epistles and once again, with this book, their expertise in navigating around The National Archives produced a mine of information. I am, as ever, very grateful to them both. Mr Peter Hunter, the current Housemaster of The Park at Harrow School, provided me with information about Gott's childhood.

Mr Gerry McCardle of the Army Historical Disclosures Section of the MoD provided information from Gott's file that allowed me to fill in gaps in his early life.

Lieutenant Colonel Tom Gowans corrected my initial text and, as always, his suggestions and comments were well judged and very welcome.

Lieutenant General Sir Christopher Wallace KBE DL, the Chairman of the Trustees of the Royal Green Jackets (RGJ) Museum in Winchester, gave me unfettered access to all the relevant regimental records and he kindly reviewed a draft of the text.

Major Ken Gray, the Assistant Curator of the RGJ Museum, was unfailingly helpful and patient in finding for me all manner of obscure but important pieces of paper.

Arthur Perry provided all the maps of the Desert Campaign and, hopefully, they made my text all the more intelligible.

The photographs are either from the archives of the RGJ Museum or from Internet sources unless specified differently.

At Pen & Sword, my commissioning editor, Brigadier Henry Wilson, was his usual imperturbable self and he did all that he could to support me in the most practical way and, not least, in appointing Mrs Linne Mathews as my text editor. She is a joy to work with and made the editing process very agreeable. Her contribution to this book cannot be overstated and extends far beyond ensuring that all the commas and semi-colons are in the right place. However, notwithstanding Linne's expertise, I take ownership of all errors and omissions.

Tank Nash
Malmesbury
July 2013

Preface

The biographies and autobiographies of Second World War generals are legion. However, the story of this one, one of the three finest desert generals, was missing from the bookshelves and it was a gap that needed to be filled.

Ideally, a fellow rifleman would have written this book about thirty years ago, when first-hand testimony was still available. In 2012, seventy years after his death, all of Strafer Gott's contemporaries are dead and evidence as to his life and the manner in which he lived it can only be found in relatively sparse archive material.

During my extensive research I found that those who knew Strafer Gott and who served above, with or below him, with only few exceptions, respected, admired or loved him to some degree and their views are well documented. I resolved to write the biography of this extraordinary, brave, charismatic soldier and Christian gentleman.

This book is not a history of the war in France in 1917-18, nor is it remotely a full account of the campaign in North Africa during 1940-42. Both of those topics have been exhaustively covered elsewhere. However, I have had to trace the outline of events in those theatres in order to place Strafer Gott's role in its correct context. My account of those campaigns is therefore truncated and, for the purist, somewhat simplistic. I have, for example, made scant mention of either the Royal Navy or Royal Air Force.

I now know that it is easier to write the biography of a military 'four-letter man' such as Charles Townshend (*Chitrál Charlie*) or a flawed personality such as Alfred Pollard VC (*Valour in the Trenches*) than that of an epitome of charm like William Gott (*Strafer*) because there is markedly less light and shade.

Was Strafer Gott truly a 1st XI player or was he merely the best of a poor crop? Was his appointment to command the 8th Army justified or was it a promotion too far? Did he really rank alongside Rommel and Montgomery? 'What if' he had not been killed?

I leave it to you to judge the place William Gott should be accorded in the pantheon of British generals. However, it is without doubt that, as a human being, he is a role model for us all.

God will not count your medals, but your scars
(John Bunyan, *The Pilgrim's Progress*)
Published in 1678 and oft quoted by Strafer Gott

Foreword

by
Field Marshal Lord Bramall
KG GCB OBE MC

Inever knew Strafer Gott. Indeed I had only just joined the Army into Strafer's old regiment a few days before he was killed. He was however already a legend amongst those fighting in the Western Desert of North Africa and over the years his memory has continued to prove a source of pride and inspiration, not only to those lucky enough to have known him personally but also to many others, particularly those in Rifle regiments who have served since that time.

This well-researched and very readable first biography of Strafer now sets out for the benefit of a wider public the details of his remarkable all too short life, from his background and boyhood to the awful climax when he was killed when flying back to Cairo, having been personally selected by Winston Churchill to command the 8th Army.

In the First World War the young William Henry Ewart Gott, never known by any other name than 'Strafer' (for a reason explained on page 7), was commissioned into his regiment, the King's Royal Rifle Corps, when not yet eighteen. He fought with them in Flanders and France in 1916-17. In the bitter fighting north of Ypres he was decorated for gallantry and after being wounded was taken prisoner. The reader can follow his career through the interwar years when he was studying his profession and developing the military skills, through to his putting them into practice in such a remarkable way in the Western Desert early in the Second World War, with his meteoric rise from lieutenant colonel commanding a battalion to lieutenant general commanding an Army corps at the young age of forty-four, all in the space of two years and under really taxing and often adverse circumstances.

Although well reported upon in the interwar years, which continually emphasised his professional dependability and his excellent personal qualities of courage, integrity and the ability to get the best out of people, it was not until the end of 1938 that, having by then been earmarked for accelerated promotion and having taken over command of a battalion of his own regiment that had urgently to be put on a war footing for operations in the desert for the defence of Egypt, his full potential and exceptional powers of leadership came to be realised.

Within a year war had been declared and Strafer was to become the key figure in that most interesting and nerve-wracking period of British military history, with the pendulum of battle against first the Italians and later the Germans under Rommel swinging backwards and forwards between the borders of Egypt and deep into Libya, until the Axis forces were finally held and comprehensively defeated at El Alamein 100 miles from Cairo. Throughout these tense years Strafer consistently showed great enterprise, resolution and flexible tactical skills to meet the fast-changing situations, as well as considerable personal courage. Indeed, the book makes clear, among British and Commonwealth troops, he acquired a reputation not dissimilar to that which Rommel achieved with his Africa Korps – always in the forefront of the battle, always calm and one to whom other commanders instinctively turned for advice and direction when they themselves were uncertain as to what was the right thing to do. No one knew the desert better than Strafer.

It is, of course, interesting to speculate as to what would have happened if Gott and not Bernard Montgomery had been in command at the Alam Halfa battle and the final battle of Alamein. In Chapter 19 the author draws on contemporary observers and latter-day historians in examining this matter. However, no matter how well informed the speculation may be, it can never be conclusive and Gott's potential, had he not been killed, still remains a matter for speculation.

So we are left not with what might have been, but with the fascinating story of the performance and memory of a highly skilled professional soldier and remarkable human being who gave everything, including his life, for his country under very difficult circumstances, and would ever be looked upon by those who knew him best and served under him as all that was best in the profession of arms.

This book provides most valuable and interesting reading, not only for those who are serving today or who have served in the British Army but to all students of military history who should realise that the key factor in all battles is the human factor and particularly the character and resolution, as well as the professional skill, of the commanders fighting them.

Bramall
Field Marshal

Chapter 1

7 August 1942, 1415 hrs

I t was hot, very hot. *Much too bloody hot*, and the swarming flies did not help.

The Bombay Bristol was sitting silently upon the desert airstrip at Berg el Arab, about 12 miles behind the front line in northern Egypt, on 7 August 1942. Its young pilot, little more than a boy, stood fretfully in its shadow. It was standing operating procedure (SOP) in 216 Squadron RAF that engines should be kept running and 'turn round' should be as brief as possible. An aircraft on the ground was very vulnerable to the predatory German fighters and not least those of Jagdgeschwader 27[1] and its group of high-scoring pilots.

It was so hot that flying had been restricted throughout the Desert Air Force to essential missions.[2] The problem was that the temperature had reached 45°C and aircraft did not function well in such extreme heat and the resulting thin air. The cruel and unremitting sun burnt everything in, on and even under the Western Desert that August day. The azure sky was unblemished by cloud.

Sergeant Pilot HG James had arrived from Cairo on a routine mission to deliver mail, rations and passengers, and to collect wounded and return mail. A messenger had run to meet his aircraft and he said, 'Switch off your engines, you've got to wait here for General Gott.'

'No, I can't switch off. These Bombays are a bugger to start in this weather,' protested James, known universally then and now as 'Jimmy'. However, it was an order and although Jimmy James complied, it was with serious misgivings.

It seemed an age before two staff cars arrived at the strip and the occupants, having dismounted, surrounded a tall officer. Jimmy presumed that this was the General Gott who had become one of the best known of the desert generals and whose meteoric rise from lieutenant colonel in 1939 to lieutenant general in 1942 was fast becoming the stuff of legend.

Seventy years later, Jimmy James remembered the atmosphere that had enveloped the group. He said it was apparent that the officer who was the centre of attention attracted nothing short of affection from those around him. He very clearly recalled the body language and the laughter making the situation informal and friendly. This, Jimmy had concluded, just had to be the famous Strafer Gott.

The aircraft was loaded with the fourteen wounded, a medical orderly, two civilians, two ground crew and a wireless operator. The General detached himself from his acolytes and walked over to the waiting young sergeant. Sergeant Jimmy James, his uniform soaked in sweat, went to salute but remembering that his hat was in the aircraft said, 'Sorry Sir, I can't salute. I haven't got my hat.'

'Don't worry about that, my boy,' smiled Gott.

'Are you the Captain? Are we ready to go?'

William Henry Ewart Gott climbed aboard the aircraft and Jimmy busied himself, ensuring that his passenger was comfortable in the furnace-like heat of the cabin. The General assured his young pilot that he should not 'worry about me – I'll sit anywhere.' Jimmy, when reminiscing, remarked that Gott was 'the least pompous general I ever met and although I flew many VIPs, none ever matched his presence and sense of warmth.'

The usual pre-flight checks were quickly completed with the help of 22-year-old Sergeant James Lawless,[3] the Canadian Co-pilot. One of the ground crew who was new to the job secured the rear doors. He was not familiar with the aircraft and, in the event, this trivial detail was to be significant. It was a relief when the Bombay's engines somewhat unexpectedly spluttered into life. Sergeant Jimmy James pointed the aircraft down the strip, accelerated hard and with one general and two pilots aboard, a total of twenty-three souls set out for Cairo.

The events of the next hour would change the lives of those twenty-three forever and alter the course of history.

Chapter notes
1. An elite German fighter squadron.
2. Air density decreases with temperature. Warm air is less dense than cold air because there are fewer air molecules in a given volume of warm air than in the same volume of cooler air. As a result, on a hot day, an airplane will require more runway in order to take off, will have a poor rate of climb and a faster approach, and will experience a longer landing roll. In combination, high and hot, a situation exists that can well be disastrous for an unsuspecting, or more accurately, an uninformed pilot. (www.pilotfriend.com/training)
3. Sergeant (later Flying Officer) James Lawless was shot down and killed over Leewarden in the Netherlands later in the war.

Chapter 2

In the Beginning
1897-1917

Who was this William Henry Ewart Gott (WHEG)? He was a Yorkshireman. Gott is an old Yorkshire name from Viking roots meaning 'water course'. The word 'gutter' is derived from the same source.

William came from a family that could trace its line, residence and business in that county back to the seventeenth century. The family business was milling and as the business flourished so had the family fortunes.

William's great-grandfather, Benjamin Gott, built the splendid Armley House[1] in Leeds in 1816 and, in due course, this passed down to William Henry Gott (WHG), who was born in 1852.

WHG was educated at Harrow School and thereafter served for many years in the 4th Battalion, The West Yorkshire Regiment, eventually rising to command the Battalion. WHG was a Justice of the Peace and a leading light in the commercial and social life of Leeds. He headed the family firm and was, by any yardstick, a very wealthy man. In 1894, relatively late in life, he married Anne Rosamund Collins, who was nine years his junior. There were three children of this union. They were Anne Rosamund (b. 1896), William Henry Ewart (WHEG, b. 13 August 1897) and John Archibald (b. 1900).

By 1897 the family had moved to 3 Montpellier Crescent, Scarborough, where they lived in some style with five living-in servants and it was here that WHEG was born. Scarborough is an attractive place to live and for the children the wonderful beach would have been the source of much pleasure. Fourteen years on and the 1911 Census recorded that nothing much had changed, although the living-in servants had been reduced to four.

In 1911, at the age of fourteen, young William, like his father, went to Harrow School. He was following in not only his father's footsteps but also those of a controversial soldier/journalist and rising politician who was to have an impact on his life thirty-one years hence. This was WS Churchill who, in

3

1911, was President of the Board of Trade. Churchill had been sent to Harrow twenty-three years earlier, in 1888, and in 1893 left to attend the Royal Military College, Sandhurst.

William joined thirty-nine other boys in a house called 'The Park', the Housemaster of which was Mr EM Butler, himself an Old Harrovian. Butler is a name to conjure with at Harrow. This was a schoolmaster to his very bones, with Harrow in his blood, not least because his father and grandfather had both been headmasters of the school. Butler went on to become the Chairman of the Harrow Association (the alumni association) after his retirement.

Boys who attend a boarding school are much influenced by their housemaster – less so today, but a century ago it was a key relationship that shaped young lives. There was at Harrow, as in most public schools of the day, an ethos of 'muscular Christianity'.[2] Young Gott came from a churchgoing family who inculcated in him Christian values, which EM Butler among others underscored. Years later, when questioned about his former pupil, Butler observed:

> The boys all knew him as 'Father Gott' and even in those days, with his quiet influence for good, all the boys turned to him.

William was a natural leader, an attribute obviously evident from an early age. He was also a practising Christian and this was manifest in the manner that he conducted his life. He was not a distinguished scholar; good enough, but not outstanding. Neither was he an accomplished games player, but he did excel in shooting and by 1914 had found a place in the Harrow VIII. A boy with his background would have been familiar with firearms, if only shotguns. At school he was exposed to full bore competition shooting and he took to it like a duck to water. Mr PD Hunter, the current Housemaster of The Park, advised:

> The Park Head of House's book for the period traces his progress up the divisions, and he is recorded as shooting for the House, e.g. in the summer of 1913 he made up the House Pair with JAA Wallace. 'Conditions were good.' The House made 80 out of 100. The firing in kneeling position was at 100 yards and lying at 200 yards. Gott scored 39/50, Wallace 41. This is recorded as 'far better than last year and constituted a record'.[3]

In 1914 war clouds were gathering and William had to decide what would follow school. His father, with a lifetime in the militia, supported him when he opted to take the entry examination for the Royal Military College (RMC), Sandhurst.

The early summer was passed in Scarborough waiting for the examination results, which, happily, were positive. Before summer was over and William could take up his place, the long-anticipated war was declared. The British Expeditionary Force sailed for France and soon thereafter the stark horror and misery of modern war became apparent as Britain's 'contemptible little army'[4] faced the enemy. Nevertheless, the whole of the United Kingdom was struck down with 'war fever' and young men swarmed to enlist, anxious not to miss a war that allegedly would be 'over by Christmas'.

William Gott joined the RMC, Sandhurst, on 23 October 1914. It was not to be a long stay as the Army's massive expansion had generated an urgent requirement for officers to lead the new and vast volunteer army. Pragmatically, the training at Sandhurst was drastically curtailed to hasten the throughput of gentleman cadets and their metamorphosis into officers.

The casualties mounted and junior officers were disproportionately represented on those endless lists. The bold, vigorous attitude bred into generations did not serve them well when trench warfare developed. The spitting venom of enemy machine guns and the lethal but random selection by artillery shells demanded a degree of caution; good luck helped too.

William's documents, completed on his entry to the RMC, show that he opted to be commissioned into The King's Royal Rifle Corps.[5] Every cadet is given a choice of regiment on entry. However, that is but an aspiration because it is the regiment that decides whether or not to accept that cadet. His performance at RMC would be a factor in this decision. The probability is that Father Gott, a retired lieutenant colonel, had made enquiries on his son's behalf and his military path had been smoothed.

The document now held in The National Archives has a column headed 'Rate of contribution £' and against Gott's name is the notation '£150'. Other cadets' rate of contribution ranges from £60 to £150. This indicates that the RMC did not provide free training even in wartime and some sort of means test operated to establish the individual's fee.

A parallel is that of the soldiers who enlisted in the Honourable Artillery Company (HAC), who were each required to pay a subscription on admittance to the Company. This was to the vast amusement of other line battalions, who found it extraordinary that there were, in the two HAC battalions, men who had actually *paid* to be subjected to shot and shell.

William had selected an elite. The KRRC, known usually as 'The 60th Rifles', had little doubt as to its merit. It was a highly selective regiment that traced its line to 1755 and its formation in colonial North America as the 62nd Royal American Regiment. It wore red coats in barracks but in the field was, perhaps, the first to adopt irregular camouflage. The Regiment took especial pride in excelling at skill at arms. The generic title of the members of KRRC was 'rifleman', in much the same way that all members of the Royal Artillery are 'gunners' and all Royal Engineers are 'sappers'.

William Gott spent barely fifteen weeks as an officer cadet and he left the Royal Military College on 17 February 1915. He was commissioned into the 60th but his training had been cursory and entirely inadequate for the test that lay ahead. He was just seventeen and a half years old.

It is the nature of these things that Gott had been trained by veterans of the previous war, in which the British Army had singularly failed to distinguish itself in South Africa when fighting what was, in effect, a civilian militia. Some of his contemporaries stayed on at the college for up to a further two months.

A fellow officer and contemporary, commissioned at the same time, was one Anthony Eden.[6] He was destined to rise to political eminence and, in due course, would have an impact on Gott's life, although there is no evidence that they ever served together. Nevertheless, Eden, speaking of his fellow rifleman some years later, remarked that Gott was 'so obviously a born leader of men'.

It is a difficult transition from officer cadet to commissioned officer, even in peacetime. The young man joins a close-knit group with its own customs and standards. He has to establish relationships with his fellow officers but above all else has to establish his dominance over the soldiers placed under his command. For this transition to take place in a unit preparing for active service makes the process all the more demanding.

The recently commissioned officer has first to adjust to his new, instant authority. But he has to judge the manner in which he is going to exercise that authority. In peacetime there is plenty of time for brother officers to guide the young man down paths of righteousness. They can and will explain the culture peculiar to that regiment or to that particular officers' mess. The senior non-commissioned officers can be relied upon to give unswerving support to the subaltern as he tries to find his way, albeit sometimes with a shrug of exasperation at the inadequacy of their young leader.

Cognisant of Gott's extreme youth, the War Office did not expose him to trench warfare immediately and he was retained in England for about eighteen months. He was posted to the 6th Battalion, KRRC, stationed near Sheerness. It was here that his military education was furthered, allowing him at the same time to find his feet and gain confidence in his role.

The 6th Battalion, KRRC was a depot and training battalion. William took on the role of training some of the hundreds of thousands of civilians flocking to the colours – some willingly, others rather less so. As a platoon officer he was part of a military sausage machine that took civilians in at one end and just a few weeks later, regurgitated men who at least looked a bit like soldiers. During this period the men under William Gott's command were new riflemen. They were less well educated but invariably older and vastly worldlier than their painfully young officer. It would take pronounced powers of leadership if Second Lieutenant William Gott was to succeed.

Early in his commissioned service William Gott was given the nickname 'Strafer'. 'Like most nicknames it was rather stupid but it stuck to him all his life.'[7] The origin was the phrase '*Gott strafe England*', a slogan used during the First World War by the German Army meaning 'God punish England'.[8] So, Strafer it was, and thereafter he was rarely ever called anything else. Accordingly, and in recognition of this, this text does *not* encase his nickname in quote marks. Perhaps his mother called him William, but if she did then she would have been in the minority.

This is a graphic use of the phrase that gave William 'Strafer' Gott the distinctive nickname by which he was known for the rest of his life.

Not long after he was commissioned Strafer attended a course at Hythe in Kent. This was the home of the School of Musketry (later the Small Arms School) and the record shows that on completion of the course he was rated '1st Class'. The probability is that this grade reflected his prowess with small arms.

In May 1916 he was sent to Ongar to attend a Pioneer Course. Attending any course in the UK was the next best thing to leave for the students from France, who could sleep in between clean sheets secure in the knowledge that there would be no call to stand-to in the small hours. The Royal Green Jackets Museum retains in its archive Strafer Gott's notebook from this course and in it he has dutifully recorded the myriad need-to-know realities of trench life, of which, as yet, he had still to experience.

The notebook meticulously records the key points on loopholes, water supply, refuse disposal, latrine construction and siting, demolition, fuses, machine-gun emplacements, defensive positions, alarms and flares and much more. Captain Bray RE, the course instructor, had an assiduous student in Strafer Gott and many of the principles he learned then were still relevant in his next war. Again, Strafer was graded '1st Class'.

In the summer of 1916 Strafer received a posting order. It had been long awaited and he found that he was to join the 2nd Battalion, KRRC. The KRRC had expanded rapidly since 1914 and eventually mustered twenty-five battalions and, of these, seventeen were deployed overseas. Each had to have at least a nucleus of seasoned regular soldiers and thus some of the most experienced men of the 60th were posted away to start up these new battalions. The wealth of expertise and experience had been spread across all of Kitchener's vast New Army and the sage advice of old soldiers was not always available.

The 2nd Battalion, KRRC was a unit that had distinguished itself in the war to date but had suffered frightful casualties, not least among the junior officers. The attrition suffered by this battalion is recorded in its war diary crisply, without emotion: 'three killed, seven wounded, two missing' might be a routine entry. Because the life expectancy of a junior officer on the Western Front was measured in days, their survival was dependent in large measure on the favours of Lady Luck. The majority of casualties (58 per cent) were caused by artillery in all its forms[9] and because it is an area weapon the destruction it deals is entirely arbitrary. The other hazard faced by all soldiers in the line was the sniper. The majority of sniper victims fell to 'headshots' and William Gott being 6 feet 2 inches tall was going to be particularly at risk when he went to France. Martin Pegler commented:

> As the war became more static the British soldiers began to notice that even in quiet parts of the line the number of men dropping from bullet wounds to the head was beyond the simple explanation of being hit by a 'stray'. On average a line battalion could expect between twelve and eighteen casualties a day, most from rifle fire. From the earliest days of 1914 the German snipers dominated the front line and their prowess was soon legendary. In a vain attempt to combat the growing menace, the British used whatever they could lay their hands on to provide makeshift sniping positions but the men had no training and were often frighteningly naïve.[10]

The war diary of the 2nd Battalion, KRRC comments that, on 22 May 1915, 'Corporal Beard was badly wounded by a stray bullet and Captain Heseltine had his periscope broken.' This entry underscores Pegler's remarks on stray bullets. There is nothing remotely 'stray' about a round that hits the lens of a periscope; it is simply very good marksmanship. That same day, 124 replacements arrived to fill dead men's shoes. The war diary of the Battalion for 2 September 1916 has the following entry:

> At 2.00 am the Germans attacked our trenches – standing up in line in the open and throwing bombs. They were beaten back by rifle fire and by bombing ... the rest of the morning was quiet.
>
> In the afternoon our Stokes[11] put a barrage on the W[est] side of the wood. Some Germans who were working in a shell hole near A Company tried to return to their lines but rifle fire caused them some casualties. The 1st Bn relieved the 2nd Bn this day. Just before relief

news arrived that the enemy was reported to be massing in WOOD LANE – E of HIGH WOOD as if for an attack.

No attack took place and the relief took place without incident. The Bn marched back to BLACK WOOD, in reserve, where it bivouacked.

Casualties: two killed seven wounded. Lieut Bristowe and *2/Lt Gott arrived for duty.* [Author's italics.]

Nineteen months after he was commissioned Strafer had arrived in France and was soon in the thick of it. The Battalion was on active service and facing an implacable enemy. There was precious little time for social niceties and the anticipated lifespan for a junior officer engaged with the enemy on the Western Front was judged to be three days or less. His place was at the head of his men and by being so placed he became a priority target to enemy machine-gunners and snipers.

Strafer would have to tackle the constant moves, the Spartan living conditions and the professional, social and practical issues that faced him in his usual calm and thoughtful way. He was mature beyond his years and was swiftly accepted and absorbed into the brotherhood of the KRRC.

Just four days after his arrival, the Adjutant, whose duty it was to write the war diary, recorded that the Battalion remained in Mametz Wood[12] until the afternoon, when it moved up into the line opposite a feature known as Wood Lane. C and D companies were in the first line, with B and A in support near the bank. Final preparations were made for the impending attack and food ammunition and water were all carried forward. The diary comments sombrely: '1 OR wounded'. This activity must have caused Strafer mixed feelings of excitement and apprehension as he was swept along by events. The Army has always been noted for requiring people to 'hurry up and wait' and this phenomenon was to be seen when the next twenty-four hours were spent in blissful inactivity, although the inactivity probably heightened the tension.

On the morning of 9 September orders were received that the attack was to take place at 1645 hrs. By unhappy mischance, Second Lieutenant (Acting Captain) LA Blackett was wounded when an enemy shell splinter detonated a bomb (grenade). The measure of the officer attrition is that Blackett, a second lieutenant, was commanding C Company. This was by no means a first in the 2nd Battalion, KRRC and Second Lieutenant Lee replaced Blackett.

At 1645 hrs on the dot, British guns opened fire and the Battalion went 'over the top' with great 'dash'. The assault was entirely successful on the left and here C Company carried its objective 'without much loss' and made contact with the 2nd Battalion, The Royal Sussex Regiment. On the right, D Company was stopped by machine-gun fire and two platoons from B Company who went to assist were also pinned to the mud. The Commanding Officer ordered Lieutenant Munro, commanding B Company, to mount another attack. This attack was made from a less than satisfactory base line. It was supported by heavy fire from Stokes mortars and Lewis guns, which saturated the enemy line and, surprisingly, the occupants surrendered. The remainder of D Company and half of B then carried their objective and made contact with the 5th Battalion, The King's Liverpool Regiment on their right.

Quite where Strafer was in all of this is unknown although this was certainly his baptism of fire and an unforgettable day in his life, but his Battalion had a butcher's bill to pay. One officer (Second Lieutenant AS Hawke) was killed, five officers were wounded, twenty-four Other Ranks were killed, eighty-three were wounded, and thirty-six were missing.[13] Among the dead were Company Sergeant Major[14] Hedge and acting Company Sergeant Majors Hyde and Dowden. They were described in the diary as: 'all most excellent and promising WOs and SNCOs. Many other excellent NCOs and riflemen were among the fallen.' The capture of fifty-nine prisoners and two machine guns was but small recompense.

After this engagement, by an indirect route the Battalion made its way to Baizieux, a tiny hamlet, which even today has a population of less than 300, and in this area it licked its wounds until 25 September.

On 25 September the 2nd Battalion, KRRC moved to Lozenge and Mametz Wood, to the recently taken German trenches east of Eaucourt l'Abbaye, part of the of German Flers line, where it took over from the 1st Battalion, The Black Watch.

A 'bombing attack' was ordered and 130 yards of enemy trench and five prisoners were captured. The next day Brigade Headquarters wanted more of the same and further bombing attacks were mounted over the following two days. The aim of these attacks is not clear, perhaps just to irritate the enemy. However, these apparently aimless attacks had a cost. One officer was killed and three wounded; twenty-one men were killed, eighty were wounded and a further eight were listed as 'missing'. The gains were not permanent but the casualties were. The bombing capacity of the Battalion was now much reduced as most of the trained bombers had been killed or wounded.

With little achieved the Battalion withdrew to Millencourt to bivouac; it stayed two days and then moved again, in French buses to Valines. There was a constant flow of reinforcements and, for example, on 6 October seven new officers reported in for duty.

The 2nd Battalion, KRRC enjoyed a month out of the line. The riflemen played football and rugby against the 2nd Battalion, The Loyal North Lancashire Regiment, cleaned their kit and generally took it easy until 29 October, when they moved to Bresle. They did, however, put in useful training on the latest

10

type of grenade, the Mills type 23,[15] which was just coming in to use. The Adjutant summed up this quiet period by saying, 'The long rest and period of training since 28 September have had a most beneficial effect on the men and the general efficiency of the Battalion.'

By the end of November the weather had taken a turn for the worse. For several days Strafer Gott and his battalion had been ensconced in old enemy trenches near Eaucourt l'Abbaye and it was a most disagreeable place to be. The dead had not been buried, the parapets were broken and the trenches were knee-deep in water. The cold did at least ameliorate the stench of decaying cadavers.

The shelling was a constant and, for example, it killed four riflemen on 27 November. The attrition was unremitting and as men were buried so reinforcements trickled in to fill the gaps. Strafer had by now lost any rose-tinted spectacles that he might have brought with him to France and he saw trench warfare for the dirty and dangerous business it really was. He learned the importance of keeping his head down, his feet dry and the incredible morale-boosting benefit of hot shaving water. He learned to live with the stench of the latrines and of unburied corpses. Above all else he came to appreciate the quality of the men with whom he served.

A church service and fervent prayers that the war would soon end marked Christmas 1916. The prayers were not to be answered and 1917 would prove to be catastrophic for the 2nd Battalion, KRRC.

Very early in 1917, and given Strafer's proven prowess as a marksman, it was entirely appropriate that he was selected to attend a course at the 4th Army Sniping School.

The pioneer of Army sniping, from August 1915, was Major H Hesketh-Prichard DSO MC. Until this point the Germans had indeed dominated the trenches. Their snipers were skilful and lethal marksmen who killed clinically and efficiently. There were battalions who contested this domination but some sort of organised response on a wider scale was required and Hesketh-Prichard was authorised to commence sniper training. He conducted some of the instruction 'on the job' and, on that basis, it was one of the more dangerous courses available. Hesketh–Prichard's students wrested the initiative from the enemy and by mid-1916 the balance had changed.

Thereafter, and having completed the course, the very high probability is that Strafer spent some of his time sniping and leading a sniper team. If he was employed as a sniper then this quiet and charming young man will have accounted for any number of enemy soldiers, although the Battalion war diary is silent on the subject of who shot whom. Sniping was a hazardous occupation, as counter-sniping was becoming a trench art form and unskilled snipers did not make old bones.

11

Initially 1917 proved to be rather quiet and the war diary records only routine administrative matter, including the constant movement of the Battalion. There was an unremitting need to furnish very large fatigue parties. These parties were employed on either digging new or repairing old trenches, or 'humping and dumping' stores. Fatigues were utterly loathed. 'Hated' is perhaps a more accurate word and most soldiers, from choice, preferred to be in the line.

It was back-breaking work, almost always subject to shelling. Every man knew that in the next few days there would be yet more fatigues to do and the task was never-ending. The entry for 4 March says, 'The whole Battalion on fatigues for road mending and wiring the Corps line'.

The next day it was more of the same.

Life in any infantry battalion, and 2nd Battalion, KRRC was typical, was not all spent in the front line. There was a roster system in place and a tour of three days in the first-line trenches was followed by three further back 'in support' and then three days even further back in reserve or 'resting'. Resting was a very loose phrase because, in that role, the unit did not 'stand slack' but was invariably employed on these hated fatigues.

It is alleged that a large body of men were observed involved in strenuous labour at night, in pouring rain, with thick mud underfoot. A general who chanced upon them enquired of his aide, 'Who are those men, a labour battalion, I suppose?'

'No, General,' the Aide-de-camp[16] replied, 'it's that battalion you withdrew from the line – they are "resting".'

The opportunities for a bath were infrequent and, when available, were faithfully recorded. Strafer Gott was named in the war diary on 1 March as being responsible for the synchronisation of watches before the 1st Battalion, The Northamptonshire Regiment relieved the Battalion on the night 2/3 March prior to it taking over billets in Becquincourt from 1st Battalion, The Loyal North Lancashire Regiment. This was only a brief respite and the crop of dead and wounded caused by enemy artillery increased on 8 March when a single shell 'fell amongst a party killing four riflemen and wounding three officers.'

It was Strafer's hand that kept the diary during March 1917, an indication that he was employed in Battalion Headquarters. On 31 March the war diary was signed by 'WHE Gott Lt'.

During the spring of 1917, the 2nd Division held a soccer tournament, during which the 2nd Battalion, KRRC beat the 1st Battalion, The Royal Sussex Regiment 7-1 on 13 April, and 1st Battalion, The Loyal North Lancashire Regiment fell to the firepower of the 2nd Battalion, KRRC 2-0 a week later. Strafer was admitted to hospital on 29 April; this must have been sickness because the Battalion had not been involved in operations for some weeks and he had not been wounded. On the same day the Battalion had a lengthy train journey to Roisel (near Péronne). The move was to make the Battalion available to labour on a railway.

The work on the railway continued; it was hard, physical work for the men but much less so for the officers. As the weather got slowly warmer there was time for the officers of 1st and 2nd battalions KRRC to play cricket, a match won by the 2nd Battalion by four wickets. The Battalion moved several times and by late June it was close enough to the coast for the diary to observe on the unwelcome presence of jellyfish in the sea.

Life for Strafer and his comrades had been well ordered and comfortable for several months. The Battalion was rested and although 'war is hell', in early July 1917 it was bearable.

This was all about to change – and much for the worse – when the 2nd Battalion occupied vulnerable positions east of the river Yser, near Nieuport.

Chapter notes
1. The house is now the clubhouse of Gott's Park Golf Club.
2. The Victorian era gave birth to the concept of 'muscular Christianity', which laid great value upon the merits of vigorous and energetic activity in combination with a positive Christian outlook. Charles Kingsley was one of the proponents of the 'culture' and he gave his name to the goal of physical health and strength and the demonstration of robust, active Christianity.
3. Letter to the author, January 2012.
4. An Army order issued by Emperor William II on 19 August 1914 pronounced: 'It is my Royal and Imperial command that you concentrate your energies, for the immediate present, upon one single purpose and that is that you address all your skill and all the valour of your soldiers to exterminate the treacherous English and walk over General French's *contemptible little army*.' Horn, Charles.
5. The National Archives – Sandhurst entries October 1914.
6. Eden had poor eyesight and initially had been rejected for Army service. However, when the Army was obliged to reduce its medical standards Eden was a beneficiary of the lower standard and he was commissioned in the King's Royal Rifles, served on the Western Front and won the Military Cross (MC) at the Battle of the Somme in 1916. After one attack at Delville Wood, Eden's unit, 21st Battalion, KRRC, suffered 394 casualties, of whom 127 were killed. Eden, at merely nineteen, was appointed Adjutant, an important job for a very junior officer and he may have been the youngest adjutant in the Army.

    By 1918 Eden was an acting major, filling the post of 'brigade major', chief of staff, to a brigadier general. He was still only twenty and his military career had been nothing less than meteoric. Eden remained a 'rifleman', at least in spirit, for the rest of his days.
7. Erskine, Major General GWEJ CB DSO, unpublished manuscript, RGJ Museum archives, Winchester.
8. The German-Jewish poet Ernst Lissauer (1882-1937) was the creator of the phrase that ran counter to mainstream Jewish opinion. Lissauer also wrote the poem *Hassgesang gegen England* (lit. *Hate song against England*, better known as *Hymn of Hate*). The term is the origin of the verb 'to strafe' and thus 'strafing'.
9. Mitchell, Major TJ & Smith, Miss GM, *Official History of the War, Casualties and Medical Statistics,* IWM, 1997.

10.   Pegler, Martin, *Out of Nowhere – A History of Military Sniping*, p80.

11.   Named after its inventor, Mr FWC Stokes (later Sir Wilfred Stokes KBE). Designed in 1915, the Stokes mortar consisted of a smooth metal tube fixed to a base plate supported by a light bipod mount. The bomb was dropped into the tube and an impact-sensitive cartridge at the base of the bomb would make contact with a firing pin at the base of the tube, thereby throwing the bomb. Three inches in size, the cast-iron mortar bomb itself weighed around 10Ibs. It was fitted with a modified hand grenade fuse on the front, with a perforated tube (with minor propellant charge) and impact-sensitive cap at the back. The Stokes mortar could fire as many as twenty-two bombs per minute and had a maximum range of 1,200 yards. It was the standard issue for the British Army for several decades and was the most widely used mortar among the Allied armies. A hundred years later, mortars, in use today, are based upon the design of the Stokes mortar.

12.   Mametz Wood was the site of fierce fighting during the Battle of the Somme in July 1916, when 38th (Welsh) Division attacked and took the wood, but suffered 4,000 casualties in the action.

13.   Soldiers listed as 'missing' sometimes turned up; others were wounded and taken prisoner. However, for the remainder, 'missing' invariably was a precursor to 'killed in action'. Usually this was because the soldier's body had either not been found or identified. This categorisation often gave false hope to families of the soldier.

14.   The Company Sergeant Major is the senior soldier of about 100 that comprise a company. His rank is Warrant Officer Class 2. He has an especial responsibility for the discipline of the Company.

15.   The grenade or 'bomb' in 1916 was the Mills No. 5. However, the No. 23 was a later refinement by the designer William Mills (later Sir William, 1856-1932). As many as 75 million Mills bombs were manufactured in the First World War. A later variant, the 36 grenade, was standard issue for almost fifty years.

16.   A junior officer, an Aide-de-camp (ADC) was typically a captain, who acted as the personal assistant to a general. The young officer was usually 'specially selected' and the hope was that his exposure to a senior officer would further his military education. His duties were usually mundane and concerned with the General's personal administration and comfort. Nevertheless, the appointment to be an ADC was expected to be a career enhancing one.

Chapter 3

Battle of Nieuport –
Prisoner of War

O n 10 July 1917, the 2nd Battalion, KRRC was the left-hand unit of the 2nd Infantry Brigade of the 1st Division, which was holding a forward position about 1,400 yards long on the east bank of the river Yser between Ypres and the sea. The 1st Battalion, The Northamptonshire Regiment was on the right of KRRC. The sketch map on page 16 illustrates the situation as at 0800 hrs 10 July 1917.

The vulnerability of the 2nd Brigade and its component battalions is quite evident from the sketch map. It would have been usual to have a substantial obstacle – like the river Yser – in front of the position rather than behind it. With the river to the immediate rear of 2nd KRRC, the unit's forward movement of food and ammunition and the evacuation of the wounded became vastly more difficult.

The KRRC held the area of sand dunes, the extreme left of the British line down to the sea. This was ground in which it was difficult, nay impossible, to dig substantial defences. The Battalion was deployed with C Company on the left, D and A companies in the centre and B Company on the right. Strafer Gott was the Battalion Intelligence Officer and his place was in Battalion Headquarters, about 350 yards behind the line and near the Field Dressing Station.

At 0600 hrs on 10 July, the sporadic German shelling turned into a full-scale bombardment and included shells of 15-inch calibre – the size of the guns on a battleship. One German battery fired 1,500 rounds, each of 250Ibs. Casualties mounted and the Battalion did not have the support of sufficient counter-battery fire to suppress the German artillery. German aircraft strafed the trenches from a very low level. The Royal Flying Corps (RFC) was noticeably absent from this parade. It was now evident that all of this activity was the precursor to a serious German attack that would be mounted by German marines.

The German bombardment was well directed. Among its targets were the three temporary bridges across the river, named 'Mortlake', 'Kew' and

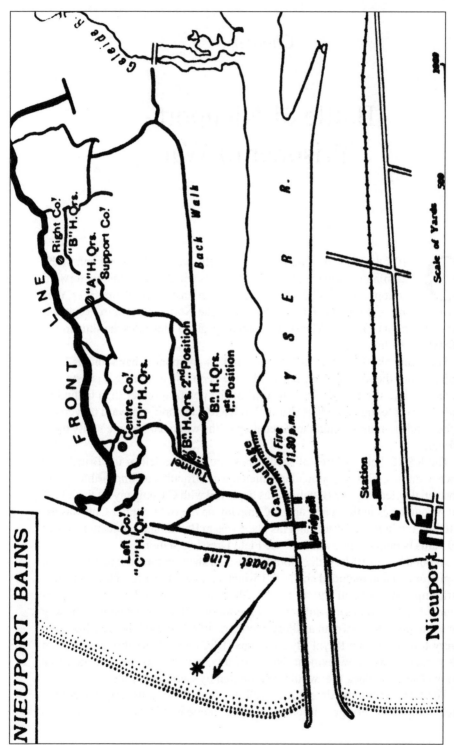

The Battle of Nieuport, 10 July, 1917. This map shows clearly the vulnerable position of 2nd Battalion KRRC and its reliance on the three bridges for the resupply and evacuation of the wounded. (The RGJ Museum archive)

'Richmond'. At 0830 hrs on 10 July, Mortlake was severed and became impassable. By 1255 hrs, Kew had been destroyed. Richmond survived until 1655 hrs, but with its destruction there went the last and only possible means of withdrawal for the 2nd Battalion, KRRC.

Casualties were taken in all the forward companies and communications were cut with D Company. At noon Strafer volunteered to go forward to obtain a situation report from D Company. It was the role of the Intelligence Officer to keep the Commanding Officer informed of the progress of the battle but this hazardous foray would entail a dash of several hundred yards across shell-swept ground and it was apparent that he faced almost certain death. The Commanding Officer, Lieutenant Colonel Abadie, remarked in the presence of several people that he would 'put Gott up for a VC'.

Young Gott plunged out into the maelstrom of shelling and by extraordinary and happy chance, against all the odds, he not only reached D Company and spoke to Captain Clinton, the Company Commander, but made the return journey safely too. He reported to the CO that Clinton and his officers were all in good order. A little later, Second Lieutenant Taylor arrived at Battalion Headquarters from B Company. He was wounded and reported the deaths of Lieutenant Munro and Second Lieutenant Heberden. The former had been buried when his trench in the soft sand had collapsed upon him. B Company was now without any officers and so, at 1400 hrs, Gott again volunteered to go out, this time to establish the situation in B Company.

The shelling was intense and it was an act of cold courage and the greatest gallantry.[1] However, now good fortune abandoned him and, on his journey, Gott was cut down by a bursting German shell and suffered shrapnel wounds to his left arm and leg.

Strafer Gott could almost be described as 'lucky' because, being wounded so relatively early in the action, he missed the carnage that was to follow. After the war, probably in 1921, he wrote a memoir of the events that followed.[2] He starts it by saying:

> On 10 July 1917 during the preliminary bombardment of the German attack on our positions near Nieuwpoort [Nieuport] Bains I was hit by shrapnel while crossing a piece of open ground, where the trench had been blown in. The time was about 1430 hrs and my orderly[3] at once assisted me to a dugout, partially demolished, which was fortunately nearby. Here we found two signallers who tied me up.

He decided to make his way back to the Field Dressing Station but, very weak and suffering from the onset of shock, Strafer Gott realised that the safest route was far too long and so he opted to take the shortest but more hazardous one.

Eventually and by now in great pain, bleeding profusely, he met a group of soldiers who helped him to the Dressing Station. He said succinctly, 'Here Doc Ward tied me up, put on a tourniquet and put me to bed.'

The bombardment restarted; part of the Dressing Station was blown in by blast and the falling debris broke the leg, in two places, of Rifleman Jenkins, Gott's orderly. Colonel Abadie,[4] the Commanding Officer, accompanied by two other officers, visited the Dressing Station and Abadie said to Strafer, 'You'll be all right; we'll get you down as soon as possible.' As it happened, Lieutenant Colonel Abadie only had a little time to live; he was killed soon after.

At 1500 hrs Colonel Abadie moved his headquarters to the tunnel shown in the sketch map on page 16. The tunnel was about 6 feet high and 3 feet wide. It ran for about 100 yards and had air holes at intervals of 30 yards. The tunnel was a haven for about forty men from an Australian tunnelling company who were lightly armed and had no officer in command. Colonel Abadie promptly put them under command of Second Lieutenant Gracie. He was the Signals Officer and it was he that drew the sketch map that was appended to the war diary and is reproduced here.

A lull in the shelling allowed the movement of rations and ammunition but at 1815 hrs the bombardment was renewed with greater intensity. Although the Dressing Station was still intact, Captain Ward RAMC was slightly wounded. Strafer had been wounded by mid-afternoon and so, lying on a stretcher, he did not witness the slaughter that was to follow.

The German infantry launched its assault and managed to get round the left flank onto the beach and, from there, to infiltrate the core of the Battalion's position. These German marines appeared in a communication trench that ran parallel to the tunnel. They threw grenades down the air holes and then, at the rear end of the tunnel, they applied 'liquid fire'.

Colonel Abadie made for the front end of the tunnel, apparently with the intention of making a last charge. He went out into the open, calling upon the party to follow him. In the narrow space behind him, crowded with ammunition boxes, passage was difficult. Before the officers who were trying to get past to follow him could get through, both entrances had been blown in. An Australian standing at the bay outside the entrance last saw Colonel Abadie firing his revolver, with which he killed five Germans before he himself was shot. His body was afterwards identified on the spot where he fell.[5] His body was roughly buried and never recovered.

At 1900 hrs and before the final collapse of the Battalion's resistance, a machine gun was heard firing close by the Dressing Station and it was clear that things were not going well for the KRRC. 'Doc' Ward told the RAMC orderlies to rid themselves of arms and equipment and to surrender if and when the Germans reached the Dressing Station.

There was the sound of rifle shots and exploding grenades close by and clearly the enemy barrage had lifted. Shouting was heard – ominously it was in German – and then as Gott watched he saw the stretcher-bearers move out to surrender. Captain Ward went out to confront the Germans; he was unarmed and covered in the blood of his patients. There was a brief parley and then the doctor called out for Gott and Taylor (the wounded officer from B Company). They went to the door and outside they saw about twenty Germans – all shouting.

Organised resistance had ceased. By now Strafer and the other wounded had been captured and removed by the Germans but the story of the 2nd Battalion, KRRC was not yet over.

There were men trapped in the tunnel and by the time they had dug their way out it was nearly dark. Second Lieutenant Henry RA went to reconnoitre and, on his return, reported that they were completely surrounded by the enemy. Rifleman Chaplin made his way to the Field Dressing Station and came back to report that the wounded had all gone. The survivors in the tunnel were four officers, fifteen riflemen and about twenty Australians. The enemy became aware of their presence and, intent on eliminating them, entered the tunnel by the rear (western) entrance and pursued the survivors as they stumbled in darkness up to the front (eastern) entrance.

The party exited from the tunnel at the forward end. Their escape was owed to two of the riflemen, sadly unnamed, who most gallantly delayed the enemy by blocking the tunnel with ammunition boxes and speculative rifle fire. The small party managed to get to the riverbank and by swimming and using the shattered remains of the bridges gained the far bank. Not all of them completed the crossing safely; some drowned and others succumbed to enemy small arms fire. Thirty-two officers and men survived from this party.

The situation had turned into a complete rout and the Battalion was destroyed, with heavy losses. Only seventy-six officers and men escaped by swimming the river. A total of 3,126 all ranks of 2nd and 97th brigades were killed, wounded or taken prisoner in this action.

The following page shows an extract from the after-action report; it makes grim reading. The arithmetic is meticulous but if it is at variance with regimental sources, it is because different criteria were used in the compilation of statistics at regimental and brigade level and it will be noted that it refers only to losses 'East of the river'.

The occupants of the Dressing Station were stripped of their gas masks (and in some cases their watches) and moved toward the German lines. Strafer made a painful but well organised journey to an enemy dugout and, on the way, men stationed along the route for that purpose offered him water. At his destination he was told to lie among eight wounded Germans, who studiously ignored him. After a while he rose and went to get fresh air. It was the last he knew until he woke up ...

19

5. CASUALTIES. The following numbers of all ranks were East of the
River, not including Machine Gun Company, Trench Mortar Batteries,
and Tunnelling Company.

	East of YSER.		Rejoined.		Casualties.	
	OFF.	O.R.	OFF.	O.R.	OFF.	O.R.
1st Northamptonshire Regt.	20	508	0	9	20	499.
2nd K.R.R.Corps.	20	524 801.	3	46	17	478 465.
TOTAL.	40	1032 1099	3	55	37	977 964.

6. AIRCRAFT. Hostile aircraft flew over our lines during the lulls
in the bombardment, and when the enemy infantry attacked they flew
very low over the whole area firing machine guns. The bridges
over the YSER were barraged by them with machine gun fire. They
directed Artillery fire by very lights and they are reported to have
opened machine gun fire on slightest movement East of the River during
the preliminary bombardment.

7. OUR ARTILLERY. The Divisional Artillery was firing continuously
throughout the day. Counter Preparation was ordered at 10.45 a.m.
and was continued more or less throughout the day, though later some
of the heavy artillery was employed on neutralising fire, but
without causing much diminution of enemy's fire.

There can be little doubt that the enemy has adopted the same
tactics as have been so successfully employed by us in attack
lately, but with the extra advantage that we were provided with
dugouts which were not shell-proof, with trenches never
very good and much damage, and that our aeroplane arrangements were
so incomplete that the enemy were at entire liberty in the air,
and we obtained no information of any value from our own Air Service.
For the same reason the Counter-Battery work appeared far less
effective than is generally the case.

(sd). G.C.KEMP,
Brigadier General,
Commanding 2nd Infantry Brigade.

14th July,1917.

*The after action report of 2nd Infantry Brigade of 14 July 1917. The arithmetic tells the story
of the destruction of Strafer's battalion. (The RGJ Museum archive)*

lying on the ground outside the dugout with a crowd of Germans
standing around looking at me. My wounds had been bleeding again
and I was soaked in blood.

The Germans gave Gott at least the same treatment as they gave their own.
However, the next twenty-four hours were miserable in the extreme as he made
his way slowly, under escort and under British shellfire to the rear. Gott
observed:

Two men carried the stretcher and were relieved about every 100 yards
by two others who followed in rear. Soon after the start we met Sgt

Cooke (C Company) and other British soldiers carrying down a wounded rifleman. There was a little shelling on the way down and at one point we took cover for about five minutes behind a concrete dugout near a gun emplacement, while at another the trench was blown in and my bearers had to climb out and afterwards ran with me for a little way.

We next reached Westende and here I was taken down into a cellar, where there were several wounded and a doctor was operating. He gave me a morphia injection and I was then put on a horse ambulance, which held about six stretchers. We jolted along on an uncomfortable pavé road to Middlekerke, where we were taken out and I was put into an empty room. Here I remembered that I still carried the BAB Code.[6] It was in my left pocket and there I commenced to tear it up with my right hand, throwing small balls of paper about the room. After about an hour I was taken out into the street and here I lay on the pavement with some other wounded. Another ambulance arrived with several trailers behind it. These are on two wheels and hold three stretchers abreast. They are roofed with a tarpaulin and sometimes as many as six are linked up behind one ambulance.

Into one of these I was put with two Germans on my right. One could talk French and would keep up a constant flow of conversation with me. He told me the centre fellow who was very quiet was a Sturmbannführer[7] and I think that the latter had got something to keep him out of the firing line for many months. Meanwhile, I still had a large part of the code; most of it I managed to stuff under the tarpaulin and out on to the road, but I had to be very careful that the others did not observe me. I was very annoyed with the fellow who could talk as I was feeling ill and it was very hot and stuffy in the trailer.

Meanwhile, Strafer had arrived in Ostend and he and the others were taken into a big house near a square adorned by an equestrian statue. He was laid upon a palliasse in a room containing some forty wounded British. Some were in a bad way and Strafer recorded:

One side of me was a man who had been gassed and who made the most awful noise in his attempt to breathe while the other was a man whose face and hands were burned absolutely black by liquid fire. After a while my palliasse and those of about ten others were placed on bedsteads. I then ate part of the [unintelligible] code that had the name etc. and finally all they got was a few torn fragments, of which I don't think they could make anything.

On the reasonable supposition that he would be static for a while Strafer took off his boots and, initially, welcomed the appearance of a German soldier bearing a plate of black bread and some pieces of various cheeses. He realised that he was not hungry but the German insisted he keep some of the cheese. Realising that he ought to eat, Strafer made a start and quickly discovered that the cheese was, by a considerable margin, the most disgusting he had ever tasted.

Soon after his rejection of the cheese he was carried upstairs to a makeshift operating theatre. It was a crude affair and it functioned on a conveyor-belt principle. There were two wooden tables each covered with a palliasse. On the floor were a dozen men, all wounded to some degree. Two doctors were working here together with a host of medical orderlies. Strafer was placed upon the floor with the others and his clothes were removed. A doctor looked down at him and said in English:

> 'You say you are an officer, how do I know that you are?'
> I showed him my lieutenant's badges on the sleeve of my tunic and he then apologised and said that they had to be careful as men sometimes said that they were officers. He also told me that about twenty-five years before, he had been taken prisoner by the British while fighting for the Boers in South Africa. He also said that there was someone there who said he was a second lieutenant but who didn't look like one. I told him what to look for and he came back and said that it was all right.
> On each side of the tables were several stretchers and as a man was lifted off on one side another was put on from the other. The palliasses on the top were soaked with blood. I was given chloroform and did not come downstairs to my old place until the next day.

The diary is annotated Wednesday 12 July at this point and reports that the wounded were loaded into motor ambulances and taken to Ostend Station, where an improvised hospital train was waiting. The coaches on this train had been gutted of their individual compartments and, in the resulting large open space, brackets had been fixed on the sides for stretchers. Germans already occupied these upper berths and so the latecomers were put on the floor. A German, clearly badly wounded and barely alive, decided to talk to Strafer, who said:

> Much though I disliked speaking to any of them I thought it as well not to make myself more objectionable than necessary. He called me 'Tommy', which was what all the Germans called our men, just as we called them 'Fritz' or 'Jerry' when our side of the lines. He could not see I was an officer as I was without my tunic and covered with a

blanket. He asked me my age, which I told him was twenty (though really rather less but for the sake of the Army I didn't want to seem too young), how long I had been at the front and so on. I think he was surprised I had been there so long.

After about one and a half hours we reached Bruges. Here we were placed on our stretchers on the platform and several civilians came and stared and one took a photo of me with a big camera. I must have been quite a sight!

The wounded were transferred once more to motor ambulances and another uncomfortable journey over uneven pavé followed. The destination was a large hospital called Marine Lazaret II, originally built as a lunatic asylum. Gott was put in a ward with ten British soldiers and he was only too pleased to see that sheets – clean sheets, no less – were provided.

Gott spent a few comfortable hours with his companions; most were his near contemporaries. They were surprisingly deferential to their former adversary but when, once more, the Germans discovered that this very large but very young man, not much more than a boy, was an officer he was told to get out of bed and go to a nearby single room. Strafer got out of bed and promptly passed out. He woke in his new single room to be told by a German orderly that he had 'fallen down twice and that it had taken four of them to carry me in, as I was so big.' He did not need to be told he had fallen because his shins were bruised and painful. Clearly he had fallen into some object.

Gott's diary is annotated 'July 12 - July 18' and at this juncture goes into some detail about the cuisine in his current residence. He opined:

> I was agreeably surprised by the good quality of the food and thought I was much better off than I expected. However, a rude awakening awaited me in Germany. The doctor came every day but otherwise I saw no one except the fellow who brought my food. The half loaf at supper was to last for twenty-four hours and at dinner I very often had stuff like 'gooseberry fool' only made of plums. After about two days I was visited by a German naval lieutenant … a wounded inmate of the hospital … the sailor wasn't so bad. He had been badly hit about four months before in an attack on the Belgian front at Dixmude. Before the war he had met an English cruiser at Alexandria and had seen a lot of our officers. He talked about sport and said he regarded the war as such.

The Germans took away Strafer's uniform, telling him that it was 'to go for repair', which seems somewhat unlikely. However, a suit of civilian clothes and a cap were delivered from the Belgian Relief Committee in the town. These were made for someone of about 5 feet 6 inches and were practically useless for a man who stood 6 feet 2 inches. The trousers were very thin and the coat was also an insubstantial affair; both were made of a blue cloth. The jacket buttoned up to the neck – well, it would have done so on a smaller man. The cap was in brown and there was also a cheap green shirt, which curiously buttoned down the back, like a hospital smock.

Strafer was told that this assortment of clothing was to be kept for him until he left the hospital. His sartorial concerns in part satisfied and having successfully disposed of the signal code, Strafer's next priority was to retain the £70 in notes, a few loose coins, £5 in gold and, incredibly, a compass, which somehow he had managed to conceal. He said:

> When searched at Ostend I had also managed to keep my compass (a new one with a reflector and floating in glycerine) concealed.

His memoir does not explain the mechanics of hiding the money and a fairly bulky compass when he was being moved about, presumably in hospital pyjamas. He did concede that his letters, a few small-scale maps and the remains of the BAB code had been taken. It is presumed that his contraband was hidden in his ward or with the aid of fellow prisoners.

He offered twenty francs to the German who carried out the entirely inadequate search and whom Strafer had expected to confiscate everything. In his words, 'I thought he was going to collar the lot.' To his surprise the German soldier refused to take the money, saying that Strafer would need the cash in Germany. This was a welcome little flicker of chivalry in a barbarous war.

Strafer had been shaved and had had his hair cut by a boy barber in Bruges. He gave the barber his loose coins. The barber, in response, said that he would keep them as souvenirs and then produced from his pocket a shilling, which had been given to him by an English captain RN at Kiel during the visit of the British fleet before the war.

On 21 July Strafer and about thirty other prisoners were taken in ambulances to an ambulance train, destination Germany. He noted approvingly that the train was 'quite comfortable and equipped with bunks with sheets'. Among the party were Sergeant Foster of D Company, 2nd KRRC, Lieutenant GE Mathews of 1st Loyal North Lancashire Regiment and Second Lieutenant Hope of 9th Battalion, The Border Regiment. Both officers had been captured at Nieuport.

Mathews had moved into a forward position the night before the German attack to make preparations for his company to relieve a company of the 60th. He was in the wrong place at the wrong time and unfortunate enough to be made prisoner. He was also seriously wounded in the right arm. Hope's battalion had been in the line to the right of the Northamptonshires and the young officer was shot in the stomach.

There were ten in each coach and a German medical orderly was on hand to give minor aid. The train, by now fully loaded and staffed, left Bruges on 21 July and arrived in Hamburg at 1000 hrs on 23 July.

Strafer thought that the journey was interesting, 'amusing' even, as the train crawled its way across northern Germany. A German medical sergeant, 'Dr' Von Kluck, who was alleged to be nephew of Count Zeppelin, paid several social calls on young Gott and, after chatting to him, pointed out the different objects of interest. Along the route some of the stations had flourishing Red Cross stalls and the local ladies were engaged in giving out fruit and sweets to the wounded – not all the wounded, however, and they took care to limit their ministrations to their own countrymen.

The train arrived, panting slothfully and noisily, at Hamburg's impressive station, where displayed prominently was a huge banner bearing the slogan 'Hearty welcome home'. Strafer, who read German, just knew it did not mean him.

There was yet another transfer by ambulance, which took the British wounded to an establishment named as the 'Barachen Lager Eppendorf' – a prison camp. It was here that, for first the time, he started to experience the gnawing frustration of captivity.

Hitherto he had been just one of many wounded and the Germans, to their credit, had not discriminated between soldiers in field grey or khaki in providing medical care. Now Strafer was firmly designated a 'prisoner of war'. He described his new home as being:

> About 150 yards long and about 60 yards wide. About 1/3 of this space was allotted to the German staff and railed off. It was surrounded by a wooden fence, about 9 feet high with three rows of barbed wire sloping inwards on the top. In the camp were about 300 prisoners, of whom there were about fifteen British officers and 120 men. There were fifteen foreign officers and 150 foreign soldiers – Russians, French, Belgians, a few Serbs and Romanians.
>
> The huts were made in pieces and could easily be taken down and were therefore not too weatherproof. As there was no vacancy in the officers' hut I was put in one with twelve British Other Ranks. I had an iron bedstead without springs, a 'biscuit' mattress. My servant Rifleman Jenkins was in the next hut to me with a broken leg. Mathews and Hope were there also. At 7.00 am the German orderly would shout out 'Aufstehen', which is their reveille. The orderly for the day, one of the hut occupants, used to fetch the coffee (made of acorns) and the daily bread ration, about six or seven very thin slices

of black bread. At 9.00 am he brought the tea (made of herbs), a tiny piece of butter and a spoonful of jam. At about 09.30 am, the German Medical Orderly dressed the wounds. The doctor made his rounds at 11.00 am. At 12.00 noon, dinner was brought, for each [of us] a cup of soup made of berries, herbs or anything vegetable and a bowl of greens with an occasional potato.

On Sundays each had a very small piece of meat and one other day in the week there might be a rissole or tinned fish.

Strafer Gott was a growing young man and the diet was hopelessly inadequate for anyone, let alone someone of his size. He was permanently hungry and his gnawing ache of hunger he shared not only with all of his companions but also with great swathes of the German population. His memoir focuses a great deal of attention on food – understandably, given his constant hunger. As a result, food became something of a fixation.

The British naval blockade was, by this stage in the war, having a significant effect on many Germans and especially city dwellers. The winter of 1916-17 was known as the 'Turnip Winter' because Britain's pyrrhic victory at Jutland had driven the German High Seas Fleet from the oceans of the world and its seaborne imports had ceased. Starvation, to some degree, was the long-term result. The appellation 'Turnip Winter' was adopted because turnip, that most unattractive of vegetables and one usually fed to cattle, was now being consumed as a substitute for the more sustaining potatoes and meat, which were in increasingly short supply. Emergency feeding arrangements were made to feed the hungry civilian population.

The hunger was not universal and farmers were strongly criticised for keeping the food they produced for themselves. The German Army had to cut the rations for soldiers and this had a direct effect upon Gott and his fellow prisoners.[8] The ever-hungry Strafer got to know his fellow officers and a Second Lieutenant Chevis KRRC arrived in another batch of prisoners and was billeted in Gott's hut. Chevis, who was only twenty-six, was wounded in the thigh and this made him lame. He had been the Colour Sergeant and so responsible for much of the administration of the company in which he and Gott had served together in 1916. The two men knew each other quite well and Gott was absolutely delighted to see him.

The domestic arrangements did not last long and within a week Hope and Gott were moved into the foreign officers' hut while Mathews, who was still in bed, went to the British officers' hut. Gott's new home was just another hut, of which the first third was for eating and the remainder for sleeping. The three British officers and a Romanian captain occupied the furthest part of the sleeping accommodation.

Gott had come from a comfortable upper middle-class home and had attended a school commensurate with that status. He was mildly xenophobic, although probably no more than most young Englishmen of his age. This antipathy was fuelled by the manner in which his foreign companion ate. The Rumanian captain would pick up his plate and lick it when he had finished. Gott, ever the Englishman, would rather have left gravy on his plate than ape the Rumanian. He commented in his memoir that 'the Russians always squabbled about the amount of food and the way it was divided.'

At about this time someone stole forty marks from Strafer and he had little doubt that the miscreant was a Russian captain. This loss of money was serious because it inhibited his capacity to buy extra food when it was available. At a price, vegetables and sometimes fish could be purchased. In the circumstances it is little wonder that a recurring subject of his memoir was food and its scarcity.

Evenings were spent playing a local version of rounders. The ball was a rolled-up handkerchief and the bat was an open hand. Strafer described it as 'comic'. Chevis struggled to play the former game but enjoyed the cocoa that followed – that is, until in August 1917, when he was sent to a camp at Augustabad. Gott regretted his going and prison life became just a little bleaker. Strafer moved huts yet again, this time into the British officers' domain. There were diversions and he commented:

> About twice a week we could go out for a walk on parole. For this we put on uniform – I had to borrow some and had a Royal Flying Corps forage cap, much too small. We were not taken into the city but went by tram to the country and then occasionally walked to a pub and had some beer and returned. Several German soldiers would go with us. We also went to funerals, which took place once a week and were generally for Russians. The cemetery was one of the largest in Europe and we used to go by tram or elevated railway. Sometimes the tram would go through the city on the way back and so we saw a little of it.

The food might well have been in short supply and of poor quality but compared with prisoners of war before and since, Strafer's life did have its compensations. On 5 September 1917, he was overjoyed to receive a parcel from Holland and soon after a post card and letter from home. At the end of the month two more parcels from home arrived unexpectedly and thereafter they trickled in intermittently. The arrival of mail was similarly sporadic. Prisoners were allowed to write two letters on four sides of notepaper and four postcards a month but they had to be conscious of the ever-present censorship of all mail. If any correspondence was to get through it had to be drafted in the blandest terms.

The arrival of a parcel was a signal to activate the small kitchen installed in one of the huts and the cooking of food, from tins, was done by the more energetic prisoners. However, the feasting could not start until the German Postmaster had opened the parcel and removed any item that could fall into the category of 'contraband'. Biscuits were issued at once but all tins had to be opened in the presence of the Postmaster and the contents thoroughly inspected before they were released. This was an entirely reasonable precaution on behalf of the Germans although, to date, they had not experienced any attempted escapes.

Strafer Gott planned to change that state of affairs, and soon.

Chapter notes

1. Most of those under an effective artillery bombardment do not live to tell the tale. However, even in controlled exercise circumstances and when observing from a deep and protected bunker, the horror and destructive power of artillery fire is unforgettable.
2. The memoir, which has never been published, is incomplete, very detailed but not particularly fluent. Nevertheless, it is an important source document and is in the possession of the RGJ Museum, Winchester.
3. Gott's courage is matched by that of his servant, Rifleman Jenkins, who, it appears, accompanied him on his two life threatening sorties. But no one suggested that he, too, might win a VC.
4. Lieutenant Colonel Richard Neville Abadie DSO was gazetted to the King's Royal Rifle Corps on 10 March 1900. It was as a major that he won his DSO, which was promulgated on 14 January 1916. He took command of the 2nd Battalion, KRRC on 23 August 1916. His body was never found but his name is to be seen on the Nieuwpoort Memorial to the Missing.
5. Hare, Major General Sir Steuart KCMG, *Annuls of the King's Royal Rifle Corps*, Vol. V, p.220.
6. The BAB must have been a signals code and its details were apparently contained in a pamphlet or notebook, but no information as to its use could be found.
7. It is interesting that Gott should use this word because Sturmbannführer was an SS paramilitary rank, equivalent to major, only adopted in 1921. This perhaps serves to date Gott's memoirs to 1921-22. It may be that the individual was a major and Gott used a modern word to describe him.
8. Chickering, R., *Imperial Germany and the Great War 1914-1918*, p.141-2.

Chapter 4

The First Escape

Incarcerated with Strafer was one Sam Hall, a lieutenant in the 5th Canadian Mounted Rifles and a citizen of the USA by birth. He was aged thirty and about 5 feet 6 inches in height, squarely and strongly built. He had been wounded in the head and captured at Arras in May 1917 and, for him, four months as a POW was more than enough.

In September 1917 Strafer and Sam struck up a friendship. They discussed any number of schemes that would get them out of the camp and on the way to freedom. Most ideas were little more than 'pie in the sky' but, eventually, their plans hardened and a workable strategy emerged, although it was dependent upon Strafer being fit enough to see it through. The wound to his arm was still very painful and it had developed boils around the scar. The escape attempt would have to be put off until the wound was a little better but before it started to get cold and when the nights were longer. On that basis early October was selected as the target date. To wait longer would be to risk the transfer of Sam Hall to another camp, which had already been mooted.

There was some planning to do and the first item on the agenda was clothes, the second was equipment. The absurd civilian suit given to Strafer in Belgium was kept in the luggage room next to the guardroom. This room held all clothes and uniforms not actually in wear. A German NCO was responsible for the security of this room – a task with few stresses.

Strafer's small suit would do for Hall if only it were possible to gain access to the locked room, but then something appropriate had to be found to fit his own very much larger frame. Strafer Gott went straight to the top and asked to see the Commandant. Granted an interview and speaking in his schoolboy German, Gott explained that the only clothes he had were the prison uniform of white and blue and, if he was to be transferred to another camp, what should he wear? Could he buy a civilian suit?

The Commandant could reasonably have been expected to say that he was indifferent to Gott's situation and that if Gott had to travel in white and blue then so be it. As it happens the Commandant was most accommodating and agreed that, indeed, a suit could be purchased at Strafer's expense but would be retained in the 'suit room'.

A German soldier was detailed off to go into town and buy a dark suit for someone 2 metres tall 'off the peg'. Several days and 100 marks later, a black suit with a chalk line was produced. Gott had no tie but there was no objection to him purchasing a black one.

A fellow officer donated a white shirt and a German orderly was persuaded to purchase a green homburg hat. The laundry woman purchased two thin cardigans for twenty-eight marks each – she had no clothing card, which was then required by current regulations but got around the issue by telling the shopkeeper that the cardigans were for her sons who were at the front. The escape plan advanced swiftly and, in Strafer's words:

> The two suits of clothing were still held by the Germans. I said that the clothes were getting damp and asked leave to buy a suitcase to keep them in. This was purchased for twenty marks; it was made of imitation leather. I had it locked with the two suits and shirts in it. They took it off to the luggage room. Other officers had a suitcase containing spare uniforms and underclothes sent from home in this room and when they needed them used to send in for them. No one else had *verboten* articles. We waited until the German NCO in charge of this room went on leave for a day or two and left another to do his work. We then sent for my suitcase, saying I wanted to get out a shirt. The new German had not been told (as we hoped) of the civilian clothes and allowed the suitcase to be brought across. We then took out the two suits and concealed them under our mattresses and filled up the suitcase with bottles and pieces of wood to give it a bulge and then returned it to the luggage room.

The establishment in Hamburg was a hospital camp and all of the POWs were required to wear the long blue and white striped coat reaching to the knee and loose trousers of the same material. The voluminous coverall was, as it happens, an aid to escaping.

The means of getting outside the wire exercised Gott and Hall and the initial plan of digging a hole under the fence was rejected as 'too difficult'. The agreed solution was to go over the wire and not under or through it. Key to the exercise was a hut at the far end of the camp (see sketch map, page 31). The two young men intended to gain access to this restricted part of the camp by way of one of the two gates and climb onto the roof of the hut adjacent to the wooden fence. The fence was crowned with three rows of barbed wire and it was a formidable

30

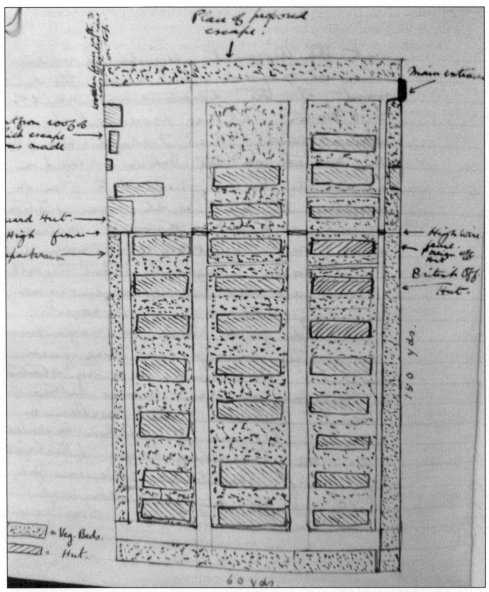

Plan of POW camp, first escape, October 1917. This plan of the camp is extracted from Strafer's post-war memoir. His handwritten annotations read from bottom left to middle right, starting at the bottom: Hut. Veg beds. [unintelligible] High fence. Guard hut. Hut from the roof of which escape was made. Wooden fence with three rows of barbed wire on top. Plan of proposed escape. Main entrance. High wire fence. Foreign officers' hut. British officers' hut.
(RGJ Museum archive)

31

obstacle to climb. However, Gott and Hall were not climbing; they were simply going to jump into the field beyond.

Unfortunately the hut was close to the guardroom and in view of the sentries. A daylight exit would be impossible but, at night, an electric lamp shone outside each hut and there were three arc lamps suspended from poles at the top end of the camp. One of these was only about 20 yards from the planned exit point. Strafer explained:

> There were three gateways in the wire fence separating our part of the camp from the German part. These were left open during the day and were in view of several sentries. ... At dusk they were supposed to be shut. But we knew that one was usually left open a little longer as it made things easier for the Germans. Our plan was to put on our civilian clothes and put our German ones on top, then to walk round the camp until we reached the open gate, seize a suitable moment to slip through and get in the shadow between the high fence and the selected hut ... climb onto the roof and jump to the ground outside, leaving our German clothes inside the camp. I had the compass, a change of socks, two Belgian sausages about 9 inches long made of a sort of salt bacon, about twelve round large thick biscuits, two slabs of chocolate, a tin of Horlicks malted milk tablets and a small flask of brandy. All of this had come out of my own or other peoples' parcels.

The aim was to cross the Dutch frontier at a point about 120 miles from Hamburg. To this end the two officers had only one map and this was taken from a German grammar textbook. It showed the juxtaposition of Bremen, Oldenburg, and Meppen, all of which were broadly west and a little south of the camp. The course of major rivers was also shown. Sam Hall had a second compass, which Strafer noted was 'not as good as mine'. He carried a similar supply of food.

The two put on their civilian suits and the German prison garb on top. They slit open the lining of their jackets in order to enlarge the storage space and filled the enlarged pockets with food. At about 1930 hrs the pair approached the gate through which they had to pass but spotted a German soldier sitting in an open window opposite their selected jumping-off hut.

The attempt was aborted.

It had been previously arranged that Second Lieutenant Swaine of the 7th Battalion, The Northamptonshire Regiment, and Lieutenant Harvey RFC would place dummies in both beds. This was to persuade the Germans that all were present when they conducted the routine headcount at 2130 hrs and turned out the lights.

The next day the same approach was made but with more luck. The gate was open, the sentries were looking the other way and like wraiths the two officers moved silently through the gap and into the shadows. The German uniforms were dumped and Strafer recorded:

> Hall gave me a shove up onto the roof of the hut. I got my knee in the main gutter, which gave a great crack. The roof was of tarred tarpaulin or something of that sort and it crackled under my weight. However, the hut was used for storing coal and so no one was likely to be inside. I lay flat on the roof and looked around. The sentry up and down that walk was not in sight and so was probably at the bottom of his beat and the sentry at the gate was just visible and looking the other way. Fortunately the big arc lamps were not yet on. I gave Sam Hall a pull up and then leaning over jumped over the wire and landed on the ground outside. Sam soon followed, making as he came an awful noise but he said I had made worse.
>
> We hurried across a field onto the main road. We had now to go through Hamburg and so it was necessary to walk back along the road in the direction of the camp gate. If we had been heard we should probably be intercepted. We walked along under some trees and passed the danger point safely. No alarm had been given and for the time being we were free!

Strafer makes no mention of it, but jumping from the roof of a hut up and outwards does present the potential risk of a sprained or broken ankle, or worse. As it was, both landed safely and fortune favoured the brave.

The route was west-southwest and the city of Hamburg was on the proposed line of march. Strafer described what happened next in his memoir.

Hall covered his face with his hand when first they met a passing civilian but soon there was a stern test when they passed one of the camp staff. Hall looked straight ahead, the German soldier did not spare them a glance and the confidence of the fugitives soared as a result.

It was now dark; streetlights were burning at intervals with deep pools of shadow in between. The road was lined with trees, all now shedding leaves at winter's approach. As the escapees got closer to the city centre, noisy, well-lit trams clanked past them and the streets started to fill with people. They made every effort to keep to minor roads whilst at the same time heading west.

One busy intersection was thronged, as light as day and filled with soldiers and civilians. The theatres and cinemas were doing good business and Hamburg was not even slightly interested in two rather frightened escapees. Their traverse of the city continued and William cheerfully admitted that 'We were very scared.

A page from Strafer's post-war memoir, written after the war circa 1919-20 but never completed. (RGJ Museum archive)

We had to cross a huge lighted space near one of the main railway stations and to pass a sentry box outside some headquarters. Finally we reached the Elbe.'

The Elbe in Hamburg is a major river and in 1917 its high steep banks were part-covered with trees. Having gained the sanctuary of these woods the two officers were at once secluded from sight. There were closeted paths leading through the woods but they abandoned the cover and struck out along the main road in order to make better time.

It became apparent that this road was guarded because it was adjacent to the wharves. The presence of so many armed sentries quenched the pipe dream of stowing away on a neutral ship. Now they needed to find a bridge – there were none in sight. A long walk was in prospect.

They walked downstream until out of Hamburg and, having failed to find a bridge, turned around and trudged all the way back. A bridge hove into view; in fact, two bridges, but one served a naval college and an island in the river close by. They drank copiously from a public fountain and contemplated the bridge leading to the west bank of the Elbe. The hope was that here they would be able to stow away on a neutral ship.

The bridge was a very long and imposing structure; at each end were three arches. The centre arch was for wheeled traffic and the left and right arches were footpaths. Trams ran across the bridge and their lights revealed the policemen patrolling on both sides.

> We waited until a tram was crossing and then started across the bridge ourselves hoping that the tram would attract [divert] attention from us. As we crossed a clock struck midnight and so we had been walking hard in the city for four hours. We crossed in safety and rested in some public gardens on the outskirts of the city and close to a railway. Here we ate a very little. We then started again on our long tramp. A large board told us that our road led to Hanover and Bremen and so we were all right as regards directions for a time. For about two hours we kept to this road, which was across flat country. We crossed another river called the North Elbe, which was a good size and had a similar bridge.

At about 0300 hrs the two tired young men entered a small town and looked for somewhere to hole up. It had started to rain, 'a thin drisle' as Strafer described it. They crawled into a hedge and lay on some conveniently placed but wet straw. If they kept still and low they were safe – at least temporarily. At first light they had a breakfast of German sausage and biscuit. The hedge bordered a field and an unwelcome visitor was a ploughman. This worthy set to plough the field and his activity brought him within 10 yards of the two men lying face down in the hedge. On the far side of the field was a railway embankment and the new plan was to jump aboard a slow-moving train. However, access to the line was by way of the partially ploughed field and the presence of the ploughman prevented any movement. They lay in the hedge, damp and very cold, until dusk, when the ploughman went home to his hearth and a hot meal.

They talked very quietly during the day and speculated on the actions that the military authorities would, by now, have taken to apprehend them. To date they had seen no evidence of a search. At 1800 hrs another cold meal revived morale and they decided to separate. Quite correctly they judged that the authorities would be looking for two men, one very tall and one significantly shorter. By now their clothes were crumpled and muddy. They no longer looked like two middle-class Germans, rather more like a pair of unshaven, scruffy tramps.

A coin was tossed to determine the batting order. Strafer won, elected to bat first and he left the hide twenty minutes before Sam Hall. At 1840 hrs Strafer set out and followed a road going south-southwest. He passed two girls who spoke to him but his German was not good enough to understand what they said and so he did not respond and purposefully strode on.

It was now fully dark and, after about 2 miles, he found that the road was taking him too far to the south. He turned off the road, set off westwards over the adjacent field and skirted a small farm, passing the farmer, who was just returning home. It is not easy to walk across country at night. Fields are never flat and all manner of obstacles are concealed in the gloom. Nevertheless, Strafer trudged on and eventually his path crossed a railway line that ran southwest. It was the Hamburg-Bremen line and he hoped that it would provide that slow train to Bremen.

A path ran parallel to the railway line and Strafer followed it through woods and round the edge of fields. It was easy walking and he was looking for a point at which he could jump onto a train. He found the ideal spot above the track and waited for a goods train. Several rattled past; they were apparently empty but travelling far too fast. Strafer did not lack courage but with one arm all but useless he was not equipped to launch himself at a fast-moving train. Clearly Plan 'A' had to be abandoned. It was briefly re-instituted when Strafer heard a train halt some 500 yards ahead.

Hope flared and he broke into a run. The train was in sight and just when catching it looked to be an achievable goal, the train grunted, puffed and then drew away into the night. The light from the train's firebox was reflected in the trees along the track. The train chugged away into the distance and the only sound to be heard in the forest was Gott's rasping breath.

He decided to walk along the track and reasoned that anyone he met would be a railway man and he would almost certainly be carrying a torch and thus easy to evade. Strafer walked through the night for a little over nine hours. He explained:

> I passed a few stations and fell over a lot of signal wires near one of them making an awful row. The night was moonlit and very cold. I got so cold that I finished all my brandy but couldn't get warm. I was too tired to try running and there was a wind. I sat down a few times and sheltered under an old railway carriage. At about 4.00 am I

decided to try and find a warm place and so obtain some sleep before doing any more. In a station yard I found a ladder going up to a loft. I ascended this only to wake a man who was sleeping there. I heard him mutter something and then hurried off. I entered an empty house about 200 yards from this station and lay down on a bench there. I was just dozing when a man entered and said something. I stood up, stretched and yawned and he went off. I soon followed and continued walking until 6.00 am. I then had breakfast, half a biscuit and some sausage, in one of the little compartments at the end of a truck.

I then walked on for there was a driving drisle [*sic*] and nowhere to hide or shelter. I followed a track at the side of the railway and passed several people who said '*gut morgan*'. I replied and gained much confidence. After a time I had once more to take to the metals and at 8.00 am a signalman came running out of his box shouting at me. I ran off down a steep embankment and into a wood. Here I hid until about 11.00 am but it was so cold that I decided to go on in the day, especially as I had passed people without difficulty and was also not getting along as quickly as I had wished. I could see in the distance a long line of high iron posts with wires, and near here I found the main road to Bremen.

The road ran south-west, the right direction. It offered the chance to make progress far quicker than moving across country. Strafer had not slept and had not taken any liquids for far too long. He was showing an extraordinary degree of fortitude but, even though he was a strong young man, a poor diet had weakened him and he was reaching his limit. He passed through a village and saw some prisoners of mixed nationalities standing about. The area was sparsely inhabited, with few people to be seen although from time to time someone would pass him on a bicycle and offer a greeting, in much the way of country people the world over. Strafer's memoir records:

I was now beginning to get very thirsty, as I had not had a drink for nearly forty-eight hours. But I could find no pool or stream anywhere. This was a contingency I had never taken into account.

At about 4.00 pm while going through a wood I came across a large farm standing on the main road. From the notice outside it was apparently a 'pub' as well. I looked in at the door and saw inside only an old woman. Accordingly, I walked in and in my best German asked for a beer. Knowing that many accents were different in such a large country I thought it quite safe. The old woman pointed to a door and told me to go in there. I didn't like to argue and so went in and found four German soldiers at one table and the proprietor and some civilians having tea at another. Near the door were a bar and a barmaid. I bought a bottle of beer and sat down at the third table. The barmaid brought it to me and said something I couldn't understand and so said, '*Ja, ja,*' and hoped for the best. She said, '*Ja ja*! What do you mean by *ja*?' – or words to that effect. Before I could think of a suitable answer she said, 'Where are you going?'

I answered, 'Hamburg' and then turned my back on her. Fortunately, she didn't try to continue the conversation otherwise I should have bolted. I then sat down to my beer and saw outside the window a large barn with British, French, Belgian and Russian soldiers standing about. Obviously they were prisoners working on the farm and these four soldiers were their guards.

I had evidently walked right into the lion's mouth. To leave the room I must walk past the four soldiers and so I decided to wait and see if they would go as I didn't want to call any unnecessary attention to myself. Accordingly, next time the old woman came near I ordered another beer and so prolonged my stay. However, the soldiers began to play cards and after waiting about twenty minutes I walked out without exciting any undue curiosity.

I then walked back along the road the way I had come in case I was watched and so to carry out the story that I was going to Hamburg. I walked through the woods and came back in a circuit until I was behind the 'pub'. Here I saw a prisoner, apart from the rest, who I thought was English. I said to him, 'Are you English?' and he replied in German that he was a Belgian. I could see some who were undoubtedly English nearer the house playing a concertina, but it was not safe to speak to them.

Strafer prudently consulted his compass and headed off to the south-west. He walked until dusk and found his way into a large village that he asserts confidently was called 'Schlessen'[1] and judging by a convenient signpost it was 53 kilometres from Hamburg. It was getting cold and so Strafer opted to find warmth and sleep in a barn – if he could find one.

He prowled around the village and eventually found an accessible barn on the edge of the houses. The great door was partially open and he slipped in to find that it was a potato store. By happy chance there was a pile of straw and some empty potato sacks and in his circumstances these were the makings of a comfortable bed. It was his intention to sleep for only part of the night but, in his exhausted condition, it is little wonder that he slept the night through and did not wake until dawn.

He opened his eyes, looked around. A woman was in the barn not a yard away. Gott, covered in the sacks, kept quite still and held his breath. The unknown woman took a pace and stood firmly upon Strafer's right thigh. He did not yelp and she did not react to the unusual surface she was standing upon. She moved off and several minutes later she left the barn and a much relieved, slightly bruised, Gott.

The sack-covered Strafer made to leave the barn and get on his way but found the farmyard occupied by farm workers busily engaged in their affairs. Patience was called for and he retreated to his former position and covered himself. He waited for about half an hour, the chatter in the farmyard ceased and he risked another look. The place was clear so he took the opportunity to slip quickly away.

By 0800 hrs he had made excellent progress and entered 'Rothenburg',[2] a charming small town, and at that time the streets were quiet He was passing an orchard, paused, looked about and then, like the schoolboy he had been only recently, he went scrumping. He filled all of his pockets with apples and pears and by so doing supplemented his now meagre stock of food.

The rest of the day, at least initially, was almost routine. He saw and spoke to no one. He rested in a wood for half an hour around noon and then, emboldened by the scarcity of people, he decided to push on. By 1400 hrs he thought it a sound idea to hide up in a wood that lay just ahead. There was a small village between him and the wood.

From the village came a cyclist. The cyclist and Strafer Gott were the only travellers on the road. As the rider came closer Strafer could see that it was a man and he was wearing some sort of uniform. Strafer assumed that he was a German NCO – he was not. He was a policeman.

The policeman stopped, propped up his bike and addressed William, whose German was not good enough to understand the question. He assumed that he was being asked where he was going and so Strafer replied confidently, 'Bremen'.

It was the wrong answer.

Strafer was asked for his papers; he had none and from this point the escape was at an end although he still looked for an avenue by which to evade capture.

Of course I had none and he grabbed me by the arm and told me
'Kommen mit' him. He had a revolver in his belt. On each side of the road was a high hedge. There were people about and so it was really impossible to escape him. If I could have knocked him down, which was unlikely as he was a big man, I would have had to run down a road with a hue and cry after me and I was not likely to be able to run very fast or for very long. I should be almost certain to be retaken or

possibly shot and an additional term of imprisonment for assaulting the police would have been mine.

Strafer was taken to the local pub, where his food, compass and most of his money were taken. Amazingly, while under arrest he contrived to slide his 100-mark note into his sock when the policeman 'wasn't looking'. He offered to buy the policeman a drink at the pub but the offer was declined. The policeman then took Strafer to the police station and made telephone calls. Policeman and captive journeyed on to the railway station of Sottrum and from here a lengthy trip, by public transport, back to captivity would ensue, during which Strafer was an object of some interest. The fact that he was manacled added to the vicarious attraction of the large, fair young officer. During the journey it emerged that Sam Hall had been recaptured twenty-four hours earlier. The captors were surprised that there had been two escapees and Strafer deduced that the news of the escape had not been widely broadcast.

Strafer's escort was now dressed in 'full fig' and he and his charge arrived in Hamburg at about 1400 hrs the following day. The Sergeant and his prisoner transferred to a tram to complete the final leg of the journey. On arrival at the camp the Police NCO said, 'Good day. I am very glad to have you back.' Strafer recorded that, civil though he was, 'he looked very sick.'

Dispatched onwards to the military headquarters in the city Strafer was given blue and white German prison clothing and his now very tattered, mud-stained suit was taken away. Sam Hall was brought in, accompanied by an interpreter and a German officer. The British officers greeted each other warmly and then were questioned about their clothes and their method of escape. Along the way Strafer noted that they 'slanged us both pretty freely'. He realised:

> They must have found out about the clothes. I told the truth about them and also told him that we had escaped at 10.00 pm (really 8.00 pm) as the last roll call was at 9.30 [and] they wouldn't suspect that our beds were stuffed and punish all the others in the hut.
>
> After he had gone Mathias, the German orderly who had bought the suit, crept in; he was in an awful funk. Apparently the Police Corporal had said that the clothes had never been put in the portmanteau in the clothes store. This was the condition on which I was allowed to have them bought and as Mathias bought them he was responsible for them until they were put in the clothing store. The Police Corporal had merely [said] this to shift the blame off his own shoulders. I told Mathias I would support his story and so quietened him. He then said that the next day we were going before the General and added that I had better tell him that I had escaped because I had trouble at home!

He said this would be a good excuse! I told him that I didn't require one at all and if asked would tell them that I was tired of being a prisoner. He told me that Sam Hall was going to adopt his excuse (this was untrue). I cannot understand why he went to the trouble of inventing this tale for us.

The escape of Gott and Hall had obviously caused some embarrassment in German military circles, but despite this, the next morning these two officers with an escaping pedigree were given back their civilian clothes. Strafer was nonplussed to find that his much-travelled compass was safely lodged in one of his boots.[3] The Police Sergeant had confiscated the compass along with all Strafer's money, letters and other personal effects when he captured him. The explanation Strafer gave for the reappearance of the compass was:

> My clothes, when taken away from me, were tied up in a bundle. The compass could not be put in this and so the two soldiers who took them probably put it in one of the boots, not thinking that I should ever wear these clothes again.

The two prisoners were marched through the camp, locked up and left to wait. Some five hours later the General appeared, followed by his ADC, and serried rows of Germans of every rank all the way down to the Camp Sergeant Major.

The General had evidently heard all about the case. He asked a few questions, which Strafer did not understand, and when he explained that his German was only of the schoolboy variety, the inability to communicate hastened the interview to its end.

Strafer's civilian clothing was not withdrawn – yet another astonishing oversight by the authorities. Prison clothing was re-issued along with the news that both Strafer and Hall had been awarded 'fourteen days' solitary' for their escapade. This was the maximum sentence permitted by the Hague Commission of June 1917. Hall was sent to 'Paichem'[4] and Strafer was moved to Karlsruhe. He stayed there for a month and then, with sixty others, he was transferred to a new camp at Saarbrücken.

Chapter notes
1. There is no town or village of this name or any other with a similar name.
2. The only Rothenburg in Germany is on the Polish border. He meant Rotenburg.
3. Strafer's memoir remarks, 'I promptly concealed it and after that managed to keep it through numerous searches until the end of the war. It is still in use.'
4. Probably Parchim.

Chapter 5

The Second Escape

The majority of Strafer's fellow internees had been taken at Cambrai on 3 May 1917. Cambrai was the site of the first battle in which tanks played a part.[1] Gott was not available to participate but later in his life the tank in all its forms was to figure large.

Geoffrey Fison, whom Gott had met in the 2nd Battalion and who knew some of his family, was a fellow prisoner. Gott and he formed a Mess with two officers of the RFC named Goode and Ibbotson. Another move was initiated and after a cold, all-night journey with a long wait at Zweibrücken, Gott's party arrived at the new camp. They were searched and although Gott had his civilian suit on under his prison clothes, these were not detected. Goode carried his compass and that was also preserved. Patently, the Boche was not adept in the Searching Department.

The camp at Saarbrücken consisted of a three-storey house that had been a school or municipal office, with a yard about 100 feet x 30 feet. The Germans occupied the basement and the prisoners slept on the first and second floors. On the top floor were the dining and reading rooms. The windows were all secured and painted over so that the inmates could not see out. Ten were billeted to a room. The beds were iron with solid bed boards covered by straw-filled mattresses.

The first two months at Saarbrücken were uncomfortable. It was now winter and on the North German Plain that can be very bleak. It was unremittingly cold; the food in the midst of this Turnip Winter was meagre, unattractive, uninteresting and not very well cooked either. Food parcels from the Red Cross were not getting through and the poor diet had a deleterious effect on all the prisoners. Strafer wrote:

> Before long we were all very weak. I had about three parcels in the two months but, when this was divided between four, it didn't make much more than five small meals. On Christmas Day we had a small tinned tongue and cake. I would eat the whole lot now as a snack and scarce notice it. Most of the time the others had nothing extra and soon we were even worse off.

The year changed, but 1918 brought no alteration to the prison routine. There was a roll call at breakfast, another at 1130 hrs attended by the Commandant, when Strafer observed acidly, 'He came and generally threw his weight about.' There was a further roll call at 1830 hrs and finally a headcount when the prisoners took to their beds.

Strafer recorded that he and Ibbotson regularly walked round and round the yard, and sometimes 'shovelled' (presumably snow) for something to do. He added, 'Most people never came out at all and hardly dressed themselves on account of the lack of food.'

Gott was now in a very weak condition and admitted that he had to hang onto the banisters for support when walking up and down stairs. Strafer Gott was actually starving. Notwithstanding, Strafer, Ibbotson and Greenslade decided to escape and devoted time to establishing a viable plan. At this point Strafer's invaluable memoir abruptly ceases. A gap of ten blank pages has been left and presumably he planned to return to the narrative. However, when it recommences it is only from early November 1918.

During 1918 Strafer made a further escape, the only source for the details of which is *Recollections of Strafer Gott* by General Sir George Erskine, a fellow member of KRRC. This is an unpublished manuscript, written in an almost illegible hand, which is now held in the archives of the RGJ Museum. At the time of writing (probably in 1954) Erskine was a major general and General Officer Commanding (GOC) British Troops, Egypt and Mediterranean Command. He reported that during the winter of 1917-18 Strafer Gott made his quite extraordinary second escape:

> He managed to retain possession of his prismatic compass by a variety of hiding devices. He possessed a grey flannel suit, which he wore as underclothes. He collected a small store of food and watched very carefully the movement of the sentries round the cage and discovered that there was one patch that was in comparative darkness and unvisited by sentries for about five minutes every half an hour.
>
> He evolved a method, which was more or less a pole vault to clear the wire. Considering that Strafer was no athlete and obviously could not practise the act beforehand, it was a remarkable achievement. The plan was for several people to escape simultaneously since the method could not be repeated.[2]

This all sounds highly improbable but, amazingly, the plan worked! There is no doubt that Strafer got out but the method by which he made his second escape really does strain creditability, although Erskine can only have got the story from Strafer.

Strafer picked the right time, on a dark night; in just the right spot he made his first ever pole vault – he sailed over the wire, as did several of his companions. It begs the question was there just one pole passed backwards and forwards or multiple poles? It was decided that they would each make their own way to freedom and Strafer struck out for the Dutch border. Erskine says vaguely and inaccurately that the border was 'several hundreds of miles away' but gives no indication where the pole vaulting had taken place, other than to make fleeting mention of 'central Germany'. It was probably Saarbrücken.

This escape followed much the same pattern as his earlier foray. He travelled by night and laid up by day. It was now winter and the grey flannel suit offered scant protection from the bitter wind. Young Lieutenant Gott made steady, cautious and incident-free progress. Eventually, lying in a hedgerow, he found himself overlooking the frontier between Holland and Germany. He could see in the distance a wood that appeared to mark the border. However, in between was a large flat expanse of farmland that was extensively patrolled. He lay up to look for an opportunity to make the crossing. For three days he watched and waited, getting colder and hungrier.

It was clear that he had to eat and his only option was to retrace his steps back to a village he had passed through on his journey. He was completely unaware that a German soldier of the Frontier Guard Force had recently deserted and he was similarly unaware that a full-scale search for that fugitive was in progress. Blithely he made his way to the village inn and ordered a meal. It was delivered steaming hot and Strafer, who was ravenously hungry, began to tuck in. He had had only a few wonderful mouthfuls when a sergeant of the Frontier Guard Force entered the inn and surveyed the occupants. Seeing a scruffy, unshaven, apparently fit young man he asked for Strafer's papers. The game was up – the Sergeant thought he had bagged a deserter but actually he had got much bigger game. Strafer was returned to the cage and spent the remainder of the war either in solitary confinement or in special camps reserved for recidivists like him.[3] At some stage he was returned to Saarbrücken and was there until early November 1918.

His POW experiences were recorded after the war but were silent on this second escape. The record – almost certainly made at the insistence of his commanding officer – resumed on 8 November 1918, when he noted:

> We all left Saarbrücken and moved by rail to a new camp, which was being formed at Coblenz.[4] We walked to the station carrying as much as we could … early on a wet morning and very hot and tired I was when I got there. We were put into a third-class corridor coach. Seven in each carriage, two sentries sitting by the windows, four prisoners and another sentry standing in the doorway and so they weren't taking any chances.

It is a wonder that even at this late stage prisoners like Strafer were closely supervised. But soon the degree of supervision reduced as the calamity facing Germany became evident to their captors. The train stopped at Trier and picked up a further fifty prisoners and then travelled up the beautiful valley of the Mosel (which Strafer incorrectly identified as the Meuse). He commented on the scenery and the vineyards on the hillsides. The train steamed purposefully but slowly on its way and, when about a mile out of Coblenz, it ground to a hissing halt. It was about 1800 hrs and the train sat in complete darkness for three hours. One of the guards explained it would not be safe to take enemy prisoners into the city as it was 'in revolution'.[5]

The prisoners realised that the war was nearly at an end and this 'revolution' was manifestly an endorsement of Germany's deep social problems. They offered no sympathy to their captors and actively welcomed the news of discontent. At about 2100 hrs a company of soldiers from the fort arrived and took over the custody of the prisoners from the Saarbrücken detachment.

It was raining. Strafer described it as 'a thin drisle' and, carrying all they could, the prisoners were marshalled into a column and marched about 2 miles to their next 'home'. It was an ill-organised march and very quickly the column 'became very strung out'. The situation made escape very easy but Strafer observed:

> I did not try, however, as I realised that the end of the war was near and I had made no preparation and had only recently recovered from a bad attack of 'flu.[6] Symes, 7th London Regiment evaded the sentries but was caught next day. We arrived at the Kartuse Fortress and found all in great confusion.[7] The fort is about 100 years old and is on top of a high hill on the left bank of the Rhine; it was protected by a moat and a double rampart. ... On arrival at the fort we found that in the absence of the company sent to fetch us the revolutionaries had captured it (the fortress) and it now belonged to a Soldiers' and Workmen's Council.

The scene inside the fortress was one of complete confusion and Strafer remarked that the Commanding Officer of the fortress was put on trial by the mob – but not harmed. There was no roll of prisoners and although there were two missing – one escapee and one who was sick and had been left at the station – inexplicably, a headcount found two bodies too many. Strafer found a place in a room for three alongside Ted Goldy, a chum. The following morning a semblance of order reigned but it was only skin deep and when the German officers appeared they were all shorn of their epaulettes. This was apparently on the order of the Soldiers' and Workmen's Council. The major, who had

45

previously been in command, had disappeared and one of the subalterns was placed in command.

> We were told that the Council had no time to put people in prison and death was the only punishment they gave and that is what we should get if we gave any trouble. Consequently, the Senior British Officer (SBO) an officer called Ficklin told us to keep quiet for a few days until we saw how the land lay.

It would be a considerable understatement to say that the situation in Germany was volatile. Anarchy held sway and in Coblenz the revolutionaries were firmly in control. The British POWs could only wait, while seizing on any scrap of news. On 12 November a German newspaper was obtained and it gave the terms of the armistice – the POWs were particularly interested, none more so than Strafer, to read that all prisoners were to be sent home at once. The SBO now asserted his position and 'interviewed' the Council. This ad hoc organisation, having previously threatened death, now agreed, rather lamely, to release all the prisoners but made the valid point that outside of Coblenz they had no power. They said that if Strafer and his comrades left the city then the chances were that they would be hindered or even stopped by the German Army, the defeated components of which were moving east and clogging the roads. The Council was also concerned that the unarmed prisoners would be molested and they themselves would then suffer for it when retribution was exacted by the Allies, who were due in Coblenz on about 9 December. About this same time, the Danish Red Cross sent a message from the British Government telling the POWs to wait where they were until transport could be sent up the river to collect them.

Life did not get any easier and food was in painfully short supply. The reserves of food and luggage that had been left at the station before the march up to the fortress had been looted and the remnants gave no comfort. Winter had set in and it was very cold. Some coal was found in a cellar but the lumps of coal on the top soon gave way to coal dust and burnable coal could only be found by burrowing into the dust, clouds of which quickly enveloped the burrower. Initially the prisoners were allowed to walk around outside with escorts but after a couple of days they were let out to roam freely at will. Many stayed out all day long enjoying the spectacular scenery where the Rhine and the Mosel meet at a place known, since 1216, as Deutsches Eck (German Corner).

> Our first difficulty was money. Most of us had none. I had a new stick of shaving soap from England and Ted Oddy, a large piece of soap. And as these were very short in Germany we decided to sell them.

> Together we walked all over the town into shops large and small trying
> to get ten marks for the two. I was the best German scholar and so did
> all the talking. Eventually we sold them for five marks. By then we
> were tired of walking and so we entered the largest hotel in the town,
> the Coblenz Hof – a magnificent place on the riverside just by the
> bridge of boats. We called for the wine list and found the cheapest
> thing was a liqueur at two marks fifty per glass. We had two of these
> and sat in big armchairs in a civilised room for the first time in many
> months.

They sat and wallowed in comfortable warmth for two hours. The next day they
resumed their quest for cash and tried, unsuccessfully, to cash a cheque at a
German bank. The fact that Ted Oddy knew the manager of the London branch
unsurprisingly cut no ice at all. The pair were told that perhaps a cheque could
be cashed 'in a few weeks' time'. They were hungry and that few weeks'
timeframe simply did not fit in with their digestive difficulties. Despair was
alleviated when a German Army quartermaster, of his own volition, cashed
cheques to the value of about £200 for the officers – albeit at an 'iniquitous rate
of exchange'. Strafer lunched daily, for six marks, at a modest hotel in the city,
having decided that the Coblenz Hof was beyond his means. His memoir runs
to an abrupt end and his final words are:

> The food wasn't bad and here one day we had a hash that looked like
> lamb but the bones were too big and yet it couldn't be mutton.
> Eventually we found out it was dog! Near the fort had been a big
> school for war dogs and after the revolution ...

Strafer's handwritten account then stops abruptly, in mid-sentence.

He did not return to his memoir and so his joyful return to England is
unrecorded. The memoir is detailed and rather bland. Nevertheless, it is
something of a regimental treasure to The Rifles, the successors of the KRRC.

The Allies reported that, by 9 December 1918, they had repatriated 264,000
prisoners. Among this number was Strafer Gott, who apparently got home in
some comfort by means of a Rhine steamer.

Many other POWs of all nations had been released en masse and turned
loose to find their own way to Allied lines. There was no provision for clothing,
food or shelter. Many officers and men released in this ad hoc manner died from
exhaustion. Others were luckier; they were met by Allied troops and sent back
through the lines in lorries to reception centres where they were refitted with
boots and clothing and dispatched to the ports in trains. Upon arrival at the
receiving camp the POWs were registered and 'boarded' before being
dispatched to their own homes. All commissioned officers were required to write

a report on the circumstances of their capture to ensure that they had done all they could to avoid capture. It was this instruction that triggered Strafer's memoir.

After a lengthy leave Strafer Gott had to decide what to do with his life. He was twenty-one years of age, fit, well educated and affluent. He had tried the Army and over the previous two and a half years he had been variously very cold, wet, frightened, shot at, shelled, wounded and captured. He was very well acquainted with the pangs of hunger. He had made two escapes and been re-captured twice. He had been a fugitive sleeping in hedges, barns and ditches. All in all, his military service had not generated much in the way of laughter but a great deal of discomfort.

Strafer Gott, the pragmatic, sober-sided Yorkshireman decided that, notwithstanding the privations of his service so far, it was to be a soldier's life for him and he opted for a regular commission. This must have been on the supposition that military life could only get better!

As they say in Yorkshire, 'Thar's nowt so queer as folk'.

Chapter notes
1. Battle of Cambrai, 20 November to 7 December 1917.
2. Frustratingly, there is no explanation of how the vaulting pole(s) were obtained.
3. Erskine, Major General GWEJ, CB DSO, unpublished memoir, RGJ Museum archives, Winchester.
4. Coblenz is the English and pre-1926 spelling of Koblenz.
5. By November 1918, civil disorder and strikes were rife across Germany. The High Seas Fleet, blockaded in port after the Battle of Jutland, was in a mutinous state. The highly effective blockade of all German ports that had strangled imports of all material had, in turn, led to severe food shortages.
6. Strafer makes passing reference to 'a bad attack of flu'. He was fortunate to survive because, between Jan 1918-December 1920, there was a pandemic of virulent influenza that killed 50-100 million people worldwide. Most of the victims were young, healthy adults but any malnourishment increased their chance of succumbing to the disease. The death toll made the estimated 16 million casualties of the First World War almost pale into insignificance.
7. The name Kartuse is not recognised. The fortress in Koblenz (as it has been spelt since 1926) is Ehrenbreitstein.

Chapter 6

Between the Wars
1919-39

T he interwar years did not involve the British Army in any major campaigns. There was, however, the unpleasant business of confronting the IRA (up until 1922), the permanent peacekeeping activity on the North-West Frontier of India and the intractable problem of keeping Arabs and Jews from each others' throats in Palestine. However, for the most part, British soldiers settled into garrison routine around the world and life was interspersed with exercises and lots of sport. Strafer Gott did not hear the sound of guns for more than twenty years, but then nor did most of his contemporaries. Promotion was agonisingly slow and by no means assured.

During these twenty years Strafer grew from a callow but decorated subaltern to a vastly experienced and capable lieutenant colonel commanding the 1st Battalion of his regiment. He did not keep a diary, fought no campaigns and did not attract public attention. The consequence of this is that Strafer's lifestyle, achievements and development can only be traced through the scant and formal medium of his confidential reports.

Strafer died on the eve of his forty-fifth birthday; the twenty years of 1920-40 accordingly represent the bulk of his adult life and cannot be lightly disregarded. During this period he did not fire a shot in anger. Any 'Cold War warrior' will testify to the frustration of the constant training for a war that never comes. No doubt Strafer felt the same, grateful not to be at risk, but …

During these twenty years he did not seek to effect change upon the Army, wrote no papers of significance and busied himself solely with the affairs of his current appointment. He passed through the Staff College but was not sufficiently high on the order of merit to be called back, later, to instruct in that hallowed establishment. He made no attempt to change Army philosophy, nor its tactics or the training for those tactics.

In due course one BL Montgomery would touch briefly on his life. This officer was made of different material to Strafer Gott. He was quick-witted, self-centred, single-minded, aggressive, socially inept and very ambitious. Montgomery did, most definitely, seek to alter the way the British Army went about its business. Later in this book these two men will be measured against each other.

In recording these twenty important years there is a strong temptation for the biographer to speculate on what Gott might have thought, said and done. This temptation has been manfully resisted.

* * *

Strafer Gott returned to England on 3 December 1918. The Rhine steamer had got him as far as Amsterdam but then he spent a frustrating couple of weeks waiting to be transported back to Blighty. He went on leave and was reunited with his parents and siblings.

The England to which Strafer Gott had returned was bankrupt and in a state of deep depression. An army of 3,500,000 was very rapidly being reduced in size by 90 per cent and millions of young men, released from khaki, sought employment. The 'land fit for heroes' (a phrase coined by the public was a paraphrase of David Lloyd-George's original ringing words) was actually anything but.

The KRRC, like every other regiment, was faced with the difficult task of downsizing and this would involve the discharge of thousands of riflemen at all levels. It would be a painful and emotional process, not least because Civvy Street was so uncertain compared with the comparatively well-ordered life available in the Army.

Strafer was posted to 3rd Battalion, KRRC, a battalion that had moved to Aldershot in June 1919, arriving on the 6th and in time for a regimental dinner – the first since 1914. 'Over 150 officers were present'. [1] That number would have been far too many for any of the regimental messes, which were designed to seat perhaps sixty at most. The very high probability is that the event was held in the Royal Aldershot Officers' Club. Its ballroom, with a spectacular sprung floor, would have been ideal.

Aldershot was a rather drab, red-brick garrison town that styled itself with some accuracy as 'The home of the British Army'. Strafer lived in Blenheim Barracks in the North Camp area. This was one of the Victorian infantry barracks that ran in a line from The Queen's Hotel (long since renamed and currently known as The Holiday Inn), along Duke of Connaught's Road (now expunged from the map and built over). The 4th Battalion, KRRC was next door, in Malplaquet Barracks, but the officers of both battalions messed together in Blenheim Officers' Mess. These barracks were all named to celebrate the victories of the Duke of Marlborough and built in the 1890s. By the standards of the day they were fairly modern.

Blenheim Officers' Mess, like all the others, was a vast rambling building and poorly heated. Nevertheless, it was the centre of social life for about twenty young men like Strafer. The Royal Aldershot Officers' Club was only a brisk, fifteen-minute walk away and the dances held there were far less formal than similar events held in the officers' messes.

The low-lying and boggy fairways of the Aldershot Command Golf Club,[2] which stretched over Cove Common and Laffan's Plain, were within easy reach and the clubhouse was but five minutes away on the Farnborough Road. Trains to London ran regularly from Farnborough and Aldershot. There was point-to-point at Tweseldown and, all in all, there were worse places to be. Post-war garrison life was quite agreeable for Strafer Gott.

An anti-gas course was held in Aldershot at this time and Strafer was a student. It is most unlikely that he was a volunteer and probably, as every battalion had to have its quota of gas-trained officers, the Adjutant picked his name from the hat. Nevertheless, he did well and was graded 1st Class.

The 3rd Battalion was warned off for service in India and there was a flurry of activity that always surrounds a unit move. India was an attractive posting and there was always the possibility of action on the North-West Frontier, although the Battalion was destined for Mhow and not the mountainous north.

From July-September 1919 the reformation of 3rd and 4th battalions was put in place. As a first step:

> All of the non-regular members of both battalions were posted
> elsewhere and their replacements were drafts of twenty to fifty men
> from the Depot, twice each week. These riflemen were men returning
> from war leave or re-enlistment furlough and the majority of them
> were on short-service engagements of two, three or four years, with
> little or no war service.[3]

The turbulence in these two units must have been very confusing but, in the case of 3rd Battalion, KRRC, Lieutenant Colonel HC Warre, the Commanding Officer, had matters firmly under control. This period was Strafer's first taste of peacetime soldiering and it was in the starkest contrast with his previous experience. In 1916-17, keeping track of the soldiers in his platoon, let alone getting to know them, would have been difficult, but in peacetime he had to know his soldiers even better than their mothers did.

In September 1919 the Battalion's advance party left for India to prepare the way for the main body and this small group departed from Aldershot on 6 October. The main body followed on but a rail strike disrupted the movement plan and the military train from North Camp Station was cancelled. This modest station, little more than a halt, has a place in military history as it had been the departure point for hundreds of thousands of Tommies during the recent war.

No trains called for a rapid rethink and so fifty-seven lorries were used instead to lift the men and their baggage to Southampton. There was lots of work here for Strafer and his NCOs. The Battalion embarked on SS *City of Sparta*[4] for the lengthy voyage to Mhow[5] via Bombay. It was exciting, exotic stuff for a young man who was still only just twenty-two.

For Strafer Gott the sea voyage of just under a month and the sights seen along the way would have left a strong impression. The voyage would also have served to cement regimental friendships and in combination they probably reinforced his attraction to the Service. Strafer arrived in India on 2 November 1919 and there he remained until September 1925.

On 30 January 1920, *The London Gazette* promulgated the award of the Military Cross (MC) to Lieutenant WHE Gott KRRC. Strafer was still painfully young, but into his short life he had already crammed a lifetime's worth of experiences. He was self-reliant, mature and had established a capacity to command other men, which he would build on in the years ahead. His reputation in the 60th was high and George Erskine remarked:

> When Strafer got back to England after the war he was naturally something of a hero in his own circle. We began to hear of his behaviour at Nieuport with 2nd Battalion and his aggressive behaviour as a prisoner – all of this was recognised by the award of the Military Cross.[6]

For generations young officers have been told of the necessity to 'get their knees brown' and so here was that opportunity for Strafer. The Second-in-Command was Major (Brevet Lieutenant Colonel) Majendie and among the other officers was Lieutenant SCF de Salis, who became a close friend and was destined to command 1st Battalion, KRRC some twenty years later. Sydney de Salis was to play an important part in the Gott family's life.

Garrison life in India was very agreeable. There was the opportunity to play sports of every sort and the daily routine, although formal, was nevertheless relaxed. The regimental history records that Strafer shot an ibex in Baluchistan whilst other members of the Battalion slaughtered elephants, tigers, stags, crocodiles – in fact, anything that swam, flew or ran. When not shooting for game, the 3rd/60th got down to range shooting, which, as riflemen, was their corporate raison d'être. They excelled and swept the board at all the rifle meetings under the captaincy of Strafer Gott. He had a track record as a marksman and although he is not recorded as having won any significant personal honours, the camaraderie of the shooting team would have been ample reward.

He was selected for attendance at a Lewis gun course; he did well and his record has just the cryptic entry 'Qualified'.

Polo was another activity, and it was taken up and played enthusiastically by Strafer, whose father provided the funds for this expensive sport. He was good enough to be a member of the team that won the Mhow Polo Cup and the Dhār Cup in 1920. The following year, the 3rd Battalion, KRRC was a beaten finalist in the Infantry Cup. Those officers of the Battalion who could afford to maintain a hunter supported the Quetta Hounds and Strafer fell into that category. Riding to hounds takes a degree of skill and no little courage: Gott was well equipped in both.

On 22 January 1921, aged twenty-three, Strafer was promoted to captain [7] and appointed second-in-command of his company, accordingly moving very slightly up in the military hierarchy. He was younger than the average for both promotion and appointment. Later that year, Colonel Warre reported upon him in his confidential report and wrote that Strafer was a 'thoroughly capable and steady officer. He has force of character and intelligence and is zealous in the performance of his duties.'[8] This report is certainly nothing to write home about and it graded him as probably no more than an average officer.

'The need for urgent economies in the defence budget' has been the unremitting cry of HMG for countless generations and in August 1921 Sir Eric Geddes was tasked to identify savings in public expenditure. Inevitably and, as always, defence was one of the prime targets and his recommendations were swingeing. Defence expenditure of £189.5 million in 1921-22 was to be reduced to £111 million in 1922-23. The size of the reduction in funding was bound to lead to massive reorganisation and not least in the Corps of Infantry. All regiments with four battalions – one of which was the 60th – were to reduce to two battalions immediately.

A draft of 450 men from 3rd KRRC was sent to 4th KRRC at Quetta to await the arrival of 1st KRRC, and the 1st Battalion, KRRC was ordered to India to 'absorb' the 3rd and 4th battalions KRRC.

In September 1922 Lieutenant Colonel Bernard Majendie sailed with the skeletal battalion as he had been selected to command the 'new' composite 1st Battalion, in which Strafer Gott was to command C Company. Majendie was a high-grade officer and he was faced with a daunting task. He was an excellent role model and the manner in which he went about his difficult job had an influence on the attitude of Strafer Gott. 'Can do' was very much Majendie's style, as it was Strafer Gott's, and the young man's early appointment to command a company was to prove invaluable training in command and administration.

He was very junior and very young, at twenty-four, to hold such an appointment and it was an early confirmation of his all-round quality, especially as there was a surplus of officers prior to the absorption process, several of whom were his senior. An option would have been for him to be adjutant – but the post was not vacant. Company commander was upmarket on adjutant and Gott would have been only too delighted.

One of the new subalterns arriving with the 1st Battalion was George Erskine (always known as Bobby). He had not seen Strafer for three years but said:

> I was delighted to find myself in Strafer's C Company. Bernard Majendie commanded, and amalgamating the battalions of the 60th was not an easy job for anybody. Each battalion thought it was the only one that knew anything about soldiering. Frightful arguments ensued over trivial matters of dress and etiquette but under the firm and wise [unintelligible] of Bernard Majendie we were soon all pulling together.
>
> Strafer was the ideal company commander. He was younger than the other company commanders but was determined to have the best company. I really enjoyed working with him. The day was a strenuous one. Strafer saw to that.
>
> PT, or runs, or Khud climbs before breakfast followed by a very full morning's work, which was always well organised and interesting – whenever possible he got the whole company out of barracks for a few days, or a few weeks. We marched enormous distances, packed our kit on camels or mules in the dark. We dashed up and down hills and generally tried to teach ourselves mountain warfare. … Strafer was very keen on 'musketry', as we called it in those days, and insisted on great care … [unintelligible].[9]

Erskine was sent away on a weapons course and returned to the Company several weeks later, vastly enthused by all matters musketry. Together, Erskine and Strafer set out to train the Company to a level so that every rifleman was either a marksman or a first-class shot. Strafer's sniper training back in 1916 would have been put to good use and to the probable irritation of the other company commanders, Gott and Erskine succeeded in their aim.

Colonel Majendie had to cope with a constant drain on his manpower and as the engagements of his soldiers expired so they were swiftly repatriated. The 147 riflemen who left in December 1920 were followed by a further similar-sized batch during 1921. The home battalion was engaged in Ireland and had to find replacements for the 1st Battalion in India.

All young officers are influenced, for good or ill, by their commanding officers and Strafer's attitude, skills and abilities were undoubtedly enhanced by Colonels Warre and Majendie.

After Gott had been in command of C Company for a year Colonel Majendie completed the routine confidential reports on all of his officers and he said of Gott that he was 'an officer with good capacity for command and leadership, most popular with all ranks and a good influence. Possessed of tact and good temper. Is reliant [*sic*] and energetic.' [10]

This report is hardly enthusiastic and gives no indication of any potential this young man might have had. Gott's contemporaries were a high-quality group of officers and the probability is that he did not to stand out in their company as being exceptional in any way.

The report, like the one quoted previously, falls into the 'average' category. However, it is interesting to note that over an officer's career the same adjectives are usually used to describe him. The fact is that one's personal qualities and personality do not vary much over the years; the only variable is 'performance'. The individual's growing experience, confidence and widening skill base, in turn, affect that performance.

This was the first time Gott's ability as a leader had been mentioned in his documents, but it was by no means the last. Equally significant were the observations on his popularity and his equable temperament – the latter being one of his prime characteristics.

Erskine looked back fondly to a period when their first and overriding priority was soldiering and the training for operations. The welfare of the riflemen was the second priority. The Battalion conducted its affairs very formally when on parade, but off parade all officers were equal – well, almost! A 'slight'[11] degree of deference was paid to age and service and the Colonel could never be anything other than 'Colonel'. The atmosphere in the Mess was very convivial and Erskine remarked:

> There were no cliques and no rank consciousness. In the Mess we wore no badges of rank on our mess kit to emphasise that rank had nothing to do with our relation to each other within the Mess. The only criterion was that we did our job loyally by each other and conformed to an unwritten standard, which was a high one.

Elsewhere in the Army every regiment was adapting to peacetime conditions, with varying degrees of success, and seeking to resurrect the best of their old traditions, tempered by the experience of a bloody war. Erskine and Gott were fortunate to be members of an elite and Erskine commented that they served with:

> a strong element of officers who had done well in the war and who knew how to create a peacetime army. It was a combination of these two qualities that mattered. Bernard Majendie, our Colonel, had the

standard he required already ... but this put a further edge on his appetite.

It would seem that Strafer watched, listened and learned from the talented officers with whom he served. Erskine named some of them and identified their particular strengths. He observed, shrewdly:

> Strafer watched all of this and in his own sweet way extracted the best of the ideas around him. That summer of 1923 at Quetta was packed with interest and during this time WHEG established himself as a fine regimental officer who found no difficulty in obtaining, in very full measure, the confidence of his Company and the respect of everyone around him.

As 1923 drew to a close the Battalion moved to Rawalpindi and George Erskine was appointed Adjutant of the 1st Battalion, an indication of his merit because that is a prestigious job, usually reserved for the brightest and best. The change of appointment meant that the two men still worked closely together but their professional relationship had altered subtly, although for the rest of Strafer's life Erskine was his devoted acolyte and admirer.

From the mid-nineteenth century the British Army in India devoted much of its energy to an extraordinary schedule of unit moves, which involved great cost and enormous human effort. With hindsight one does wonder what these exhausting peregrinations achieved. The road from Lucknow to Peshawar is a thousand miles of an almost geometrically straight road. It was along that Grand Trunk Road that regiments and battalions marched north-west or south-east from cantonment to cantonment under a hot sun: 12 miles a day – sometimes 15 – all of this through clouds of choking dust, accompanied by myriad flies that together made the exercise an unattractive way to spend a summer's day.

At the day's end a bivouac area was reached and first and foremost the horses had to be fed, watered, groomed and made comfortable. This was before there could be any thought of pitching camp or getting food; the needs of the men, although below those of the horses, were nevertheless well above those of the officers. In the order of priority the officers came last.

Rawalpindi was a large and popular station, which housed three British battalions. The 1st Battalion, King's Royal Rifle Corps was, initially at least, part of the Abbottabad Brigade. However, British battalions moved between all three brigades, in a regular circular migration. Thus it seems that, notwithstanding the passage of at least eighty years, the culture of the Army in India had changed not one whit. Erskine advises that 'Baggage was moved by bullock cart and the men marched between staging posts.' The Ist Battalion decided that it was a 'two-stage battalion' and instead of marching 15 miles per day it would cover 30. That takes some endurance in temperatures hovering around 100°F and to be successful *all* the participants had to complete the day's journey. The 60th did not find this a problem. However, Strafer looked for even more strenuous challenges:

> He produced a scheme to march to the [illegible] hills via Abbottabad. It was a long way round and a very rough mountain track, quite impassable ... Such expeditions were very good training and we made the most of it. [12]

Inevitably the personalities changed. Two officers departed for the Staff College, the CO's tenure expired and with deep regret the Battalion saw the departure of Bernard Majendie. Other officers were routinely posted elsewhere on promotion or on appointment. New blood arrived from England but life in the 1st Battalion, KRRC did not miss a beat.

By 1924 Strafer began to think that he too needed a change of scene. An opportunity arose when the KRRC's territorial battalion required an adjutant. Although he was by now an experienced company commander, he nevertheless accepted the post with 13th Battalion, City of London Regiment (13 CLR), which had previously been titled 3rd (Volunteer) Battalion, KRRC. He took up his new job on 18 September 1925[13] and relieved Major MV Manley MC of The Border Regiment. This was not a career move – he was in effect moving sideways and downwards.

Service with the TA was at the other end of the military spectrum to that of service in India. The upside was that the job was in London; most young officers can bear the bright lights and Strafer was no exception. He was in reach of his family and the job was refreshingly different. Very different.

The Regiment was spread across the metropolis of London in small packets – a platoon here, a company there. These small groups by dint of the geography operated almost independently. It was the Adjutant's task to administer this miscellany of small packages and develop a cohesive whole. Not the least of the problems was that the Regiment was underfunded and ill equipped. It has ever been thus. The unit rarely assembled as a regiment – usually only at annual camp, held at one of the major training areas in the summer of each year.

The job of adjutant, especially in a TA battalion, required an incumbent to have a flexible attitude, a sense of humour and a capacity to cope with professional frustration on a daily basis. He also had to serve the countless demands of his commanding officer, who was himself usually a volunteer and a part-time soldier.

It seems that Strafer Gott was thought to be such a man. To succeed he had to accept that members of the TA viewed soldiering as 'a hobby, a bit of fun'. He had to realise that whilst they were prepared to 'fix swords – charge'[14] on Sunday afternoon, by Monday morning they had to be back delivering the mail, driving the taxi or dealing with customers in the bank.

Strafer buckled down to the job, adjusted to working every weekend and, in the summer of 1926; Erskine came to see him when the Regiment was 'in camp'. George Erskine swiftly found himself co-opted and remarked wryly, 'I had my first taste of soldiering with the Territorial Army.'

Gott's tour with 13th Battalion, City of London Regiment took him out of the KRRC spotlight and no records have survived of these two years other than one of his confidential reports that said:

> As Adjutant of 13 London Regiment in 1925/26 he has carried out his duties most creditably in every respect and it is largely through his zeal, knowledge and energy that the Battalion has made a marked improvement.[15]

On the face of it that is a perfectly satisfactory report but it is rather less than an efficient, hardworking and enthusiastic adjutant would expect from his CO. The report is a bit thin and it would have been helpful if the reporter had specified just what the 'marked improvement' was. This report was not likely to hasten Captain Gott to a major's crown, nor does it mark out Captain William Gott MC as a rising star. The move to London had not been professionally productive.

Gott completed his lengthy tour with the TA and it was not until 1928 that he moved back into the family circle and joined the 2nd Battalion, KRRC, at Jellalabad Barracks in Tidworth, as a company commander. Photographs taken at the time show that the pencil-slim young man of 1919 had blossomed into a large, full-framed, robust-looking officer.

Tidworth was an agreeable station. The Mess was identical to those of the same vintage in Aldershot, having been built to the same design. However, it was no warmer! The training areas were on the doorstep and the 2nd Battalion had all the space of Salisbury Plain upon which to practise its battle drills. Within easy striking distance were Andover, Amesbury and Salisbury. London was 'getatable'. There was cricket, golf, polo, hunting and shooting, in its many forms. Strafer settled into his new command and breathed a sigh of relief at being back with regular soldiers.

In 1928 Strafer's father, Lieutenant Colonel William Henry Gott, was seventy-six. He was a distinguished man and was summarised by *The Times* on 28 August 1929 which said that he was:

Educated at Harrow and Cambridge, he was a JP, for the West Riding, Lord of the Manor of Armley, and had served for many years in the 4th Bn (Militia) West Yorkshire Regiment. He is the head of a family, which had taken a prominent part in the affairs of Leeds and the West Riding for over 150 years.

The Colonel was a Yorkshireman to his bootstraps and, like all Yorkshiremen, had no doubts as to his place in the order of things; indeed, there was a view then, still firmly held today, that God is a Yorkshireman. The Colonel reviewed his domestic and financial affairs and, no doubt after a degree of consultation with his three children, decided to dispose of the family seat of Armley House and move to a house called Woodlands, in Selling, near Faversham, Kent.

Armley House was gifted to the City of Leeds. It was renamed Gott's Park and today houses a golf club. This was a momentous change in family life and why the elderly couple would want to abandon their lifetime associations in Yorkshire for Kent is unexplained. At least Strafer had his parents a little closer.

Major G De Pree was a newly commissioned officer when he joined the 2nd Battalion, KRRC in Tidworth. Later (in November 1983) he recalled[16] the period when the Battalion was part of 7th (Experimental) Infantry Brigade, which was a guinea pig formation for all the latest War Office ideas – both good and bad. These came from in-house 'experts', foreign attachés and military correspondents. The 2nd Battalion evolved into what eventually became a motorised battalion. De Pree, who was clearly somewhat in awe of Gott, wrote:

> Strafer was in it right from the beginning – even trying out our new petrol cookers, which continued to blow up in our faces years later in the desert. He commanded C Company, one of the three rifle companies, which still marched on foot. The Company Commander had a charger, but this animal was usually led by a groom. The Machine Gun Company was mechanised with Carden Loyds [17] and personnel carriers.

Strafer's sunny personality and sense of fun made him a key member of the Mess in Tidworth and he 'lived in', as was the custom for unmarried officers of his rank. This was reflected in a confidential report written on him in 1929. In the view of his commanding officer he was:

> Invaluable as a regimental officer and can be entirely relied upon to run any kind of activity in the Battalion. Good organiser, a great asset in the Officers' Mess, highly popular with his brother officers and radiates good tone.[18]

This is a much more useful report and it recognises not only the efficiency but also the personal qualities of a man who had been generating affection from his comrades for some years. The report went on to say:

> He is well above the average for his rank and age in military knowledge; he will make a splendid staff officer and battalion commander. I very strongly recommend him for promotion to brevet[19] major for the good of the Army.

The contrast between this report and those that had preceded it is enormous. In part this is a reflection upon the earlier reporters who did not identify in sufficient detail the key aspects of Strafer Gott's personality and its impact upon those around him. The system was not perfect and every officer was dependent upon his commanding officer's penmanship for recognition. Nothing much has changed in the last eighty-three years; the written opinions of commanding officers still remain on an officer's personal file in perpetuity and they provide the basis for, and a road map of, his career.

It is of note that while he was still a captain, his card had been marked as a future battalion commander. This was and is not unique, but it is, certainly, unusual. This latest report is at variance with those that preceded it and is markedly more complimentary.

Strafer's morale may well have been boosted by this glowing testimonial but bad news arrived around the same time because in August 1929, his father died. Perhaps Colonel Gott had foreseen his demise the previous year when he had gifted Armley House. Judging by his will, originally drafted in 1903 and amended by two codicils dated 1914 and January 1928, the Colonel had taken great care to preserve his estate for his family. He put his affairs in order and 'save and except settled land', his estate was valued at £75,757 – a vast sum of money in 1928.[20]

On 8 January 1930, Captain GWEJ Erskine married Miss Ruby de la Rue at St Margaret's, Westminster. He paid Strafer the compliment of asking him to be his best man and the day was another building block in their friendship. It was a rather grand wedding, as befitted the son of General George Elphinstone Erskine (1841-1912) of the Bombay Cavalry.

Strafer Gott knew that if he was to achieve professional success then attendance at the Staff College in Camberley was a prerequisite. Entry to the Staff College was by way of a competitive examination and the unqualified recommendation of his commanding officer. The course lasted a year and on its completion graduating officers were distributed across the face of the Army to fill staff appointments, some more prestigious than others. That most recent report was a valuable vehicle in Strafer's journey to Camberley. The examination would be a stern test of a candidate's intellect and professional ability. Gott started to prepare for the examination and that now took priority over the active social life of Tidworth garrison. Major De Pree, who was there, observed:

> During this time [early 1930] Strafer was working for the Staff College ... so he was pretty busy but always very approachable and, above all, amusing. Whether it was in the cold dawn by a lonely clump of trees on Salisbury Plain or in the Mess, his sense of humour and of the ridiculous are the most vivid memories of him ... no need to go to the theatre to see and hear Tom Walls, Ralph Lynn and Robertson Hare.

On 18 December 1930, Strafer's younger brother John married Evelyn Grahame in St Baldred's Church, North Berwick. Interestingly, Strafer was not the best man but Rosamund, the groom's elder sister, was a bridesmaid. John had married into an army family and his father-in-law was a serving lieutenant colonel.

Meanwhile, in Germany, a man called Adolf Hitler was working hard to establish a place for himself in an increasingly militant Germany. Only a little more than a decade had passed since the end of the war but the savage reparations demanded of Germany by the Allies had, in accordance with the 'Law of Unintended Consequences', given birth to an aggressive, self-confident country likely to be difficult to accommodate in the future.

The Staff College examination was taken in the summer of 1930 and after some anxious moments came the news that Strafer Gott had passed. In January 1931[21] Strafer reported to Camberley and threw himself into a hand-picked society that would be part of the rest of his life. His contemporaries were the brightest and best and to excel in their company was going to be difficult. The instructors had, in their time at Camberley, similarly been the brightest and best. It was, and is, a meritocracy.

Strafer took on the role of Secretary of the Drag Hunt and he was thought to be 'painstaking and very efficient'.[22] This job was not part of the course but nevertheless; 'extra-mural' activities at Camberley were closely watched and reported upon.

Reading between the lines Strafer Gott acquitted himself well enough at the Staff College but was a no more than a 'middle-of-the-road' student. His instructors took the view that he was 'an officer of the very good solid type'. That is hardly a ringing endorsement and perhaps best left unsaid. However, he was also described as 'cheerful, attractive, with a strong personality backed by strength of character, self-confidence and determination'.[23] That is very much better.

Strafer's personal qualities did not pass unnoticed and he was judged to be 'ready to accept responsibility, energetic and hard-working, thoroughly loyal and reliable'.[24]

Writing a report on another person calls for skilled penmanship, empathy and the capacity to detect, as yet, untapped potential. In the Army, the reality is that a senior reports on his juniors and their futures can stand or fall on his ability to produce objective, shrewd and fair judgments of their performance. Often a report tells the reader more about the reporter than the reported. At the Staff College Strafer was fortunate, because officers with the requisite skills compiled the reports written on him. Thus it was observed that he was:

> Popular and imperturbable. He works well with others and has the personality and temperament that enables him to get the best out of others and inspire their confidence ...

If ever there was a description of a leader then this is it. However, there are caveats because Strafer was also said to be:

> Better at tactical and administrative work than at dealing with bigger problems. A rather slow but methodical thinker with a sound judgment and plenty of common sense. Rather lacking in imagination and breadth of view, expresses himself clearly and well – verbally and on paper. The former without any sign of nervousness.[25]

In summary, the Staff College view of William Gott was:

> A tall and strongly built, physically fit and active officer. His professional knowledge is good all round: sound and practical. He should make a good staff officer and a *better commander*.[26] (Author's italics.)

How very perceptive was that last phrase.

They seem to have got Strafer's measure but, even in this academic forcing house, there was no suggestion that he lacked intellectual ability. 'Slow but methodical thinker with sound judgment and plenty of common sense' is not in the least derogatory.

It had probably occurred to Strafer Gott that, at thirty-four, his unmarried friends were starting to get a little thin on the ground but, as yet, the right girl had not come along – although there was a girl called Pamela Kays who had attracted Strafer's attention.

The Kays family lived in Farnham, Surrey. Farnham is no great distance from Camberley and Pamela's father, Brigadier-General Walpole Kays CMG, had been most civil when first they met – well, he would be, as he too was an officer of the 60th. The Brigadier, although long since retired, nevertheless kept up to date on regimental affairs and he was well briefed on this young fellow Gott and his prospects.

Hummm ... seems to be a good chap; might do well.

The Staff College course was completed at the end of 1931 and, on graduation, William Henry Ewart Gott would now bear the highly valued post nominal letters 'psc' (always lower case) after his name in military records. A new avenue of employment had opened up for him and he would move through the Army in either regimental jobs, serving with soldiers, or on 'The Staff', in which he would be engaged in 'helping the units whether they liked it or not', in the words of a cynic of old.

Professional matters were far from his mind when he gave away his sister Rosamund at her marriage to Mr William Wade-Dalton at St Peter's, Cranley Gardens in Kensington on 10 February 1932. The groom hailed from Yorkshire, so that was all right.

The Times recorded the part played by 'Captain Gott 60th Rifles' and so that brevet majority, anticipated and hoped for, had not yet materialised. The Reverend Charles Gott, an uncle of John, Rosamund and William, officiated at the marriage and the family was present in full force. Mrs Gott, the bride's mother, gave her address as 2 Brechin Place, South Kensington.[27]

When the successful students were given their new postings there was disappointment for some and Strafer was probably one of that number. The top-graded officers left for the War Office to fill jobs close to the hub of things or to major overseas commands but again close to the centre of power. Their appointments were a reflection of their performance at Camberley.

At the other end of the scale, in 1933 Strafer was dispatched to a minor headquarters in Calcutta. Here he was to be DAA & QMG.[28] In this job he was responsible for managing, coordinating and controlling all the administrative and logistic issues in the Command. In effect he had his fingers in a multiplicity of military pies, some of which posed issues of which he had absolutely no practical knowledge at all. He learnt quickly and realised that applied common sense was actually more useful than poorly exercised expertise – fortunately, he had common sense in abundance. Major ML Buller MC endorsed that common sense approach when he recalled:

> When we were in Calcutta there was a great deal of talk about the length of time some officers had to wait to be promoted. The Rifle Brigade, our sister regiment, was notoriously slow. This was a good deal their own fault, as they had refused accelerated promotion into other regiments. Strafer roundly condemned such an attitude. He made all allowance for reluctance to leave one's regiment, but he said it was 'one's duty, if selected for the good of the Army to go elsewhere, to accept and do all one could to raise the standard of some other regiment, however poor one privately thought it and never to patronise it.' He was a very great man in every way and I wish so much that I had served more with him.[29]

India was a turbulent country. By 1933 the demand for independence was growing ever louder and, on the North-West Frontier, Indian and British troops of the Indian Army were engaged on constant, low-intensity operations. The Indian Army was in urgent need of reform as it had changed little in the previous fifty years. There was a lot to do even though Calcutta was far from any fighting.

Officers serving in India were permitted to return to the UK on leave and in 1933 Strafer took three months, from 17 June, to come home, when he caught up with family life and its affairs. He spent some time in Farnham, an agreeable little market town with certain social attractions in the shape of Miss Kays.

He was made brevet major in January 1934, about five years after his recommendation.[30] It was 'nice to have' but had no practical benefit as he was promoted a substantive major six months later. [31] On 1 January 1934 he took up a new appointment as General Staff Officer, Grade 2 (GSO 2) P&A District.[32] In this job Strafer had responsibility for operations and the training for operations. He answered to a lieutenant colonel, a GSO 1. The new job went well, very well and in 1934, Strafer's annual report, written by the GSO 1, was unequivocal:

> Outstanding, possesses character, brains and a logical reasoned outlook. Liked and respected by all, is doing excellently in his present appointment. Well above the average of his rank and there are possibilities in this officer.[33]

There are two key words in that short paragraph and the first of these is 'outstanding'. This is a word usually applied very sparingly indeed in an officer's report and its appearance here is significant. The second word is 'excellently'. Excellent and its derivatives are also used infrequently but when they are employed it is similarly significant. The report concluded: 'In the interest of the Service he should be transferred to a similar appointment at a command headquarters at the end of his two years.'

Change was in the air, especially on the domestic front. During his tour in Calcutta Strafer had been writing regularly to Pamela Kays. He took three months' leave from 21 May 1934 and sailed home, but he had something on his mind. The leave was extended until September. Clearly, something was in the air.

The 'something' was the announcement of the engagement of Strafer and Pamela on 7 June 1934.[34] Their marriage followed three weeks later at St Andrew's Church, Farnham, at which Uncle Charles, once again, officiated. Captain Sydney de Salis KRRC was the best man. Strafer had made a good choice and he and Pamela were devoted to one another.

Major and Mrs Gott travelled out to India and moved into married quarters.

It was as well that she came from an army background because there is a culture gap between leafy Farnham and hot, dusty, crowded India. That said, life in the sub-continent between the wars was very comfortable. The Gotts could well afford house servants and they lived in some comfort and style.

On 31 May 1935, an earthquake of 7.7 Mw occurred about 100 miles from Quetta – a major British garrison town that housed the Indian Staff College, among other units. A Colonel Bernard L Montgomery was an instructor there at this time. The city of Quetta was destroyed and loss of life was estimated at 30,000-60,000. This was a national catastrophe and the Army was the prime component in the rescue operation.

The carnage was more concentrated and grotesque than anything Bernard could have witnessed in the Great War; indeed, the scale of the disaster was so great that the Army Commander ordered the entire city to be ringed with barbed wire and sealed off like an amputated limb.[35]

The 1st Battalion, The Queen's Royal Regiment based in Quetta, was heavily involved in the operations that followed the disaster and six months later its regimental journal carried the following report:

> It is not possible to describe the state of the city when the Battalion first saw it. It was razed to the ground. Corpses were lying everywhere in the hot sun and every available vehicle in Quetta was being used for the transportation of injured. … Companies were given areas in which to clear the dead and injured. Battalion Headquarters were established at the Residency. Hardly had we commenced our work when we were called upon to supply a party of fifty men, which were later increased to a hundred, to dig graves in the cemetery.

The extreme heat of an Indian summer aggravated the awful situation because bodies had started to putrefy at the moment of death. This attracted a plague of flies that feasted on the dead – the stench turned the stomach. It was a gruesome task to recover the corpses of European and Anglo-Indian victims and then, after the briefest of funerals, conducted by Army chaplains, bury them in hastily dug graves. Indian casualties were assembled for mass cremations in accordance with their religious needs. All civil communication systems were destroyed and the Royal Signals set up telephone and radio links to fill the void.

Strafer was serving some distance from the disaster area but nevertheless his headquarters had a responsibility to assist in the coordination of the military response. It was a case of 'all hands to the pumps'. Much of this work fell on his shoulders although the relief work was essentially a major logistic task. As a staff officer this crisis was in Strafer's particular bailiwick and the aftermath of the Quetta earthquake was longstanding and harrowing for everyone involved.

While Strafer was engaged in Quetta's disaster, his previous confidential report had rung some responsive bells. As a result, he was warned of a move at the end of the year to another Grade 2 staff job but in the much bigger Command Headquarters in Calcutta. The Gotts took home leave some few weeks after the earthquake and the contrast must have been very marked on their return to a green, tranquil and well-ordered Farnham.

Gott seems to have had the capacity to charm everyone who came within his orbit. He did it naturally, easily and unconsciously. It was a characteristic upon which a succession of people remarked. It was, of course, a valuable leadership tool. Soldiers *want* to like their commander and if he is naturally likeable, then so much the better: the product of this 'likability' is a desire, generated among the soldiers, to please their leader and never to let him down.

In 1935 Gott was acknowledged to have 'a thorough knowledge of staff and regimental duties'. That is an unremarkable observation given that he was in his third Grade 2 job after Staff College. It was not all work and no play because it was noted that Gott 'played polo and led an active life'. However, his confidential report went deeper and vouchsafed that he had:

> An outstanding personality. He combines common sense, a sense of proportion and a sense of humour to an uncommon degree, knows his own mind and can get all things done without friction, deservedly popular with both staff and regimental officers, has an active brain and is a most conscientious and thorough worker and entirely reliable.[36]

This report focuses upon Strafer's personality and by now his file was starting to show the same traits being identified by several reporting officers.

Strafer now moved on to a pure 'Q' or logistic job as DAQMG[37] Headquarters, Baluchistan District,[38] on 12 February 1936, replacing Major FC Simpson of the 17th Dogra Rifles. This was an area he was familiar with having previously served in Rawalpindi with his regiment back in 1923. Pam Gott had her first house move on posting, with all the domestic upheaval that entailed. Army wives are a breed apart and need to be. They have to be self-reliant, practical and stoic. It seems that Pam Gott was all of these. Strafer thrived in this new appointment, sufficiently so that in his next report his commander was very brief. He wrote:

> I classify Major Gott as outstanding and consider that his rapid advancement is in the interests of the Service.[39]

There was that word 'outstanding' again. The Gotts' period in India was drawing to a close because Strafer was due to return to regimental duty in 1938. However, the job in Baluchistan had to be completed first and by now with his

66

confidence matched by his experience the new DAQMG excelled. He was riding very high in the esteem of his superiors and his report in late 1937 summed him up as being an:

> exceptionally confident officer, much above the average. In every way outstanding. Excels in the three senses – common – proportion – humour. Has more general interests and is more a man of the world than the majority of officers.[40]

The final sentence of that report is intriguing. We know that Gott was an enthusiastic full bore shot and that he played polo. Similarly he was a gregarious person and an amusing companion off parade. The probability is that marriage had widened his horizons and he was acute enough to realise that, as a European war was a possibility, he should prepare himself for it.

In December 1937 the Gotts moved back to the UK. The sea voyage gave them a chance to refresh themselves before Strafer assumed the command of Headquarters Company, 2nd Battalion, KRRC. The Battalion had been stationed in Salamanca Barracks, Aldershot, since 1935 and had its corporate feet comfortably under the garrison table. This time, instead of Strafer living in one of the drafty messes of yore, he and his wife moved into one of the Victorian era, married officers' quarters with which Aldershot was well furnished. However, the MOQs were pretty drafty too.

Strafer's ability had been recognised in the stygian depths of the Military Secretary's Department in the War Office and he had been earmarked as an officer with the potential to go further. However, there is a system designed to ensure that promotion is gained purely on merit with seniority just a minor factor taken into consideration. There are no short cuts for the sons of generals, or those of monarchs, for that matter.

A board of senior officers sits to sift through the reports of officers who are in the promotion bracket. This bracket is usually delineated by age in peacetime; this is to keep the rank structure and its pyramid in order. The board members individually award a score to each of the 'runners' confidential reports. The scores are then debated and an order of merit is established. It is a time-consuming and very clinical process, but it works.

There is a place for 29-year-old brigadiers in wartime,[41] as Michael Carver amply proved with Michael Calvert (thirty-one) and John Profumo (thirty) just behind, although such early promotions would be unmanageable in peacetime.

In 1937 Gott was in the promotion zone and, at thirty-nine, was hardly a young candidate but then promotion between the wars was notoriously slow. Montgomery, for example was still a captain at thirty-seven, although he was promoted to major at thirty-eight and brevet lieutenant colonel soon afterwards.[42] Gott was, if anything, ahead of his better-known and much older comrade. There are several fundamental differences that set the two men apart and these are considered, briefly, in the closing chapters of this book.

Like every officer before and since, Strafer was concerned about his promotion to lieutenant colonel. This is the most important time in any officer's career and a promotion to lieutenant colonel 'first time in the hat' is a positive marker for the future. Not only did he have a degree of professional anxiety, but he also had the additional concerns of an expectant father. Pamela was pregnant with their first child, due in late February 1937.

Diana Elizabeth appeared, a little late on parade, on 1 March 1937. Her birthplace was recorded as 86 Harley House, London NW1. This is and was a smart address in North London, not far from Regent's Park. It may have been a private nursing home but whatever the reason that persuaded Pamela to give birth there, it certainly was not the most convenient place for a father serving in Aldershot.

Aldershot, a major garrison town, was blessed with the Louise Margaret Maternity Hospital, an establishment that had been delivering the progeny of soldiers for years and was more than equipped to cope with the birth of little Miss Gott. The address 2 Brechin Place, Kensington, appeared on Diana's birth certificate as the 'residence of the informant, WHE Gott, father'. This was still the home of his mother, Mrs Gott senior.

Twenty-seven years later, on 18 November 1964, that little girl was to marry Major Charles Taylor of the 5th Royal Inniskilling Dragoon Guards. Lieutenant General Lord Norrie, about whom much more will be heard later, gave her away.

The baby safely born, the deliberations of the Promotion Board were duly published and it came as no great surprise to anyone when WHE Gott's name appeared on the list of successful officers. He was selected to take command of the 1st Battalion of his regiment in October 1938. This appointment was the culmination of his career to date. He had achieved the unspoken goal of every officer – command of his own regiment.

That all lay in the future and in the meantime there was a Headquarter Company to command and the training to equip it to take its place in the new Mobile Division. This Mobile Division looked likely to have an outing sooner rather than later as Hitler ratcheted up his demands and the atmosphere in Europe became increasingly tense.

The Commanding Officer of the 2nd Battalion was obliged to report on Strafer Gott in the middle of 1938. He wrote in the most glowing terms describing his subordinate as:

> An officer of outstanding ability. An immense help to me in the reorganisation and training of the Battalion in its new role. He has a quick brain, has sound tactical knowledge and his ability to impart it

to others is most marked. He is a first-class organiser and administrator, which was at once apparent when seeing the results of his own company. He has considerable experience on the staff in grade II appointments and all these attributes, combined with self-confidence and a keen sense of humour, make him an excellent leader and commander.

He is shrewd and can see things from a broader aspect. He has a great capacity for work and grasps essentials quickly and always puts work before everything. He is most popular with all ranks and I consider he is very much above average for his rank and age and he will make a fine commander both in peace and war.[43]

Well, you can't say fairer than that! The important and usual buzz words appear: 'outstanding', 'quick brain', 'first-class', 'self–confidence', 'popular' and 'sense of humour'. The War Office knew what it had in William Henry Ewart Gott and there was ample evidence that it had backed the right horse. The second reporting officer, who added his remarks to the report, gilded the lily somewhat. Reporting on a major he stuck his head over the reporting parapet and said:

I confirm that Major Gott is an exceptional officer of outstanding qualities. I consider that it will be in the interests of the Service to promote this officer to full colonel at an early date. This officer will make a first-class brigade commander now and I have the greatest confidence in recommending him for this appointment or for any first grade staff appointment. An officer who should be considered as qualified and capable of going a long way in the Army.[44]

Strafer Gott was certainly a high grade officer but he was, as yet, unproven as a battalion commander and to suggest that he should '*command a brigade now*' (author's italics) does seem to be more than a little over the top. As it happens, those apparently intemperate remarks were later seen to be little short of very shrewd indeed.

Chapter notes
1. Hare, Major General Sir Steuart, *The Annuls of King's Royal Rifle Corps*, Vol. V, p.2.
2. Now known as Army Golf Club. Lieutenant Colonel EH Sartorius VC founded the Aldershot Divisional Golf Club in 1883. Since then the Club has had five titles and has played over eight courses laid out in the Watt's Common, Rushmoor Bottom and Laffan's Plain areas of what was the military training area.
3. Hare, Major General Sir Steuart, *The Annuls of King's Royal Rifle Corps*, Vol. V.
4. SS *City of Sparta* (5,415 tons) was owned by the American India line and employed on the Southampton route, until she was broken up in 1931.

5. Mhow was a cantonment in the Indore District in Madhya Pradesh, India. It is located 14 miles south of Indore city towards Mumbai on the Mumbai-Agra Road.
6. Erskine, Major General GWEJ CB DSO, unpublished memoir, RGJ Museum archives, Winchester.
7. *The London Gazette* supplement, p.3,065, dated 15 April 1921.
8. Vernon, Brigadier HRW, *Strafer Gott*, p.26, original source, WHEG personal file, MoD archive.
9. Erskine, Major General GWEJ CB DSO, unpublished memoir, RGJ Museum archives, Winchester.
10. Vernon, Brigadier HRW, *Strafer Gott*, p.26, original source, WHEG personal file, MoD archive.
11. Erskine, Major General GWEJ CB DSO, unpublished memoir, RGJ Museum archives, Winchester.
12. Ibid.
13. *The London Gazette* supplement p.6,615. 13 October 1925.
14. The KRRC and, now, their modern counterparts, 'fix swords'; lesser organisations 'fix bayonets'.
15. Vernon, Brigadier HRW, *Strafer Gott*, p.26, original source, WHEG personal file, MoD archive.
16. Ibid, p.24.
17. The Carden Loyd tankettes, with a crew of two, were a series of small British tanks that were produced in several versions, of which the Mark VI was the most successful. It was so successful that it was manufactured under licence in several countries. The originators of the vehicle were Sir John Carden and Vivian Loyd.
18. Vernon, Brigadier HRW, *Strafer Gott*, p.26, original source, WHEG personal file, MoD archive.
19. There were two avenues for promotion in the British Infantry and Cavalry and these were the Regimental List and the Army List. Brevet rank applied only to the Army List. It was an award ostensibly for meritorious service, but patronage and good fortune were also factors.

   The Commander-in-Chief loosely controlled the number of brevet ranks in the Army, but there were no prescribed allocations for any particular rank. Those who were promoted to 'brevet' wore the badges of their brevet rank and were granted Army seniority in that rank. The downside was that they retained the responsibilities and pay of the lower regimental rank.

   The significant benefit enjoyed by brevets was that they were accumulating seniority in the brevet rank whilst their non-brevet fellows depended on regimental seniority only. It was a clumsy system that generated frustration and irritation and at this distance the merits of the system are difficult to discern.

   Predictably, the brevet system as it applied to the Foot Guards was different and vastly more advantageous – little wonder at the disproportionate number of general officers from the Foot Guards while the brevet system was in operation and, quite correctly, it was eventually discontinued.
20. District Probate Registry, Wakefield, Yorkshire, 6 December 1929.
21. *The London Gazette* supplement No. 33,572, p.428.
22. Vernon, Brigadier HRW, *Strafer Gott*, p.27, original source, WHEG personal file, MoD archive.
23. Ibid.
24. Ibid.

25. Ibid.
26. Ibid.
27. *The Times,* London, 10 February 1932.
28. Deputy Assistant Adjutant and Quartermaster General.
29. Vernon, Brigadier HRW, *Strafer Gott*, p23.
30. *The London Gazette* supplement No. 34,011, p.55, 2 January 1934.
31. *The London Gazette* supplement No. 34,071, p.4666, 20 July 1934.
32. The full particulars of 'P&A District' have been lost and so the significance of Strafer's appointment to this HQ is difficult to gauge.
33. Vernon, Brigadier HRW, *Strafer Gott*, p.27, original source, WHEG personal file, MoD archive.
34. *The Times*, 7 June 1934, p.17.
35. Hamilton, N., *Monty – The Making of a General*, p.238.
36. Vernon, Brigadier HRW, *Strafer Gott*, p.27, original source, WHEG personal file, MoD archive.
37. Deputy Assistant Quartermaster General.
38. *The London Gazette* supplement p.2,386, 10 April 193674.
39. Vernon, Brigadier HRW, *Strafer Gott*, p.27, original source, WHEG personal file, MoD archive.
40. Ibid.
41. The youngest officer to achieve one star rank was Brigadier Roland Boys Bradford VC MC (1892-1917). He was promoted at age twenty-five and killed in action ten days later.
42. Hamilton, N., *The Making of a General*, p176-9.
43. Vernon, Brigadier HRW. *Strafer Gott*, original source, WHEG personal file, MoD archive.
44. Ibid.

Chapter 7

And So to War
September 1939-June 1940

In 1938, 1st KRRC was serving in Burma and in that station it depended upon mules and horses for its transportation. It was an efficient battalion but even the Adjutant, Captain (later Colonel) JL Corbett-Winder, acknowledged, 'It was living in a world far removed from the reality of modern military life.'[1]

The Battalion's utopian existence ceased when it was moved to Abbassia, Egypt, and into the citadel on the outskirts of Cairo. The new Commanding Officer met the troopship at Suez and the transformation of the Battalion began that same day. Strafer 'hit the ground running':

> His first action on taking command was typical. He called together all the officers and told them that now the Battalion had to prepare for war. Games, polo, sporting and social life – all the accompaniments of peacetime soldiering – must now take second place to work, and work they did, and none worked harder than he. By the time war broke out in 1939, the Battalion was fully trained and equipped for desert war.[2]

The 1st Battalion, KRRC was to form part of the Mobile Force being established to thwart any Axis ambitions toward the Suez Canal. The Battalion had moved halfway around the world, it was adapting to its new environment, and then the CO set about changing just about everything.

More used to mule transport, communication by semaphore, signal lights and telephone, the Battalion had to make the transition to motor vehicles, personnel carriers and the wonder of radio communication. The CO oversaw in detail the training for these new systems. Gott had been through this process back in Tidworth with the 2nd Battalion. It really was a case of 'horses for courses' and Strafer Gott was the right man in the right job. Corbett-Winder said generously:

There were many difficulties, but Strafer quietly overcame them, arranging, so ably, courses in MT, signals, the new Bren gun, the sun compass, desert tactics and administration. This was an immense task, particularly situated as we were in the middle of Cairo – not the best place to train drivers!

But Strafer set about his problems with care and energetic efficiency. I can picture him now drafting his orders and training programmes with such speed and then going off to see that his orders were being carried out. And all the time *he was so deeply concerned with the effect his arrangements would have on the individuals concerned*.[3] [Author's italics]

That last sentence is worth considering again. The Army is not a democracy and a battalion functions at the will of its commanding officer. On that basis, it is neither absolutely necessary nor usually practical for a commanding officer to give his personal attention to the feelings of perhaps 650 individual soldiers. Of course it is desirable, but usually difficult, bordering impossible, to achieve. That, forty years later, Colonel Corbett-Winder should comment in this manner indicates that Gott probably went some way towards achieving the 'difficult, bordering impossible'. Speaking of him at this time, one of his young officers remarked, 'To us subalterns he was a most lovable god and we would have died for him.'[4]

By the middle of 1939 Pamela Gott was visibly pregnant, the clouds of war were gathering on the horizon and the pace of change was necessarily swift. Reluctantly it was decided that it would be best if Pamela and Diana (by now always known as Elizabeth) returned to the UK. It was, of course, a painful decision but home leave was always on the cards. In the meantime, and until that leave could be taken, Strafer concentrated on the job in hand. The activity in 1st Battalion, KRRC did not go unnoticed and only three months in command was sufficient for Gott to win the confidence of his commander, who reported upon him, somewhat prematurely, as being:

A marked personality, drive and power of command. Quite imperturbable. A good organiser. This unit has made most satisfactory progress in mechanisation. Moreover, he has himself assimilated the principles of his new role so well that he was able to train the unit efficiently to play a useful role in collective training in the Western Desert. I consider this a remarkable achievement due principally to the ability, energy and creative imagination of Lieutenant Colonel Gott. An outstanding officer whose advancement I can confidently recommend. GOC British Troops, Egypt, agrees and says it is remarkable how, due to his influence, his battalion has changed equipment organisation and role in so short a time. Lieutenant Colonel Gott maintains a high standard himself and demands it of his officers, who give most cheerfully of their best. Even though he has been so short a time in command I [would] gladly accept him as a brigadier or senior staff officer now.

That adjective 'outstanding' is now such a regular feature of his reports as to be almost routine. 'Imperturbable' and other similar words are also usual but this particular report did not mention 'sense of humour'. Perhaps this commander had just not noticed.

It is readily conceded that Strafer Gott's passage towards the upper levels of the military firmament seems to be inevitable, irresistible and thoroughly well deserved. However, the reader might at some point be expecting to find some light and shade in this biography, some indication of his fallibility, a weakness, perhaps, even amounting to a flaw in his character.

Did he ever make mistakes?

Were there times when he drank too much?

Was he ever irascible, discourteous or unthinking?

Did he use bad language?

Did he cheat at golf or cards?

Did he have poor table manners?

Was he a dangerous driver?

Did he gamble, womanise or have any other weaknesses?

If he did have any of these deficiencies then no one ever took the trouble to record it. Not one word to his detriment has even been as much as breathed.

Only the Italians and Germans were left to expose any weakness that he might have had and it would not be too long before they came into his life – in large numbers and armed to the teeth.

Given the state of the world, Egypt was a good place not to be and so a pregnant Pamela Gott returned to England with Elizabeth. She took up residence in the recently purchased family home in Waverley Avenue in Fleet. This was only about 7 miles from her parents' home in Farnham. Strafer's Adjutant, Corbett-Winder, recalled:

He was completely selfless in all his work – indeed, in all his life. When we were discussing leave arrangements for all early in 1939, the problem arose as to when the CO and Adjutant would take theirs. Typically, he detailed the Adjutant to go first. Sadly, this decision meant that Strafer never got home to England nor did he see his second daughter, Jennifer, whose godfather I am proud to be.

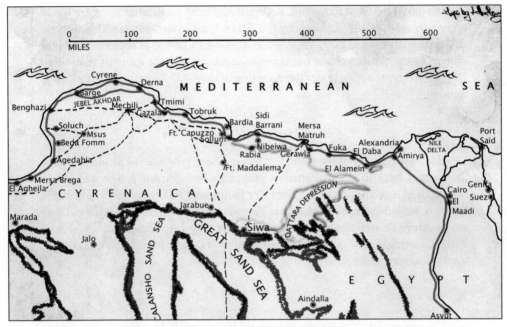

North Africa – the arena over which Strafer Gott fought. (Map by Arthur Perry)

By late summer 1939 1st KRRC was in good order, it was newly equipped and morale was high. The news that the CO was to move to be GSO1 at the Headquarters of the Armoured Division was heard with dismay all round, 'but by this time thanks to his example and inspiring leadership,' said Corbett–Winder, 'the Battalion was highly trained and ready for the battles that he always so clearly foresaw. All ranks were devoted to him.'

Strafer moved on and command of the Battalion fell to Major SCF de Salis, Strafer's great friend and former best man. At the turn of the year his other great chum, Bobby Erskine, was to take command of the 2nd Battalion. It was on 25 August 1939 that, while Gott was playing himself in at Divisional Headquarters, the 1st Battalion, KRRC drove out of the citadel and went to its allotted war station.

In 1938, garrison troops in North Africa were reorganised to counter any Italian thrust toward the Suez Canal and were established at Mersa Matruh, about 120 miles west of Alexandria. Initially this organisation was titled 'Mobile Force' but in September 1939 was renamed 'Armoured Division (Egypt)'; it was to this headquarters that Strafer Gott reported, serving under the all too fleeting command of the brilliant Major General Percy Hobart. The GOC was soon to be summarily sacked and sent to retirement by Wavell.[6] He was the first of the many generals to be removed from command during the desert campaign.

75

The move to war stations on 25 August had been predicated upon the likely early advance of the Italians to the Suez Canal, notwithstanding that no declaration of war had been made. There followed a period of considerable anti-climax as the Italians made no aggressive moves and the units of Armoured Division (Egypt) acting under the direction of the GSO 1 applied themselves to training.

* * *

Despite the inactivity of the Italians it had not been possible for Strafer to make the journey back to UK as Pamela's pregnancy ran its course. She was safely delivered of a second daughter, Jennifer Faith, on 23 October 1939. This time the birth was at the Louise Margaret Hospital in Aldershot. This little girl was the daughter Strafer was never to see. It was a long way ahead but, on 30 June 1961, Colonel SC de Salis, one of her godfathers, gave Jennifer in marriage to Captain Alick Cubitt.

* * *

By Christmas 1939, with no action in the immediate offing, some units withdrew to their earlier peacetime locations.

On 16 February 1940, Armoured Division (Egypt) was renamed and took the name that would become legendary: 7th Armoured Division – the 'Desert Rats'. The new General Officer Commanding replacing Hobart was Major General Sir Michael O'M Creagh. However, on the renaming, the GOC formed a Pivot Group and placed it under the command of Strafer Gott. This organisation was, in effect, an independent brigade and was later renamed 'Support Group'. So, setting aside his responsibilities as GSO 1 and giving the rank of colonel a miss (which was not unusual), Strafer put up the badges of brigadier. In eighteen months Gott had advanced from being a major commanding a company in the 2nd Battalion to brigade commander. This was an eye-catching speed of promotion.

The area in which operations were to be carried out in 1940 was called, inaccurately, the 'Western Desert'. It was then and is today an unattractive, rocky area about 240 miles long (east to west) and 150 deep (north to south). The northern boundary is the sea and along the coast were scattered small settlements such as Mersa Matruh, Sidi Barrani, Sollum, Bardia and Tobruk – names that would be blood-stained ere long. The coastal strip was host to most of the indigenous population and it varied in width before rising, in the south, to about 500 feet and to the escarpment above, known as the Libyan Plateau. It would prove to be a significant feature in the fighting that was to come. The escarpment allowed access to wheeled and tracked vehicles in only a few places. The Official History[7] said:

> While the whole region is desert, it is not the waste of sand that the name suggests. Except in the sandy coastal strip, there is limestone rock lying close below the surface of clay or fine sand, often breaking through in irregular patches. Pebbles, small boulders and low scrub are frequent and give a distinctive blackish colour to the desert at a distant view.
>
> To the south lies a vast and forbidding tract almost devoid of habitation other than the oases of Jarabub and Siwa, the last ports of call before the inhospitable Sand Sea. Just to the north-east of the ill-favoured Siwa, the un-navigable and impassable Qattara Depression forms a major obstacle. To the west there are no natural boundaries but the 240-mile mark is a line drawn south from Gazala into the southern wastes. The desert is also home to flies, trillions and trillions of them.
>
> The flies were everywhere – an infestation of enormous beasts that would come down and pinch the food off your plate unless you continuously waved your hands about, and this is what men learned to do. It was said that for nine months of the year you were waving your hands in front of your face then it took the next three months to get out of the habit. There was no escape, however far you went into the desert the flies followed. You just got used to it.[8]

In 1940 the Italians had two standing armies in Libya, the 5th and the 10th, with the capacity to advance and seize that absolutely vital artery, the Suez Canal. Notwithstanding the fact that Egypt was a sovereign country the British had, by treaty,[9] the right to defend the Suez Canal.

An uneasy stand-off situation obtained for the first six months of 1940 and for the British this was a useful period in which to make preparations for the attack that was fully expected. Strafer made best use of the time available and he worked to forge an identity and esprit in his Support Group.

On 10 June 1940, Italy finally declared war against Britain and France. Britain faced the reality of fighting those two armies, the Italian 5th Army in Tripolitania and the 10th Army in Cyrenaica. Colonel TE Lawrence had expressed a view on desert campaigning when he said:

> Desert operations should be like wars at sea in their mobility, their ubiquity, their independence of bases and communications, their lack of ground features, of strategic areas of fixed directions of fixed points.[10]

The Italians had massive superiority in men and materiel with 250,000 men opposed by only 30,000. There were 400 guns against 150, 190 fighter aircraft against forty-eight, and with 300 tanks, double what the British could muster. By most military yardsticks this was 'no contest'. However, the two elements missing from the equation are the quality of the soldiers and the ability of their officers. It was against this uncertain backdrop that Gott was to be tested to the limit. He excelled and in the year that followed he established himself as one of the most effective of the desert generals.

Facing the Italian threat was a weak British corps of two under-strength divisions (4th Indian and 7th Armoured) and Lieutenant General Richard O'Connor shrewdly withdrew the corps in August 1940 to a concentration near Mersa Matruh. His plan was for 7th Division Support Group to provide a covering force and to give Strafer Gott responsibility for the British front. Initially, for this task Gott had under command:

> 3rd Battalion, Coldstream Guards
> 1st Battalion, King's Royal Rifle Corps
> 2nd Battalion, Rifle Brigade
> 11th Hussars, One Squadron
> 1st Royal Tank Regiment
> Two batteries, Royal Horse Artillery
> Section 7th Medium Regiment Royal Artillery
> Detachment of Royal Engineers

This was a frail force with which to face two armies. Gott was told to harass the enemy and, if attacked in force, to impose as much delay as possible without being drawn into a pitched battle. The theory was that with these tactics losses would be light and the capacity to make a strong, armoured counter strike retained. Operations in a desert region always pose the problem of logistic support and as a sage with experience of an earlier desert war once remarked:

> Victory is the beautiful, bright coloured flower. Transport is the stem without which it could never have blossomed.[11]

The British Army had only recently, and somewhat reluctantly, abandoned the horse as a prime means of transport and in 1940 was still not comprehensively mechanised. The carriage of water, vital as it was, nevertheless occupied a disproportionate volume of cargo space in the inadequate transport system.

The Armoured Division was some 200 load carriers short. Extra mileage was thus thrown on the tracked (fighting) vehicles, adding to their wear and tear, already a matter of great concern to the maintenance units. The result was that the mobile troops in the Western Desert were tethered to their railhead by a very short administrative rope.[12]

Strafer did not linger.

Clausewitz once said, 'Never forget that no military leader has ever become great without audacity'[13] and, appropriately, Gott sent Lieutenant Colonel Combe of the 11th Hussars and his armoured cars close to the frontier with instructions to stir up the opposition. By 11 June, the 11th Hussars had reached the frontier wire, which presented no obstacle to Combe and his armoured cars. Passing into Libya they marauded in the frontier area to great effect, shooting up any target they could find and creating chaos in the Italian lines. They inflicted many casualties on the enemy and significant material damage as well. Two days later, Combe returned from his foray with seventy prisoners, having lost not a single man. The 7th Hussars relieved the 11th on the frontier.

Encouraged by this early success Strafer then struck decisively at the Italian forts of Capuzzo and Maddalena,[14] two of a chain of nine outposts that were placed along the 168-mile Frontier Wire Barrier built by Italian forces in 1931. (Maddalena is not shown on the map on page 85 but is about 40 miles south-east of Sidi Omar.) The 11th Hussars, supplemented by elements of 4th Armoured Brigade and with 1st KRRC took Maddalena without a shot being fired and Capuzzo fell, in the face of only token resistance and little bloodshed. Six Italian Fiat-Ansaldo L3 tankettes appeared briefly, but on losing one, the Italians beat a prudent retreat. Much later, Alan Moorehead commented:

> Brigadier Ewart Gott, a huge, soft-voiced man who looked more like a bishop than a soldier, commanded the Support Group. He had only recently been promoted and the opening of the desert war found him right in the front line. It was Gott who gave the order for the British to fire their first shots, Gott and his men who made our first conquest in the desert – Fort Capuzzo. For two years after that Gott never left the desert for more than a few days at a time. His name became a legend in the desert.[15]

On 16 June 1940, an Italian column between Omar and Fort Capuzzo confronted two troops of 11th Hussars. This column was clearly aiming for Fort Capuzzo and it included tankettes and lorried infantry. The two troops of armoured cars ignored an order to withdraw and two cars advanced to make contact with the enemy. They brewed up three tankettes but prudently withdrew when an enemy gun joined the battle. Colonel Combe took control of all the available assets and fought the Battle of Nezuet Ghirba. In reality the Napoleonic tactics of the Italians were inexplicable and the engagement, the first between armoured formations in the campaign, was hopelessly one-sided. The Italians fought bravely but a battalion of infantry, part of an armoured regiment and several guns were destroyed. Only 100 survived and the Italian Commander, Colonel D'Avanzo, was among the many killed during the action. These actions in mid-June had the effect of disrupting Italian movement between Bardia and Tobruk. However, it was only a temporary victory because the Italian 1st Blackshirt Division re-captured Capuzzo and thereafter this fort was to change hands several times over the next two years.

The exploits of Strafer's Support Group went far beyond the temporary taking of ground and 'between 11 June and 9 September, Italian losses amounted to 3,500 and those of the British 150.'[16] With that imbalance Strafer had imbued his troops with abundant self-confidence, developed their capacity to live and fight in the desert but above all else started the process of implanting in the Italians, at all levels, the belief that their British and Commonwealth opponents were in all respects superior. That moral superiority established by Strafer Gott in the summer of 1940 would bring rich rewards.

Strafer lived alongside his soldiers in a small, agile HQ. Matthew Halton, author of *Ten Years to Alamein*, asked him if, despite the discomfort and incessant torture of myriad flies, he had grown to love the desert. Strafer, not unreasonably, replied wryly, 'I hate it, but it's a fit place to fight a war.'

The Commander-in-Chief Middle East General Sir Archibald Wavell had no doubt as to the success of Gott's aggressive and fast-moving command and in a dispatch published in *The London Gazette* after the war he reported:

> This small force was distributed over a front of 60 miles from Sollum to Fort Maddalena. The troops continued the same policy of active patrolling, but the enemy's numbers were now very much increased, his artillery was numerous and active and the opportunities for effective action were fewer. Nevertheless, this small force continued to inflict heavy losses on the enemy with practically no loss to itself and to hold in check a force of four or five divisions for a further six weeks. A skilful use was made of dummy tanks to deceive the enemy.[17]

During his period, and while in command of the Support Group, Strafer Gott fought alongside Lieutenant Colonel JC Campbell MC RA.[18] Campbell, normally known as 'Jock', commanded the artillery component of the Support Group and he was a fierce and intrepid warrior. The two men held each other in mutually high regard and they made a formidable team. Campbell was a 45-year-old major in 1939 and in the normal course of events may well have remained a major until he retired, but war changes the lives of all the participants, including Gott, but Campbell not one whit the less.

Life in the desert for Strafer and his men was spent in an inhospitable, rugged, uncomfortable and featureless wasteland. The 2nd Battalion, The Rifle Brigade one of his infantry battalions, had a routine:

> Each company of about eighty men would use their vehicles to form a square with Company HQ in the centre. Out would come whatever rations we might have on board, mainly bully beef and hard tack biscuits. These would be emptied into a disused petrol tin with the top cut out and this would be placed over another petrol tin half-filled with sand with some petrol and oil mixed in. The petrol was set alight and that was our way of cooking in the desert. The subsequent glutinous mess would be eaten with some relish and followed with liberal helpings of tea. The water was very brackish and always a bit on the salty side. The powdered milk that was added to the brew gave the tea the appearance of curdled Devon cream.[19]

It is little wonder that the Desert Army soon had a reputation for a somewhat cavalier approach to 'Dress Regulations for the Army'. At about this time the work of a cartoonist named Jon produced a plethora of cartoons depicting his 'Two Types' of desert officers with their bizarre interpretation of uniform. One of Jon's minor masterpieces is reproduced overleaf. The heat rising from the tin can in the background underscores Victor Gregg's observation above.

Strafer was always correctly dressed, as befits an officer of the 60th and he did not adopt non-standard uniform. All photographs of him show that he was correctly conventional. However, Gott was fully aware of Jon's work and, given his pronounced sense of humour, he will have been as amused as his soldiers.

To be fair, Strafer lived slightly more comfortably than his men, but only by a small margin. He was never a feather-bedded general and sought no indulgencies denied to his soldiers. He shared willingly in their discomfort. His HQ was small and he made it a principle to be as far forward as possible in directing the battle. His proximity to the front was noted and appreciated by his soldiers and by other observers, one of whom noted:

> The troops loved him because he was always there, never lost his head and because of his passion for ranging the open desert behind enemy lines and striking suddenly and unexpectedly in the night.[20]

Strafer's attitude to desert warfare is summed up by a remark he made to and recorded by Alexander Clifford.[21] He said, 'Never fight the desert, but make it fight for you.' He also remarked, 'To him who knows it, the desert can be a fortress, to him who does not, it can be a death trap.'

"My brother says he's on a lonely gunsite in Yorkshire—
two miles from the nearest pub!"

This cartoon by Jon was one of very many published in Crusader, *the 8th Army newspaper. It was a morale booster and captured the spirit of the desert soldiers and the life they led.*

Clifford then added, 'And all through that first campaign the Italians were proving his theories for him.'

The Italians had numerical superiority and much as Wavell would have liked to attack his enemy he realised that he would have to be patient. On that basis he endorsed the use of 'Jock columns'. These were a mixture of lorried infantry, armoured cars and field guns. Their role was to harass the enemy. Jock Campbell commanded one of these columns and did so brilliantly. Whether or not he gave the columns the name 'Jock' is unclear, but it seems likely.

The Italians became increasingly proactive and aggressive and, on 13 September 1940, five Italian divisions located in Cyrenaica were ordered to cross the Libyan/Egyptian border and advance on Mersa Matruh. The 7th Armoured Division and 4th Indian Division were in this area and both prepared to stand fast. The Support Group under Gott and specifically 3rd Coldstream Guards, C Battery and part of F Battery RHA, one company of 1st KRRC, a machine gun company of 1st Battalion, The Royal Northumberland Fusiliers and a section of 25/26 Medium Battery RA were the obstacle to the advancing Italians, whose close formations were meat and drink to Strafer's gunners, but sheer weight of numbers obliged him to withdraw and this allowed the Italians to re-occupy Sollum.

The enemy was moving along the plateau about 500 feet above the coastal plain at this point and was heading for the Halfaya Pass. This key feature is about 2 miles inland from the sea and here a gentle slope makes for an easy passage down from the heights toward Egypt. The Pass is known locally as 'the great ascent'. The sketch map on page 85 shows the juxtaposition of Sollum, Fort Capuzzo and the Halfaya Pass.

It was ground that would be fought over for the next two years and it was here that tens of thousands would die for possession of a wasteland of worthless sand, rock and flies. The importance of the Halfaya Pass in this bloody contest can be seen from the sketch below.

Vastly outnumbered, the Support Group nevertheless continued to harass the enemy force to marked effect as it withdrew to the east. One officer observed on this period:

> It was during the first Italian advance and it had been going on in some of the worst conditions the desert can offer. Strafer was in command of the covering force. They, under his direction, had put up a magnificent show and had done all that was asked of them, and more. Orders had been issued for their withdrawal that night.

This pen and ink sketch shows the track up the Halfaya Pass to the dominating 500-foot high Libyan Plateau. This plateau would prove to be a significant feature in the fighting that was to come. The escarpment allowed access to wheeled and tracked vehicles in only a few places and the most important of these was the Halfaya Pass. (Jack Crippen, 1943)

83

I arrived at Strafer's headquarters at 1500 hrs in the afternoon with orders for him to stay and continue the withdrawal in contact. It was quite wonderful to see him act, tired as he was, with a highly uncertain situation as it seemed at the time, on his hands. It took him only a few moments' thought, and then out came the orders clear and simple as his always were. It was most heartening and impressive. I have always believed that that extra thirty-six hours stopped the enemy coming further.[22]

The Italians having taken Fort Capuzzo and Sollum thereafter moved forward very slowly, making only 60 miles in three days. By 16 September they had passed beyond Sidi Barrani and reached the inconsequential coastal town of Maktila, about 10 miles further on beyond Sidi Barrani. Showing extreme caution and a remarkable lack of aggression, the enemy set to work creating a defensive line of fortified camps.

This line ran 15 miles from Maktila to the rocky hill of Bir Sofafi, around which the Cirene Division established four strongpoints on the south-western ridge. This defensive line was wholly ineffective as the camps were not mutually supporting but well spread and sufficiently vulnerable to be picked off individually. The Italians, already with massive superiority albeit poorly deployed, waited to replenish their stores and receive further reinforcements.

Strafer's support group gathered itself and the 2nd Battalion The Rifle Brigade awaited his orders. Rifleman Gregg recorded:

For the last five or six months we had been living like Bedouins and the Battalion had taken on the appearance of Afghan tribesmen. Our daily water ration was about half a gallon per man for everything; we pooled it to wash in. It was common to toss up to determine as to who had the privilege of washing first. In the morning the last man in the section usually gave his wash a miss for that day. We hadn't had a proper wash for months. Our uniforms were in rags; we were lousy and covered in desert sores.[23]

During this period of independent operations Strafer Gott thrived. This was an entirely new type of warfare, waged in a theatre where there were no fronts and no flanks. Conducting operations in the desert was not unlike fighting at sea, just as Lawrence had predicted. The ground was, for the most part, featureless and unremittingly accurate navigation was a prerequisite, not just for success but also for survival. The logistic chain was constantly stretched to its limits and the storage and movement of water every bit as important as the supply of ammunition.

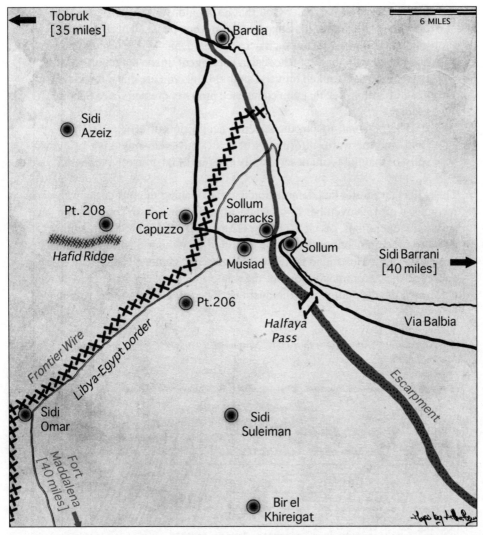

The initial area of operations, 7 Armoured Division Support Group. (Map by Arthur Perry)

Many of the places named in this book were little more than map references. There were few significant and strategically important locations. Centres of population were, invariably, very small indeed and few and far between. A water source provided riches beyond measure. The only things the desert offered in abundance were sand, burning sun and flies – especially flies.

Strafer was under constant physical and mental pressure but he remained a 'soldier's officer':

It was typical of Brigadier Gott that he should want to see personally the young riflemen of his Support Group when they had been involved in important patrols. One such occasion Sergeant AGL Goschen, who had joined with the first Rhodesian contingent, made his report to the Brigadier, who thanked him and said, 'I think you are due a few days' leave after that. See that you come back properly dressed – as a Second Lieutenant.'

The personal touch, the speedy recognition of efficiency in the field, and the warm informality of it all conveyed something of the spirit of that tight-knit desert family and one of its greatest members.[24]

The skills that Strafer had demonstrated in the opening months of the war were recognised on 15 November 1940, when, after five months of constant and very successful operations, his GOC, Major General Sir Michael O'M Creagh, wrote a citation recommending that he be admitted a member of the Distinguished Service Order.[25] This found favour with Lieutenant General HM Wilson,[26] who endorsed the recommendation six days later. General Sir Archibald Wavell confirmed the decoration on 30 November. The original citation is reproduced below.

The citation for Strafer Gott's first DSO, November 1940. (WHE Gott's personal file, The National Archives)

Chapter notes

1. Vernon, Brigadier HRW, *Strafer Gott*, p.30, original source WHEG personal file MoD archive.
2. General Sir Evelyn Barker, *King's Royal Rifle Corps Chronicle*, 1942.
3. Vernon, Brigadier HRW. *Strafer Gott*, original source WHEG personal file MoD archive.
4. Major Sir Hereward Wake, late KRRC, extracted from Vernon, Brigadier HRW, *Strafer Gott*, p.103.
5. Ibid.
6. Later, Field Marshal Lord Archibald Wavell, 1st Earl Wavell GCB GCSI GCIE CMG MC PC (1893-1950). He was Commander-in-Chief Middle East and in that capacity he fought a highly successful campaign against the Italian 5th and 10th armies in 1940-41. However, he did not have a warm relationship with Churchill who eventually replaced him with Auchinleck.
7. Playfair, Major General ISO et al, *The Mediterranean and Middle East*, Vol.1, p.115.
8. Gregg, V., *Rifleman – A Front Line Life*, p.42.
9. The Anglo-Egyptian Treaty of 1936.
10. Liddell Hart, B., *Colonel Lawrence: The man behind the legend.*
11. Churchill, WS, *The River War*, Vol. 1, p.276.
12. Playfair, Major General ISO et al, *The Mediterranean and Middle East*, Vol. 1, p.68.
13. Major General von Clausewitz, C., *Principles of War*, 1812.
14. On the Internet's YouTube there is a short sequence of the capture of this position by 11 Hussars on 11 June 1940. See www.youtube.com/watch?v=e27QJ62D8R4
15. Moorehead, Alan, *Daily Express*, 13 June 1943.
16. Playfair, Major General ISO et al, *The Mediterranean and Middle East*, Vol. 1, p.206.
17. *The London Gazette* 13 June 1946, Operations in the Sand on 13 September Middle East from August 1939 until November 1940.
18. Later, Major General JC Campbell VC DSO* MC (1894-1942). It is alleged by Mead in his book *Churchill's Lions* that Campbell enlisted in August 1914 in the Honourable Artillery Company. The archivist of the HAC is less sure and comments, 'I can find no entry for him in our HAC membership records. The only possible is a "James Campbell", who was admitted in 1915. He was in B Bty and in June 1915 lived at 12 Bellevue Road, Ayr.' If he was HAC then his membership had lapsed and thus the HAC does not claim him as its fifth VC.
19. Gregg, Victor, *Rifleman – A Front-line Life*, p.48-9.
20. Moorehead, Alan, *Sunday Express*, 13 June 1943.
21. *Daily Mail,* 11 August 1942.
22. Peyton, Colonel G., quoted in Vernon, Brigadier HRW, *Strafer Gott*, p.68.
23. Gregg, Victor, *Rifleman – A Front-line Life*, p.48.
24. Mills, G, and Nixon, R., *The Annals of the King's Royal Rifle Corps*, Vol. VI, p.104-105.
25. The Order was instituted in 1886 and is typically awarded for distinguished leadership under fire. Recipients are termed 'Companions' of the Order and carry the post-nominal letters DSO.
26. Later, Lord Wilson, FM GCB GBE DSO (1881-1964).

Chapter 8

Operation Compass
November 1940-February 1941

W avell ordered the General Officer Commanding Troops Egypt, Lieutenant General Sir Henry Maitland Wilson, to plan a limited operation to push the Italians back and Operation Compass was planned as a five-day raid to achieve this.

'First things first' was the order of the day and under conditions of the greatest secrecy the logistic arrangements to sustain a corps in desert conditions were put in place. Geography is always a factor:

> The problem of maintaining the attacking force was complicated by the great distance separating them from the Italian fortified camps, which were to be the first objectives. In order to achieve surprise this distance would have to be covered quickly. Therefore the force would have to be kept supplied with essential needs for a battle to be fought anything up to 100 miles from the existing railhead. It was necessary … to establish two forward dumps or Field Supply Depots some 40 miles to the west of Matruh about 14 miles apart – one each for 4th Indian Division and 7th Armoured Division.[1]

These depots were very vulnerable and so not only was their location covert, but every effort was made to conceal them from casual prying eyes. By dint of their location they had to be especially well guarded, as there was only the thin Support Group screen between them and the enemy. The depots were stocked with 'five days' hard scale rations and a corresponding sufficiency of petrol and ammunition, together with two days' supply of water.'[2] All through the preparatory period the Support Group was keeping up its aggressive inquisitiveness. Hardly a day or night passed in October and November without some part of the enemy's defences being visited. From time to time there were encounters between patrols or mobile columns, never far from the enemy's camps

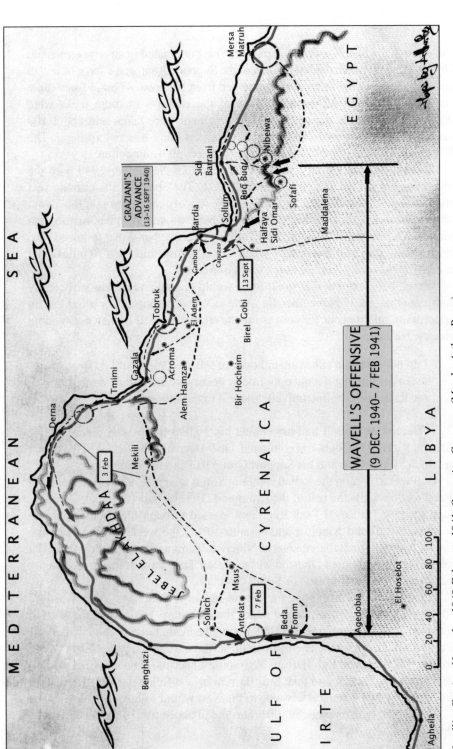

Wavell's offensive, November 1940–February 1941, Operation Compass. (Map by Arthur Perry)

and often in the Nibeiwa-Rabia gap itself. This culminated in an engagement on 19 November between the left column of the Support Group and a force of Italian tanks and lorry-borne infantry that emerged from Nibeiwa. Another force came out from Rabia but turned back. Five of the enemy's medium tanks were destroyed and others damaged: eleven prisoners were taken and about 100 casualties were inflicted. Thereafter the Italians were less enterprising. The British losses were three killed and two wounded, all by air action.

Training for Operation Compass started on 26 November 1940 with the imaginatively named Training Exercise No. 1. The object of the training was another well-guarded secret and only a very few officers knew that the layout of the exercise replicated the objectives of Nibeiwa and Tummar, near Mersa Matruh. The numerically predictable Training Exercise No. 2 that followed was, in effect, the start of the operation when Wavell's force marched 70 miles to its concentration area, about 20 miles south of Maktila.

Wavell believed that that small force would prevail and he was sufficiently confident that, on 28 November, he wrote to Wilson expressing a belief that an opportunity might occur for converting the enemy's defeat into an outstanding victory. He said:

> I do not entertain extravagant hopes of this operation but I do wish to make certain that if a big opportunity occurs we are prepared morally, mentally and administratively to use it to the fullest.[3]

By 8 December Wavell had assembled his 30,000 troops and placed Major General Richard O'Connor in command. On 9 December he launched the attack in which Strafer Gott and his Support Group had an important role.

Gott was to cordon the Italian camps at Sofafi to negate any movement from that direction while the rest of the Armoured Division and 4th Indian Division, supported by 7th Royal Tank Regiment, passed through the undefended gap between Sofafi and Nibeiwa and assaulted from the west, that is to say, the enemy rear and the Italian camps at Nibeiwa, Tummar East and Point 90. The role of the 7th Armoured Division was to screen these activities from any enemy initiatives from the Buq Buq or Sofafi direction.

Once Nibeiwa was captured a second Indian brigade, again supported by 7th Royal Tank Regiment, would attack the Tummars. Meanwhile the Matruh Garrison Force, comprising 3rd Battalion Coldstream Guards and a battery of artillery would cordon the enemy position at Maktila and the Royal Navy would bombard Maktila and Sidi Barrani. Assuming a successful outcome, the Indian Division would attack and take Sidi Barrani on the following day. Thereafter, the hope was that a general advance to the west would follow.

The sketch map on page 89 illustrates the juxtaposition of the objectives of Operation Compass.

The opening stage of the operation was called the Battle of the Camps, an imprecise title that alludes to the Italian encampments that were constructed in a loose defensive line running south from Sidi Barrani and the coast. The Italians refer to it as the Battle of the Marmarica, so called for the empty, coastal plain upon which the engagement took place.

O'Connor had under his command 7th Armoured Division, 4th Indian Division and the 16th Infantry Brigade. He had in support an aggressive but overstretched Royal Air Force, which in the opening exchanges destroyed twenty-nine enemy aircraft on the ground, and the Royal Navy in the shape of the heavily gunned HMS *Terror*,[4] *Aphis* and *Ladybird*. The Italian 1st Libyan Infantry Division was positioned at Maktila and it was to be the recipient of the combined firepower of *Terror* and *Aphis*, while *Ladybird* bombarded the garrison of Sidi Barrani.

Brigadier AR Selby, commanding a mixed force of about 1,800 men, took up a position just south of Maktila having at first deployed a formation of dummy tanks to deceive enemy aircraft. He was somewhat isolated, received no orders and, as a result, the 1st Libyan Division declined action and melted away to the west.

By 8 December the Italians had reinforced all of their forward positions and, when battle was joined, seven comparatively weak divisions were to be attacked over unpromising ground by one strong division and one armoured division.

At 0715 hrs on 9 December the 11th Indian Infantry Brigade, supplemented by 7th Royal Tank Regiment attacked Nibeiwa from the north-west. The point of the attack had been established by a patrol from 2nd Battalion, The Rifle Brigade on the night of 7/8 December. This patrol established that the garrison's supplies gained access at a point in that north-west sector and concluded that there was a route through the minefield. For the defenders this was an unexpected quarter because, from 0500 hrs, diversionary fire had been delivered from the east. The major and most effective artillery concentration had fallen on the defenders as the attack went in. Surprise was achieved and twenty-three enemy tanks were destroyed even before they could be manned. Although the assault was then fiercely resisted enemy losses were high and the Italians capitulated an hour later. The Commander was killed and 2,000 prisoners were taken. It was a stunning victory achieved at a cost of eight officers and forty-eight men.

Major General N Beresford-Peirse, Commander of 4th Indian Division, resolved to take the Tummars and called forward his 5th Indian Infantry Brigade with supporting field artillery for the task. The 7th Royal Tank Regiment was the sharp end of the attack on Tummar West and after replenishment it swiftly breached the enemy line opening a gap that the following infantry was able to exploit. Tummar West succumbed eventually after spirited defence and by early evening Tummar East was also taken.

Success followed success and the 4th Armoured Brigade moved swiftly north and northwest on Azizya, took 400 prisoners and the position. The 7th Hussars pushed on to cut the all-important Sidi Barrani/Buq Buq road. The town of Sidi Barrani fell to 11th Indian Infantry Brigade, supported by 7th Royal Tank Regiment, the Regiment that had initially blocked any enemy exit to the south. Once again enormous numbers of Italians were captured.

On 11 December Strafer Gott's Support Group entered Rabia and found it to be deserted. Strafer pressed on while the operation went from strength to strength, sweeping all before it. HMS *Terror*, *Aphis* and *Ladybird* targeted Italian convoys retreating in confusion along the coast road.

O'Connor, predictably, wanted to exploit his success and by now Benghazi was in his sights but he was thwarted when, summarily, Wavell withdrew 4th Indian Division and redeployed it to East Africa. This was less 16th British Infantry Brigade, which was placed under command of 6th Australian Division, the replacement formation but, as yet, it was un-blooded and new to the theatre. The 7th Royal Tank Regiment and additional artillery reinforced the 6th Australian Division. The seasoned and tested Support Group was of increased importance in this situation and Strafer's command played an active part in the capture of Sollum, Halfaya Pass and the retaking of Fort Capuzzo.

O'Connor decided to pursue his adversary with his armour and sent 7th Armoured Brigade along the coast and 4th Armoured Brigade along the top of the escarpment. This was sound in theory but in practice it posed acute logistical problems. In part, captured Italian stocks helped but the feeding of an army of prisoners negated any benefit.

Bardia was the next objective and likely to be a tough nut to crack. A force of 40,000 Italians defended the fortress and Mussolini had made clear to the Italian Commander, General Bergonzoli, that the 18-mile perimeter of Bardia was to be defended to the last. The perimeter had been the subject of extensive defence works and had a permanent anti-tank ditch 4 feet deep and 12 feet wide. Deep and well-laid double-aproned wire supplemented by mutually supporting concrete blockhouses added to the defensive mix. In addition there were six minefields and other mines had been strewn at random inside the wire.

The structural changes imposed by Wavell caused a change of name for his command and XIII Corps came into being. Strafer was a part of this new formation but he little knew that all too soon he would be commanding it. Christmas 1940 was celebrated in the field and everyone knew that 1941 would start with a literal bang.

The Royal Air Force made more than 100 bomber sorties against Bardia between 31 December and 2 January 1941 and the Royal Navy gunships bombarded the coastline positions at will. Strafer penned an after-action report,[5] writing:

On 31 December 1940, Support Group moved, by night, to a position astride the main Bardia/Tobruk road. At this time this area was only occupied by patrols of 11 Hussars. The task of Support Group was to prevent the enemy withdrawing from Bardia to the west and prevent any reinforcements from the west reaching the beleaguered garrison. As a result it was necessary for Support Group to face both ways. The following troops were under command:

> 11 Hussars
> 1 Bn King's Royal Rifle Corps
> 2 Bn Rifle Brigade
> 1 French Motor Company
> 1 Regt Royal Horse Artillery
> 'M' Battery, 3 Royal Horse Artillery

On 3 January 1941 Support Group probed Italian defences to the north of the Tobruk road with patrols of six tanks and carriers. It also harassed the Italian defences with artillery fire and sought to take any opportunity offered to exploit the success of the main attack by patrolling forward with the French Motor Company.

To the west the 6th Australian Division (16, 17 and 19 infantry brigades), led by its 16th Infantry Brigade, attacked Bardia on its weaker flank. (See sketch map on page 89.) This was the first engagement of the Australians but, notwithstanding the fixed defences, the Australians blew gaps in the wire with Bangalore torpedoes and bridged the anti-tank ditch with the liberal use of picks and shovels. This was a heroic feat of arms conducted under fire by inexperienced soldiers.

A breach was made in the line and 7th Royal Tank Regiment led the way as the attackers flowed through. Resistance collapsed and 8,000 prisoners were taken. The 16th Infantry Brigade captured the town of Bardia on 4 January. The following day the brigade's assault was overwhelming and the objective was seized. The 1st KRRC and 2nd Rifle Brigade were in at the kill and, meanwhile in the north, the Italians were surrendering wholesale to the Support Group.[6] After the victory Strafer expressed his view:

> Effective demonstration by carriers and light tanks can be carried out with little or no casualties if well handled by its junior commander. A similar demonstration by unarmoured infantry is a much more hazardous undertaking and, if such action is necessary, requires as much artillery and machine-gun support as can be provided.
>
> When large numbers of fugitives are escaping from a captured

objective, sufficient troops should be left to prevent their escape and collect them – a task that in broken country may well take several days.[7]

General Bergonzoli escaped to fight another day but 40,000 of his soldiers did not. This latest coup yielded massive returns. A further 25,000 prisoners were taken, together with 400 field and medium guns, 130 tanks and 200 other assorted vehicles. The Australians had 456 casualties.

After the fall of Bardia, 7th Armoured Division, with 19th Australian Infantry Brigade, moved toward Tobruk. Hitherto the coastal prizes had been little more than fishing villages with a jetty. They were, for the most part, of little use to a modern war machine like XIII Corps. Even Bardia had a limited capacity and many of its modest installations had suffered badly at the hands of the Royal Air Force and Royal Navy.

Tobruk was a different matter and its acquisition was highly desirable. The port was cut off by 6 January 1941 and completely surrounded by 9 January. The Italians sat behind their 30-mile defended perimeter and waited. Then they waited a little more because O'Connor did not rush his fences and he spent time in replenishing his force. He laid careful plans and made his move on 21 January. The Official History summed up the situation:

> The 7th Armoured and 6th Australian divisions outside Tobruk were out of reach of their Field Supply Depots at Capuzzo and Sollum; a new depot was therefore formed for each division about 35 miles east of Tobruk. The problem this time was to supply their daily need, build up the requirements for the attack and create enough reserves to tide over the time that would be required before the port of Tobruk was in working order. This meant another period of intense road convoy work, in which captured lorries played an important part.

Once again the attacking force was to be 6th Australian Division. The plan was quite simple. In order to help the tanks through the anti-tank belt a section of the perimeter, about 3 miles east of the El Adem road, was selected for an assault on a narrow front. A battalion of 16th Australian Brigade was ordered to take and hold a bridgehead. Once the bridgehead was established the remainder of the brigade was to move through the gap accompanied by the tanks of 7th Royal Tank Regiment. At this time there were heavy sandstorms, which hampered the activity of the Royal Air Force but not the redoubtable Royal Navy gunships that had moved down the coast for their next performance.

The role of the Support Group in the Battle of Tobruk was similar to that it had had at Bardia. Strafer and his force were to prevent the reinforcement or escape of the Tobruk garrison. However, Brigadier Gott was markedly more proactive than that. He ordered extensive and active patrolling to locate enemy batteries and strong points. He required his two infantry battalions to furnish him with information as to the general extent and state of artificial anti-tank obstacles and the location of wire and mines. In addition he practised what he described as 'tapping in'. This was a constant probing of enemy defences by the carrier platoons until resistance weakened sufficiently to permit an advance by the motor platoons.

Their demanding and aggressive commander kept the KRRC and Rifle Brigade battalions very busy.

The French Motor Company was detailed to light beacons on 19/20 and 20/21 January to assist the RN to carry out night shoots on the Tobruk garrison. These beacons then became a target for enemy machine guns. One was extinguished but a gallant party of Frenchmen relit it under fire. Previous experience made it imperative that Support Group units were 3,000 yards from the enemy perimeter. Nevertheless, a number of naval shells still fell among them, happily inflicting no casualties but by any yardstick this was overshooting of heroic proportions.

At 0540 hrs on 21 January the attack was launched and by 0830 hrs a platoon of 1st KRRC under the command of Second Lieutenant John Holdsworth had secured the main road crossing on the Wadi Sahal. By 1100 hrs, Second Lieutenant Tom Bird led a platoon of 2nd Rifle Brigade through the enemy defences north of Acroma Road and in both cases large numbers of prisoners were taken.

Once the Australians had breached the perimeter eventual victory for XIII Corps was assured. A total of 25,000 prisoners were taken, including 2,000 sailors, 208 field guns and eighty-seven tanks; XIII Corps suffered about 400 casualties, of which 355 were Australians.

The port facility was damaged but usable. The distillation plant was in working order, as was the power station, complete with a stockpile of coal. Only two days later the port was functioning.

This latest British success motivated the Italians to withdraw from Cyrenaica and they planned to use the coast road as the means of egress. The GOC 7th Armoured Division (O'Creagh) determined to cut off this retreat by sending a small mobile force directly across country by a shorter route to block the evacuation while, at the same time, 7th Armoured Division and 6th Australian Division harried the retreat. On the map the intercept plan looks to be obvious. However, the direct route was across an unmapped wasteland and the potential for disaster was infinite. There were also serious logistical issues as vehicles had to be taken from other divisional units to carry the fuel and ammunition required. Wireless communications had to be set up and tested.

Lieutenant Colonel JFB Combe[8] Commanding the 11th Hussars was selected to command the composite force of about 2,000 men drawn, in the main, from the Support Group such as 2nd Rifle Brigade but supplemented by squadrons of armoured cars from 11th Hussars, King's Dragoon Guards and the RAF. The force was strong in anti-tank weapons manned by C Battery, Royal Horse Artillery (RHA) and 106 Battery RHA. The move had to be executed quickly and Victor Gregg of 2nd Rifle Brigade recalled:

> Our small brigade was ordered to force-march over an inland area of the desert. Before we knew where we were the blue flag was fluttering in the breeze 'move forward'. The column was on the move, and it was chaos. Some of the lads were still throwing bedding rolls and the other stuff that we carried into the back of trucks and carriers, while other men who were in the middle of eating the evening meal swallowed what they could and ran to their vehicles. We set off toward the setting sun, then, as darkness fell, so the column swung south into uncharted terrain. It was unmapped, with no tracks, and even the local tribesmen rarely set foot there. We relied entirely on compass bearings. The route ran south of Jebel Aktar, and with every hour the going got rougher and in those days we did not have four-wheel drive. We were led by the 11th Hussars who, to save time, had just drawn a straight line across the map – a line we had to follow without deviating. ... This type of terrain was new to us, partly mountainous with rocky outcrops and deep sandy wadis. It was soon obvious that the tanks were going to be left miles behind. We left a trail of broken vehicles behind us, but even so a good proportion of the force survived the journey and ... arrived at dawn.[9]

The trek across the desert by 'Combe Force', as it was christened, was a success and the blocking positions were established 20 miles north of Agadabia (the modern spelling is Ajedabia) and 30 miles south-west of Antelat. These blocks were occupied on 5 February 1941 and only minutes before the advance guard of the Italian 10th Army arrived.

Moreover, to complete the bottling up of 10th Army, 4th Armoured Brigade reached Beda Fomm, a very small town between Benghazi and El Agheila to the south-west and overlooking the coastal road. Meanwhile the remainder of the Support Group was positioned by Strafer to attack the main body of the Italian rear and northern flank.

The odds were weighed very heavily in favour of the Italians, who numbered about 20,000, and it was imperative for them to break though the blocks at Beda Fomm manned by 4th Armoured Brigade and the roadblock to the south now manned by 2nd Battalion, The Rifle Brigade.

There was not a moment to lose and not even time for a brew. The order to The Rifle Brigade to 'dig in' was impossible to carry out and so sangars[10] were quickly constructed from the available material on the desert floor. The vehicles were moved to the rear, including the armoured car squadrons. The gunners were even further back. This was going to be an infantry battle and riflemen were to bear the brunt. Victor Gregg remembered:

> What livened us up was the urgent shouting of the piquets[11] to stand-to. We could hear the incessant rumbling of tracked vehicles – tanks. Soon enough we saw them, the leading elements of a vast army, emerging from out of the early morning mist, a thousand yards to our front like a huge black mass of locusts. We realised that they did not know we were there. On they came until, without warning, our guns opened up and the leading tanks began to brew up – exploding and bursting into flame as the first shells hammered into them.[12]

The Italian infantry continued the advance across ground as flat as a football field; it had no chance against the Vickers and Bren machine guns that faced it. Badly blooded, it withdrew. The men of 2nd Rifle Brigade were now reinforced by elements of 2nd Royal Tank Regiment and the bulk and firepower of the tanks was a welcome bonus. The enemy realised only too well that salvation was dependent on it driving through the roadblock and a second determined assault was launched. Victor Gregg had no doubts that this was to be:

> a fixed-bayonet job. The artillery to our rear was, by now, firing over open sights. The enemy tanks were burning only yards away, in a few cases right on top of our positions. Their infantry attacked and it became hand-to-hand stuff. It went on all through the day, they attacked were thrown back, they attacked again. On and on it went until about four in the afternoon when, all of a sudden, the noise started to die down. There were no more attacks that day. Our lines were still holding, a bit thinner it's true, but still holding.[13]

The aftermath of a battle is never a pretty sight and the area around the Battalion position was no exception. There was a smell of burning oil and rubber mixed with the unholy stench of burning flesh. Explosions continued as ammunition in the Italian tanks 'cooked off'. Shrieks of the wounded went on through the night as medics sought to clear the casualties of both sides. The following day the fighting recommenced and, at about 1400 hrs, with enemy tanks on the position, hand-to-hand fighting was the order of the day. Lieutenant Colonel Renton,[14] the CO of 2nd Battalion, The Rifle Brigade, called for artillery fire onto his position. It was a bold and desperate call but it was successful. The enemy tank force was caught under a ferocious bombardment at short range and destroyed while the infantry of both sides went to earth. Victor Gregg recalled:

> After ten minutes the barrage ceased, followed by a terrible silence. The only visible movement was the trails of smoke drifting over the area to our front, and then as our senses slowly returned, the agonising noises of the aftermath of battle began to filter through, the terrible cries of the wounded on both sides.

The battle known as Beda Fromm was over and with 7th Armoured Division and 6th Australian Division now bearing down on them from the north and east the tattered remnants of the 10th Italian Army surrendered. Its commander, General Tellera, was among the many dead. There remained several clearing-up actions, such as that at the oasis of Giarabab, but the backbone of Italian resistance was shattered.

El Agheila had been occupied on 9 February 1941 and two days later Gott was suddenly summoned to HQ 7th Armoured Division, where he was ordered to dispatch a column of all arms to Marada. This was an obscure oasis not marked on any but very large-scale maps and situated 75 miles south of El Agheila in the Al Wahat district of Cyrenaica. An Italian force of about 1,200 all ranks were said to be located in Marada and Strafer's task was to harass this formation. He put together a composite force of one company of KRRC, a squadron from the King's Dragoon Guards, a battery of guns from the RHA and a detachment of sappers. Major Mathew was selected to command the column.

The approach to Marada was accomplished and the King's Dragoon Guards occupied the oasis without opposition and it was then revealed that the initial intelligence was incorrect. The nearest enemy was a further 65 miles to the east. Strafer withdrew his column, as frustrated as his soldiers, and everyone wrote off the abortive mission to experience.

By 20 February Support Group had moved back, north-east, to the Antelat area (see map on page 89), where there was a chance to catch up with personal mail, dhobi[15] and sleep.

Ten weeks after the initial advance, Operation Compass had accomplished all its aims and Wavell, O'Connor, O'Creagh and, to a lesser extent, Strafer Gott could take modest pride in a comprehensive victory. The Italian losses included 130,000 prisoners, twenty-two generals and 960 guns. Italian dead are unknown but numbered in the tens of thousands. British and Commonwealth losses were 494 dead, 1,373 wounded and fifty-five missing.

The imbalance in casualties is all the more remarkable given that XIII Corps was so vastly outnumbered yet it took the initiative and attacked continuously over 500 miles, destroying an army of ten divisions.

It is an apocryphal story but, allegedly, an officer of the Coldstream Guards remarked on the bag of prisoners by saying, 'We have about five acres of officers and 200 acres of Other Ranks.'

After the victory came the rewards and Strafer was at once recommended for a decoration; the original citation is below. Clearly there was some confusion as to Strafer's rank, probably because he was advancing up the pecking order at some speed.

The London Gazette of 8 July 1941 promulgated the award.[16] He was not alone and decorations were bestowed on commanders at all levels and, where possible, personal gallantry was properly marked. The system is not fair, nor is it always the case that the most deserving are rewarded. Many officers and men engaged in Operation Compass were content merely to have survived.

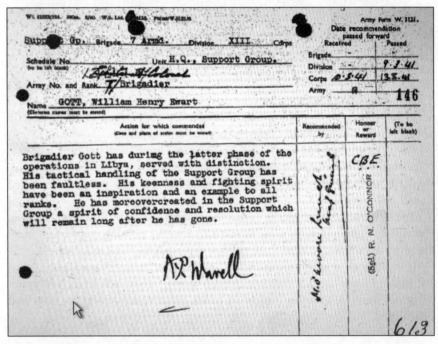

The citation for Strafer Gott's appointment as a Commander of The Most Excellent Order of the British Empire (CBE), March 1941. (WHE Gott's personal file, The National Archives)

Strafer Gott committed to paper some thoughts on Operation Compass and specifically upon 'lessons learned'. He focused in particular on the impact that had been felt by the presence of the Luftwaffe. His remarks are not high-flown matters of military philosophy but simple, common sense rules for desert fighting. He wrote:

Road movement most vulnerable by day and even by moonlight on the straight open desert roads. Roads must be avoided except at night when there is no moon. This period is so difficult for aircraft that it is worth travelling with some lights, say, one headlight on the leading vehicle of a batch of twenty or thirty. Vehicles moving by day require lookouts facing front and rear. As soon as a low-flying attack is seen the vehicle should leave the road, if possible, and the occupants scatter and lie down away from the vehicle.

Vehicles should always be dug in when time permits.

AA batteries are an enemy target and should be sited well away from HQs and troop concentrations.

Traps might well be laid for enemy aircraft, such as a few tents, abandoned motor transport, dummy wireless masts or other bait placed near a road and well dug in and camouflaged. AA Brens and Bredas about 100-200 yards away.

Avoid buildings. They are so rare in the desert that they are certain to be targets.[17]

These matters do all seem to be very prosaic and one wonders why he found it necessary to burst into print. The conclusion is that common sense is actually not all that common and he said what needed to be said.

On 28 February 1941 Strafer led his Support Group back to Cairo. The two rifle battalions were bedded down in Mena Camp, about 10 miles from Cairo, the RHA to Beni Yusuf, and Strafer's headquarters into the well-equipped Kasrel-Nil barracks.

The officers had the chance to savour the delights offered by the Gazira Sporting Club as the Support Group spent the next five weeks refitting and replenishing; the seven days' leave granted to all ranks was particularly well received.

It was not all rest and recuperation and the Commander was asked to visit 3rd Indian Motor Brigade on 19-20 March specifically to advise the formation on desert warfare, a further indication of his growing reputation, by now well established.

Strafer Gott had started 1941 in very good order. He had commanded an aggressive mobile force that had an unbroken record of success. He was recognised as a skilled exponent of desert warfare and his determination to be as far forward as possible with his troops had added to his reputation. For years, Gott had been a well-known character in the 60th now he had become an Army character, a man admired by his subordinates and one whose judgment was trusted by his seniors.

Alexander Clifford was a journalist embedded in 7th Armoured Division and he saw a great deal of Strafer Gott, of whom he wrote:

Even before that campaign ended he was planning a book on desert warfare. I met him deep in Libya at Fort Mekili and he gave me a fascinating synopsis of his ideas. His Mess was reported to be the worst in the desert, for he was too busy with war to bother about food. But this time we bartered a whole case of Italian mineral water to him against a tin of army biscuits and he was glad, for he was just about to make the incredible trip to the coast south of Benghazi to trap the remainder of Graziani's Cyrenaican Army, and water was going to be vital.[18]

It is a great shame that the book was never written. It might have been the definitive work on desert warfare, a valuable source and a great aid to understanding Strafer's thinking.

Chapter notes

1. Playfair, Major General ISO et al, *The Mediterranean and Middle East*, Vol. 1, p.262.
2. The ration of water was four pints per man per day for all purposes and eight pints per radiator.
3. Playfair, Major General ISO et al, *The Mediterranean and Middle East*, Vol. 1, p.262.
4. HMS *Terror* was a Monitor, a class of ship that is now long since obsolete. She mounted two 15-inch guns, from which she fired 600 rounds into the positions of the Italian 1st Libyan Infantry Division.
5. War Diary, 7th Armoured Division Support Group, January 1941.
6. Playfair, Major General ISO et al, *The Mediterranean and Middle East*, Vol. 1, p.287.
7. War Diary, 7th Armoured Division Support Group, January 1941.
8. Combe, Lieutenant Colonel JFB 11H (later Major General CB DSO*, 1895-1967) was promoted to brigadier in April 1941 but then was captured along with General Neame and General O'Connor. He escaped twice and his second attempt was successful. He reached Allied lines in May 1944.
9. Gregg, Victor, *Rifleman: A Front-line Life*, p.51-2.
10. Sangar is a word derived from the Persian word *sang*, meaning 'stone'. In this context it is used to describe an above-surface, fortified position, constructed of loose stone or sandbags. It is a technique invariably used when the ground is too hard to dig trenches.
11. Piquets are sentries.
12. Gregg, Victor, *Rifleman: A Front-line Life*, p.53.
13. Gregg, Victor, *Rifleman: A Front-line Life*, p.53.
14. Ibid. Lieutenant Colonel JML Renton RB was awarded the DSO for this action (LG 9 May 1941). He went on to win a bar to his DSO the following year.
15. Dhobi is 'soldier speak' for washing of clothes. A legacy of the Indian Army.
16. King George V instituted the 'Most Excellent Order of the British Empire' in 1917. Strafer was admitted as a commander of the order. Normally, the Monarch invests recipients but as far as can be ascertained there was no formal ceremony for Strafer Gott.
17. War diary, 7th Armoured Division Support Group, 24 February 1941.
18. Clifford, A., *Daily Mail*, 11 August 1942.

Chapter 9

Operation Brevity
March-May 1941

The period immediately post Operation Compass was the high-water mark for British arms in the Western Desert and in the following eighteen months victories were to be few and far between.

The defeat of the two Italian Armies may have been a high-water mark for British arms, but it is a fact of life that tides do ebb and flow. The next eighteen months of campaigning in the Western Desert would be ample testimony to that. The arrival in North Africa of the German Lieutenant General Erwin Rommel on 12 February was to herald a change in British fortunes.

General Wavell was faced with some difficult choices. He was occupying vast tracts of territory, held by exhausted troops, very thinly spread. All of his formations were in urgent need of reinforcement and replenishment. He put in place some significant structural changes, firstly creating a Cyrenaica Command and, initially, selecting Lieutenant General Sir Maitland Wilson to command it. Wilson would be 'double-hatted' as he had also to carry out the function of Military Governor in order to replicate the function of the previous Italian administration. He was soon to be replaced by Lieutenant General P Neame[1] VC, and Lieutenant General O'Connor took over command in Egypt.

The 1st Australian Corps, under the command of Lieutenant General Sir Thomas Blamey, was called forward, not least because '7th Armoured Division, which had now been in contact with the enemy for nearly eight months without rest, was to be relieved by 2nd'.[2] The 7th Armoured Division withdrew to Egypt to refit.

The 2nd Armoured Division was in a parlous condition. It was incomplete and ill equipped; it was an armoured division in name only. Strafer's Support Group was not relieved. Although it was renamed 'Mobile Force', it was incomplete. Its role was unchanged. Blamey and his corps headquarters, after the briefest stay, were then sent to Greece by Wavell and, as the Official History[3] remarks soberly:

There was now no corps headquarters to handle purely military matters and 2nd Armoured Division and 9th Australian Division came directly under Cyrenaica Command, which was virtually a static headquarters.

This highly unsatisfactory command structure boded ill for the future.

The logistic chain remained very stretched and this was compounded by a combination of bad weather and effective enemy action. The Luftwaffe arrived in the Mediterranean in January 1941 and its active presence changed everything. It mined the harbour at Tobruk and a ship carrying fuel struck a mine, took fire and caused a nearby ammunition ship to explode, further damaging two small but vital minesweepers that were being repaired.

Benghazi was a regular recipient of German attention from the air that was sufficiently efficient as to render the port unusable and efforts to establish Benghazi as an advanced base failed. In combination, and despite the possession of Benghazi, it was a long, hard, dusty and fly-infested drive along the coastal road – some 450 miles from Tobruk to El Agheila, the furthest extent of the British gains.

General Neame was painfully aware of the deficiencies of Cyrenaica Command. He knew that the defence of his parish would depend upon fast-moving, armoured operations. The 2nd Armoured Division was not going to provide that as, in effect, it was little more than a brigade equipped with tanks that were worn out even before any operations started.

Wavell acknowledged the weakness of the British position and he gave Neame the latitude to withdraw to Benghazi and beyond if it was necessary, to preserve his force. In the meantime Strafer was holding an 8-mile front around Mersa Brega, 40 miles north of El Agheila. He was exposed and a priority target for Rommel, who now had 5th Leichte-Division in North Africa and under command. The 15th Panzer Division was on the way.

On 21 March Rommel made his move, much to the dismay of Wavell, who expected a period of inactivity to last until early May. The inadequacies of the British and Commonwealth forces in El Agheila and Mersa Brega were brutally exposed as the Axis force swept aside the opposition and took possession of two important water sources. In part, the Germans' success was achieved by the bluff of dressing soft-skinned vehicles up as tanks with the addition of a length of telegraph pole.

The British retreat only served to reduce the degree of defeat. General O'Connor had no doubt whom he needed now and he sent for Strafer, who flew in to Tobruk on 7 April accompanied by his brigade major. The 2nd Division Support Group was a shambles and, in 'Army speak', Strafer 'gripped it'. He worked unceasingly, visited all his units, spoke to all the commanding officers and as many of the men as possible and in all of them he imbued his own sense of purpose. His reputation had preceded him, his equable, unflustered manner was just right for the circumstances and his leadership was welcomed. Then he led the rejuvenated Support Group and other remnants of 2nd Armoured Division into action south of Tobruk. Strafer managed to delay the enemy and this allowed the garrison more time to strengthen its defences. He then conducted a skilfully managed withdrawal back to the Egyptian border by mid-April.

The citation below makes clear that Strafer had rescued a very difficult situation. However, his stay with the 2nd Armoured Division was of necessity very short as his talents were in demand elsewhere.

The first page of his citation for a bar to his DSO is reproduced below.[4]

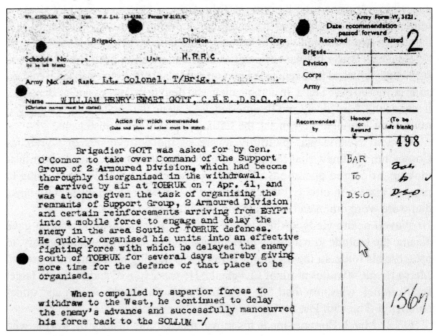

Citation for bar to DSO, April 1941. (WHE Gott's personal file, The National Archives)

The citation continued with these words:

Sollum/Halfaya area where their advance was finally checked.

He continued in command of the troops in the frontier area, conducted an attack on the enemy in the Capuzzo-Sollum area in May, which achieved its object in the first instance.

He remained in command of the front, acted as second-in-command of 7th Armoured Division in the operations in June and subsequently remained in command of all the mobile troops in the forward area.

Throughout these operations, he has shown great tactical skill, power of command and inspiration and organising ability.

On 7 April, Strafer's old battalion, 1st KRRC, carried out any number of demolitions as 9th Australian Division withdrew to new defensive positions. That night, 6/7 April, the advanced Headquarters of Cyrenaica Command was in Maraua and the plan was for it to move back to Tmimi. However, General Neame and General O'Connor did not arrive at the new location and Brigadier AF Harding,[5] the Brigadier, General Staff, feared for their safety. He reported their absence to Wavell and it was later confirmed that, accompanied by Brigadier Combe, the two generals had taken the wrong desert track and by heading north instead of east, they had run into a German patrol.

The situation was dire and it would get worse.

At Tobruk, 18th and 24th Australian Infantry brigades were preparing the defences of the port. The 9th Australian Division, less 24th Brigade but with the Support Group in company, straddled the coast road with its left flank at Acroma.

Major General Gambier-Parry, GOC 2nd Armoured Division, had established his headquarters in Mechili and he had taken under his command 3rd Indian Motor Brigade (commanded by Brigadier Vaughan) as well as the remnants of several other units. Gambier-Parry was ordered to withdraw to El Adem that night. However, during the preceding day the enemy encircled HQ 2nd Armoured Division and twice invited Gambier-Perry to surrender, offers he courteously declined. He agreed with Vaughan that they would fight their way out.

They failed.

On 8 April, General Gambier-Parry, Brigadier Vaughan, and most of the Indian Motor Brigade and the entire Division Headquarters were taken prisoner. It was just as well that Strafer and what remained of 2nd Armoured Division was still in the fight.

Headquarters Cyrenaica Command, which had evolved from XIII Corps, had been completely outmanoeuvred and defeated. It was dissolved on 14 April and its remnants were re-mustered and rather confusingly reverted to the 'Western Desert Force' under the command of Lieutenant General Noel Beresford-Peirse.

The 9th Australian Division moved into the fortress and port of Tobruk on 9 April and the remainder of the Western Desert Force withdrew to Sollum, a distance of about 100 miles. This left Tobruk isolated and besieged. The Australians established a Field Hospital in a complex of caves in the rocky terrain of the fortress, the entrance of which was marked by a fig tree. The tree is still to be seen and cuttings are said to have been taken from it to mark war memorials in Australia.

As the citation above shows, during this period Strafer manipulated his command with flair and skill. The German-Italian opposition, although not an entirely happy marriage, continued its advance challenged only by Gott's mobile force. He fell back and the enemy took Fort Capuzzo and on 12 April it also re-captured Bardia. Then, by the end of April, the Axis formations had not only taken Sollum but also the strategically important Halfaya Pass. This Axis advance did have the downside of extending its logistic chain and as a consequence Rommel took up defensive positions in order to consolidate his gains.

Wavell had to stop the rot and, to effect this; he planned Operation Brevity. General Beresford–Peirse briefed Strafer Gott and told him that his aim was 'to gain time, to apply pressure whenever he could and to give ground only if compelled by superior force'.[6] These words should be noted as they are important, particularly so when the success or otherwise of Brevity and Strafer's role in the operation is considered.

Strafer handed over command of the 2nd Armoured Division Support Group after his very brief sojourn in that appointment as he was to be the operational commander for this foray and he assumed command of the forward elements of 7th Armoured Division on 14 April.

He had under command three columns or groups and the composition of these was as follows:

Coast Group
2nd Battalion, The Rifle Brigade (2 RB) (minus one company)
Mortar support, 3rd Battalion, Coldstream Guards (3 Coldm Gds)
5th Australian Anti-tank Battery (5 Aust Anti-tank Battery), 2/2nd Australian Anti-tank Regiment (2/2nd Aust Anti-tank Regt)
8th Field Regiment (8 Fd Regt, RA (2-pounder anti-tank guns))

22 Guards Brigade Group
1st Battalion, The Durham Light Infantry (1 DLI)
2nd Battalion, The Scots Guards (2 SG)
3rd Battalion, Coldstream Guards (3 Coldm Gds)
4th Royal Tank Regiment (4 RTR) (24 Matilda Mk II Infantry tanks)
One troop, 12th Anti-tank Battery, 2/3rd Australian Anti-tank Regiment (2/3rd Aust Anti-tank Regt) (2-pounder anti-tank guns)

7 Armed Brigade Group
A Company, 2nd Battalion The Rifle Brigade (2 RB)
2nd Royal Tank Regiment (2 RTR) (29 Cruiser tanks)
6th Australian Divisional Cavalry (6 Aust Div Cavalry) (28 light tank Mk VIB)
7 Support Group (elements)
11th Hussars (11 H) (Marmon-Herrington armoured cars)
One troop, 12th Anti-tank Battery, 2/3rd Australian Anti-tank Regiment (2/3rd Aust Anti-tank Regt) (2-pounder anti-tank guns)

Notwithstanding the above, the Official History described the object and organisation of Strafer's command:

His force consisted of the 22 Guards Brigade Group, in the Halfaya Pass area, and four, small mobile columns whose composition varied from time to time but was based on one or more troops of 25-pounders, a company of infantry, and a few armoured cars or light tanks. These columns were located at Halfaya, Sofafi, Buq Buq and Sidi Barrani while a French motor battalion held the escarpment pass at 'Halfway House'. These dispositions [were] aimed at making the important passes and water supplies secure from anything but a strong attack. The columns from Halfaya and Sofafi at once to harass the enemy about Capuzzo and Sollum.[7]

This statement seems to be quite clear but later in the same Official History (page 160) the authors had this different view:

Brigadier Gott's plan for Brevity was to advance by three parallel routes. On the desert flank the so-called 7th Armoured Brigade Group (consisting of 2nd Royal Tank Regiment at a strength of only two squadrons, or twenty-nine Cruiser tanks in all, and three columns of the Support Group) was to advance some 30 miles from Bir el Khireigat to Sidi Azeiz and destroy any enemy encountered on the way. In the centre above the escarpment 22nd Guards Brigade Group with 4th Royal Tank Regiment (two squadrons of 24 'I' tanks in all) under command was to clear the top of Halfaya Pass, secure Fort Capuzzo and exploit northwards. ... The third or Coast Group consisting mainly of 2nd Rifle Brigade and 8th Field Regiment RA was to prevent the enemy moving out of Sollum and was then to capture the lower Halfaya Pass and Sollum Barracks and village.

Strafer Gott's headquarters was expanded to reflect the size of his new command and the War Diary remarked that the headquarters 'became very busy ... and gradually expanded to almost a division for its new aggressive role.' Lieutenant Colonel de Bruyne KRRC joined as AA & QMG[8] and Captain Hobart was appointed Deputy Brigade Major.[9] There was some light relief on 8 May and the entry advised:

Some interest was aroused by a fake rifleman, whose treacherous behaviour drew, from the gunner who spoke to him, the comment that he thought at the time he was 'a bit overdressed'. This was the first instance of the German disguise trick. It was also clear that the Germans were using our captured tanks and cars.[10]

On 15 May Strafer made first contact with the Axis force. No. 274 Squadron RAF flew standing patrols over his advancing columns and supported him. Strafer was in his element. He had an independent command and was free to roam at will. He was to be seen everywhere and his constant presence was undoubtedly a factor in the aggressive attitude of his soldiers. His first objective was the Halfaya Pass and here he achieved complete surprise. The 2nd Battalion Scots Guards and a squadron of 4th Royal Tank Regiment overran the defences, although the Italian gunners knocked out seven tanks.

Surprise having been lost, a robust response from the Germans, in particular, was expected and duly received. The defenders of Fort Capuzzo resisted the 1st Battalion Durham Light Infantry and its squadron of supporting tanks and, although the two components of the attacking force lost contact with each other the position eventually succumbed. Two days after the initial assault Capuzzo and Halfaya Pass were in British hands. Bir Wair and Musaid were also soon taken. However, the loss of tanks precluded any further significant exploitation to the north.

The Coast Group advanced across broken ground against an enemy entrenched below the Halfaya Pass. The ground favoured the defenders and despite the close support of the eight Blenheims of 14 Squadron RAF, no progress could be made. Meanwhile, up on the escarpment and on the left flank, only a light enemy screen faced 7th Armoured Brigade Group and it was able to push north towards Sidi Azeiz without difficulty.

One of Strafer's columns, almost certainly 7th Armoured Brigade Group, brought down fire upon an enemy transport convoy in between Capuzzo and Sidi Azeiz to considerable effect. Colonel von Herff, the German Commander and recipient of this fire, swiftly sent a report to Rommel that exaggerated the threat he was under.

Rommel took the report at face value and concluded that this might well be the opening moves of an attempt to relieve Tobruk and the release of 9th Australian Division. He was already in possession of intercepted signals that spoke of an attack and events seemed to confirm his worst fears. He immediately strengthened his besieging force to guard against any Australian breakout and then ordered a battalion of 5th Panzer Regiment to counter-attack the Durhams. The attack was successful and the North countrymen were driven back to Musaid 'with heavy losses'.[11]

Rommel was decisive; he threw more armour into the battle and bearing the initial brunt was 2nd Royal Tank Regiment. However, mechanical problems forced the Regiment to pull back to Sidi Suleiman. This was a serious reverse.

Strafer's force on the east or desert flank, now close to Sidi Azeiz, was ordered to relieve the pressure on Fort Capuzzo but was unable to affect the issue and the 1st Battalion The Durham Light Infantry was now expelled from Fort Capuzzo, suffering further heavy losses in the process. Fort Capuzzo was having an exciting war as it changed hands yet again, and not for the last time.

The Coast Group had persevered and taken the position below the pass and 124 prisoners, to boot. At this point the operation could be counted a limited success. The shrewd leadership of Rommel tipped the balance and he overruled Colonel von Herff's judgment of British strength and intentions. Rommel countermanded von Herff's decision to fight a 'delaying action west of Sidi Azeiz', reinforced von Herff with a battalion of tanks and ordered a further counter-attack. At Bletchley Park the battle was being monitored and, when Rommel's intentions became clear, Ultra messages were flashed to Egypt.[12]

Strafer was painfully aware that his 22nd Guards Brigade Group was very exposed in open ground up on the escarpment and very vulnerable to an armoured attack. At 2100 hrs on 15 May 1941 he signalled HQ, Western Desert Force to tell the GOC that he considered that a withdrawal to the Halfaya Pass would be prudent. Inexplicably, and even though he was the Operational Commander, he did not feel he had the authority to make this decision and passed it to Beresford-Peirse. This was curiously indecisive and unlike Strafer Gott.

There was then a delay, for reasons that remain unexplained, and it was not until 0245 hrs on 16 May that a reply was received. The GOC's message was for Strafer to hold fast until he, Beresford-Peirse, had had a chance to examine reports from aerial reconnaissance. This was a surprising response given the clear intelligence advice; perhaps Beresford-Peirse had not received it.

As it happens, Beresford-Peirse was too late; Strafer, reverting to type, had taken a decision about an hour earlier to withdraw 22nd Guards Brigade Group back to the head of the Pass and 7th Armoured Brigade Group to cover the enemy positions in and around Sidi Azeiz. The Coast Group occupied the area between the bottom of the pass and Sollum.

The armoured reinforcement promised to Colonel von Herff arrived in Sidi Azeiz at 0300 hrs on 16 May but was then incapacitated until 1700 hrs before it could refuel. Von Herff advanced on the screen of 7th Armoured Brigade Group the following afternoon and pushed the British force back about 15 miles, to Bir el Khireigat. The cruiser tanks of 2nd Royal Tank Regiment were subject to any number of mechanical failures along the way. That apart, the withdrawal was conducted in good order.

The Germans were content to halt and adopt a defensive posture on the general line Sidi Omar-Sidi Suleiman-Sollum and by doing so ceded control of the Halfaya Pass to Strafer's force. This was the sole gain and the *Official History of the War* considered that 'Operation Brevity was, therefore, a failure'.[13]

"... and precisely what do you mean by improperly dressed?"

Cartoonist Jon returns to a familiar theme but Strafer's military policemen did not have time to apply dress regulations; they were fully occupied with their principle task.

Before this judgment is readily accepted it would be as well to consider the aims given to Strafer before the operation began. He was told that he was '*to gain time, to apply pressure whenever he could and to give ground only if compelled by superior force.*'[14] (Author's italics, see p.106.)

On that basis Strafer had satisfied his given aim and then, prudently and in accord with his orders not to tackle superior forces (outnumbered in tanks by more than 2:1), he withdrew to defend the vital Halfaya Pass. His force, widely dispersed, was always insufficient to inflict major damage on the enemy and the conclusions of the latter-day historians who made the judgment were unrealistic.

It was certainly not a crashing victory but then neither was it a disaster – it is suggested that 'failure' is too strong a word. The costs of the operation were borne in the main by the Durham Light Infantry, which lost 160 all ranks. A total of eighteen tanks were knocked out or damaged. German losses were very modest: twelve killed, sixty-one wounded and 185 missing. Three tanks were lost. Against the scale of other wartime operations Brevity was little more than a skirmish. Its unrecorded benefit was that it gave Strafer further valuable experience and demonstrated his capacity to control a formation in mobile operations over difficult terrain.

It is germane that, notwithstanding the label 'failure' that was hung on Brevity, it did not reflect on Strafer and his reputation was, if anything, enhanced. The influence of Strafer Gott on the campaign was acknowledged within the Army but it was War Office policy not to publicise the exploits of any officer below the rank of lieutenant general. Sometime later, General Oliver Leese said:[15]

> There can be no doubt that if censorship had been controlled on better lines in those days Strafer Gott would have been built up just as high as Rommel.

Chapter notes
1. Neame, Lieutenant General Sir Philip VC KBE CB DSO KStJ (1888-1978). He won a gold medal at the 1924 Olympics for shooting. He was captured in 1941 but escaped in 1943.
2. Playfair, Major General ISO et al, *The Mediterranean and Middle East*, Vol. 1, p.365.
3. Ibid, Vol. II, p.3.
4. *The London Gazette* supplement No. 35,209, p.3,881, 4 July 1941.
5. When Lieutenant General Richard O'Connor and Lieutenant General Sir Philip Neame were captured on 6/7 April 1941, Harding was the senior officer left in the headquarters and on that basis he assumed command of the Western Desert Force – albeit briefly. However, it was he that took the decision to hold Tobruk. He subsequently rose to become FM Lord Harding of Petherton.
6. Playfair, Major General ISO, et al, *The Mediterranean and Middle East*, Vol. II, p.30.
7. Ibid, p.36.
8. AA & QMG is an abbreviation of Assistant Adjutant and Quarter Master General. The officer appointed has responsibility for all the Administrative and Logistic functions of his headquarters. He is, for example responsible for implementing and coordinating his commander's policy on all personnel matters, such as discipline, pay, promotion, appointments, decorations, medical, and grave registration. In addition he is responsible for all logistic matters. Thus he has a direct interest in transport and supply in all its aspects.
9. Deputy Brigade Major in this case is the appointment of an officer to assist in the planning and execution of operations.
10. Playfair, Major General ISO, et al, *The Mediterranean and Middle East*, Vol. II, p.36.
11. War Diary, 7th Armoured Division Support Group, 8 May 1941.
12. Playfair, Major General ISO, et al, *The Mediterranean and Middle East*, Vol. II, p.161.
13. McKay, S., *The Secret Life of Bletchley Park*, p.134.
14. Playfair, Major General ISO, et al, *The Mediterranean and Middle East*, Vol. II, p.162.
15. General Sir Oliver William Hargreaves Leese KCB CBE DSO (1894-1978) in a letter to Brigadier HRW Vernon and reproduced from *Strafer Gott*.

Chapter 10

Operation Battleaxe
May-June 1941

Just before the launch of Brevity the Royal Navy escorted a vital convoy that delivered eighty-two cruisers, 135 'I' tanks and twenty-one light tanks to the Western Desert Force and with this new materiel, 7th Armoured Division was to be rebuilt. Had these tanks been available for Brevity the operation would have had a different outcome.

General Paulus[1] visited Rommel in early May and concluded that the latter was dangerously deficient in fuel and ammunition. Paulus reported the situation to General von Brauchitsch, the Commander-in-Chief of the German Army, who knew that Hitler was about to launch Operation Barbarossa. Rommel was ordered not to advance further to take up defensive positions and to conserve his assets.

Rommel was painfully aware of his limitations and so he was content to limit his operations to reconnaissance in force. Strafer was ordered to maintain his grip on the Halfaya Pass and to push further west as and when it was possible. This 'further west' was in order to provide a firm start line for Wavell's next offensive move. This was to be Operation Battleaxe, the aim of which was to drive the enemy beyond Tobruk. Predictably, Wavell wanted the use of the coastal road, at least as far as Sollum, in the early phase.

The Germans were strong in armour and had 160 tanks in three battalions facing Gott, but their use was limited by the availability of petrol. On 27 May, von Herff made a speculative foray towards the head of the pass now held by the 3rd Battalion Coldstream Guards. The foray developed into a full-blooded attack and the guardsmen, supported by their gunners and 'I' tanks, could not stem the onslaught. Strafer recognised the danger and authorised the CO of 3rd Coldstream Guards to withdraw. This he did with commendable skill but the position was lost, as were 173 casualties, four field guns, eight anti-tank guns and five 'I' tanks. This was, emphatically, not the stable and firm start line Wavell required.

The Royal Navy had captured an Enigma machine on 9 May 1941,[2] and thereafter the Allied forces had an enhanced capacity to read enemy signals. The official, three-volume history *The War in the Mediterranean and Middle East* was written between 1954 and 1960, when these matters were still shrouded in secrecy. On that basis, it is understandable that nowhere in this magisterial work is there a single specific mention of Enigma or the Ultra intelligence derived from that source. Similarly, General Alan Brooke's[3] diary is also silent.

Paulus's report was intercepted by Bletchley Park and the Ultra intelligence convinced Churchill that an opportunity existed to strike a decisive blow.

Wavell had already issued his plan for the Western Desert Force to carry out Battleaxe on 1 May 1941, but realised that he needed time before he unleashed his force. Unfortunately, he was under constant pressure from Winston Churchill, who had an inflated idea of his own military acumen, and kept on insisting that Wavell attack at once. Churchill either did not understand or did not care about the enormous burden he had placed on the object of his impatience.

Wavell had vast responsibilities, his command spanning nine countries, two continents and measuring 2,000 by 1,700 miles. He had scant resources to defend this vast tract. In addition he had diplomatic duties to deal with: the French in Syria and North Africa, consultations with HM Ambassadors in Egypt, Iraq, the Governor General in the Sudan, the High Commissioner for Palestine and Transjordon, the Governors of Cyprus, Aden and British Somaliland and the political agent in the Persian Gulf. Wavell was given a headquarters staff of five officers.[4]

All in all, Archibald Wavell had a lot on his plate but he was far too wise to launch an offensive until he had his forces properly trained, aligned and equipped. He was starting from scratch with 7th Armoured Division, which had lost almost all of its tanks in Operation Compass. The armoured personnel of the old division had been scattered across the face of the Army and there was serious work to be done before what was, in effect, a new formation. The re-equipped 7th Armoured Division was battle ready. The very earliest date on which operations could begin was 10 June, but even that date turned out to be no more than an aspiration.

The problems with 7th Armoured Division were deep and multitudinous. The tank crews were unfamiliar with their vehicles, the organisation had to be formed and systems to operate it re-introduced. The enemy was made up of seasoned soldiers and pitting this brand new division against them carried considerable risk. The most battle-experienced soldiers in the Division were in Strafer's Support Group.

Wavell expected that, in the initial phase of his plan, the enemy would be engaged and defeated in the area bounded by Halfaya, Sollum, Capuzzo and

Sidi Azeiz by the 4th Indian Division led by Major General FW Messervy. All of these places were very familiar to Strafer and his men, who remained under command of the re-equipped 7th Armoured Division commanded by Major General Sir Michael O'Creagh. This division was to cover the left flank of the Indian Division during this advance and to provide support as and when appropriate.

On 8 June the GOC 7th Armoured Division took a brief leave of just two days and Strafer stepped up and assumed command of the Division. The War Diary refers to him as 'Major General' during this period. Lieutenant Colonel Campbell stood in at Support Group.

In the second phase, 4th Indian Division and 7th Armoured Division were to thrust north and take Tobruk and El Adem. Following success here Derna and Mechili were then to be taken and secured by 7th Armoured Brigade (of 7th Armoured Division) on the left and Jaxo Column from the Support Group. It was left to General Beresford-Peirse, the Corps Commander, to determine the degree of support that could be given by the besieged Tobruk garrison at any stage in the operation.

That is a vastly simplified synopsis of a complex plan that was designed to sweep away a well-equipped adversary who had had ample time to prepare his defences. The only strategically important objective was the Hafid Ridge and Hill 208, its highest point.

The 7th Armoured Brigade Group, accurately named, consisted only of:

> 2nd Royal Tank Regiment
> 6th Royal Tank Regiment
> 3rd Hussars

The Support Group was to operate in concert with it and, under Strafer's command, was:

> 1st Battalion, KRRC
> 2nd Battalion, The Rifle Brigade
> 3rd Regiment, RHA
> 4th Regiment, RHA
> 1st Regiment, Light AA Regt RA

Taken together as an entity, this was a well-balanced and powerful formation. However, these two organisations functioned as two separate commands and herein lay a fundamental problem. The Support Group had no armour and the Armoured Brigade had no artillery. The need for effective coordination is obvious.

Armley House, Leeds. Built in 1816, this was the family seat of the Gott family until Gott's father gifted it to the City of Leeds in 1929. The surrounding parkland was converted into a golf course and the house is now the clubhouse of Gott's Park Golf Club. *(Patrick Broadhurst)*

No. 3, Montpellier Crescent, Scarborough. The Gott family lived in this house from 1897 and William Gott was born here. *(Patrick Broadhurst)*

WHE Gott (centre) as a schoolboy, 1913. *(Harrow School)*

Mr EM Butler Esq., the Housemaster, The Park. Butler had a strong influence on William Gott when he was a pupil in his charge. *(Harrow School)*

WC Churchill at Harrow School, circa 1888.
(Internet source)

Harrow School.
(Internet source)

Lieutenant Anthony Eden MC KRRC. Eden, a fellow rifleman, was a firm supporter of Strafer Gott and extolled his virtues to Churchill, his father-in-law. *(Internet source)*

Lieutenant WHE Gott MC KRRC. *(RGJ Museum archive)*

Captain WHE Gott MC KRRC, 1929, serving with 2nd Battalion KRRC at Tidworth in 1929 as Officer Commanding C Company. *(RGJ Museum archive)*

William and Pamela Gott, recently married in 1934.
(RGJ Museum archive)

The officers of 2nd Battalion KRRC, serving in Aldershot in 1938; Major WHE Gott MC (centre left).
(RGJ Museum archive)

A British Matilda tank being towed up Halfaya Pass. Sollum Bay is in the background.
(Internet source)

The small settlement of Sollum, 1941. Many soldiers must have wondered if this was a place worth dying for. The escarpment and its dominance over the coastal strip is evident. *(Internet source)*

The bay at Sollum. The wreckage is the result of gunfire from HMS *Aphis*. *(Internet source)*

Hauptman Wilhelm Bach: a courageous adversary, who took and held the Halfaya Pass during Operation Battleaxe. *(Internet source)*

FM Irwin Rommel (1891-1944), who was unquestionably the finest of the desert generals. It was Strafer Gott's misfortune to find himself arraigned against such a skilled and bold adversary. Rommel was an officer of the 'old school'. He was a chivalrous gentleman and fine innovative soldier. *(Internet source)*

Lieutenant General Sir Alan Cunningham GCMG KCB DSO MC. He was briefly the GOC-in-C of the 8th Army. Auchinleck sacked him in late November 1941. *(Internet source)*

Brigadier JC 'Jock' Campbell VC DSO* MC. This photograph was taken just after the parade at which he had been decorated with his Victoria Cross. Only a few weeks later, he was killed in an accident. *(Internet source)*

Major General WHE Gott and Brigadier JC Campbell. These two good friends participated in some of the bitterest fighting in the Desert Campaign. They made a formidable team. *(Internet source)*

Major General GWEJ Erskine CB DSO. A devoted acolyte of Strafer Gott, he had served under Gott as a subaltern in India. Later, he was his Brigadier, General Staff. *(Internet source)*

Rifleman Beeley VC KRRC, one of the casualties in the destruction of the 1st Battalion KRRC at Sidi Rezegh on 21/22 November 1941. *(Internet source)*

The detritus of war: Sidi Rezegh, after the guns fell silent. *(Internet source)*

A Crusader tank passes a burning Panzer.
(Internet source)

Lieutenant General Herbert Lumsden CB DSO MC, photographed in 1943. He was an admirer of Gott and was killed in action later in the war. *(Internet source)*

WC Churchill. His selection of Gott to command the 8th Army was hasty and ill-considered. *(Internet source)*

General Sir Alan Brooke KG GCB OM GCVO DSO*. He was Churchill's principal military adviser and counseled against the selection of Gott to command the 8th Army. He favoured Montgomery. *(Internet source)*

War correspondents Alexender Clifford and Alan Moorehead. Their impressions of the Desert Campaign are invaluable to latter-day historians. Both men knew Gott and admired him. *(Internet source)*

Sergeant HG James DFM RAF. Having suffered life-threatening wounds, Jimmy James spent months in hospital. He made a full recovery and is pictured here in 1943. *(Squadron Leader HE James)*

An Italian surrenders to an Indian soldier. *(Internet source)*

Crusader MK1 with 2pdr gun. *(Internet source)*

Lieutenant General Sir Neil Ritchie KCB DSO MC KStJ. Appointed to command the 8th Army after Cunningham was sacked, he operated under the close supervision of Auchinleck. He was unable to exercise effective command over his corps commanders and was eventually replaced by Auchinleck himself in 1942. *(Internet source)*

Lieutenant General Godwin-Austen CB OBE MC. He was one of the most successful desert generals but resigned his command of XIII Corps, in extraordinary circumstances, in February 1942. Strafer Gott took his place in command and was promoted to acting Lieutenant General. *(Internet source)*

General Sir Claude Auchinleck GCB GCIE CSI DSO OBE. *(Internet source)*

Generals Norrie Ritchie and Gott confer over a map. The body language in this photograph is interesting. Ritchie, the Army Commander, is in the centre (with Gott centre right) and clearly not leading the discussion. *(Internet source)*

Major General DH Pienaar CB DSO, the recalcitrant and very difficult South African officer who did not like Gott and frequently challenged his leadership. Pienaar was killed in action in late 1942. *(Internet source)*

Major General H Klooper DSO. He was the hopelessly inept and ill-prepared defender of the Fortress of Tobruk and he surrendered on 22 June 1942. He was jeered by the soldiers that he led into captivity but was exonerated after the war and had a very successful career thereafter. *(Internet source)*

Churchill, Dorman-Smith, Gott and Auchinleck. The fateful meeting on 5 August 1942, showing an aggressive Churchill talking to Auchinleck, whom he was about to dismiss. Gott looks on quizzically and Dorman-Smith observes from the background. *(Internet source)*

Bir Hacheim, seventy years later. This was the scene of fierce fighting between the 1st Free French Brigade and the Italian Ariete Division. The small white flags on the left of the photograph are marking mines that were laid more than seventy years ago and are still lethal. *(Internet source)*

El Alamein railway station in 1942. It was a nondescript railway building that became the centre of a historic battle. *(Internet source)*

The Bristol Bombay in which General Gott was killed. This photograph was taken the day that the aircraft was delivered to RAF Lyneham by Bristol. *(Squadron Leader HE James)*

Emil Clade, the German fighter ace who commanded the flight of Me 109s that brought down the Bristol Bombay on 7 August 1942. *(Internet source)*

Emil Clade and his mechanic. *(Internet source)*

The burial service for Gott and seventeen others on 8 August 1942 at the place they died. Their burned-out aircraft is the backdrop. These were temporary graves and the bodies were all later reinterred. *(Gordon Brown)*

Squadron Leader Jimmy James DFM AFC in 2012. (*Author*)

The author at Strafer's final resting place in March 2013, placing a wreath on behalf of Strafer's Regimental Association. (Author)

Strafer's headstone.
(Author)

Strafer among his soldiers. *(Author)*

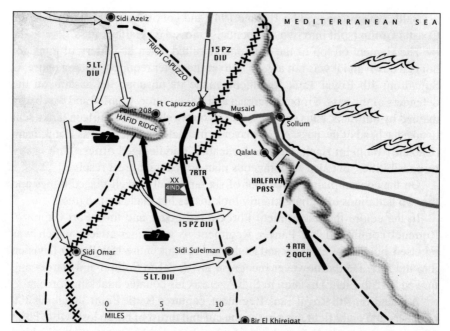

Operation Battleaxe, May-July 1941. This was a relatively minor but unsuccessful operation. Strafer Gott was one of very few to emerge from this debacle with his reputation intact.
(Map by Arthur Perry)

The so-called Escarpment Force was the 22nd Guards Brigade and the 4th Armed Brigade, in total three infantry battalions and two armoured regiments.

The Coast Force also had two components, the Halfaya Group, with one battalion of infantry, and a squadron of tanks from the 4th Royal Tank Regiment. The 11th Indian Infantry Brigade was the other component with, two battalions and two troops of 4th Royal Tank Regiment (six Matilda and eleven infantry tanks).

The RAF mustered every airframe available – ninety-eight fighters and 105 bombers. The air plan allowed for the bombing of airfields, road convoys and Benghazi. The latter target was hit on a regular basis. The Royal Navy kept up its hazardous supply of Tobruk and 'it seemed to Wavell that the British would at any rate start the operation stronger than the enemy.'[5] However, only a little later he started to entertain doubts, particularly about his armoured cars, which were no match for their German equivalent. In addition, and to compound his concerns, the 'I' tanks were too slow and the Cruiser tanks very unreliable.

Wavell shared his misgivings with the Chief of the Imperial General Staff (CIGS) General Dill in a telegram on 28 May but, nevertheless, he issued his detailed orders that very same day.

Battleaxe commenced on 15 June 1941 and got off to a poor start when the Coastal Group (split into two components) moved on Halfaya Pass.

The element on top of the escarpment halted when its battery of guns got bogged down and it was not able to deliver the cover required. After a pause, C Squadron, 4th Royal Tank Regiment, made its unsupported assault on the defenders of the pass, a mixed German and Italian force. It failed and was badly mauled by anti-tank guns, which knocked out twelve of the thirteen tanks sent to take the head of the pass. A key player in the Halfaya defence was Hauptmann (Captain) Wilhelm Bach. He was a capable, middle-aged officer with heavy responsibilities, but also a courageous man armed with great resolve.

On the coastal plain below, four of six tanks fell to well-placed mines and the two battalions of Indian infantry took losses but made no progress.

In the centre the Escarpment Force fared better and took Fort Capuzzo. Rommel committed 8th Panzer Regiment to a counter-attack, which was repulsed, but he was cautious and loathe to throw his entire 15th Panzer Division into the fray. He did however recognise the threat to Sollum and Bardia and moved his 5th Light Division to Sidi Azeiz as his counter-attacking force.

A Squadron, 4th Royal Tank Regiment, captured Battle Point 38, taking 200 prisoners and eight field guns but in the cut and thrust of battle lost Battle Point 38 to counter-attack. B Squadron, who had been held in reserve, attacked but failed to take Hill 206. The 2nd Scots Guards captured the outpost of Musaid. A total of 500 disconsolate enemy soldiers were marched to the rear.

On the desert flank 7th Armoured Brigade led the advance and Strafer's Support Group guarded the south-west. When the armour was held in front of Hafid Ridge there was no immediate artillery support because all the guns were located with the Support Group, which at this stage was concentrating its attention on the protection of 7th Armoured Brigade's flank.

Paddy Griffith summed up the situation and the problems the British encountered in his book *World War II Desert Tactics*. In this he said:

> On Hafid Ridge the British would encounter a phenomenon that would become almost typical in subsequent battles. This was the allure of an enemy position that appeared to be only lightly defended, or occupied only by vulnerable soft-skinned vehicles. The temptation would be strong for British armour to charge in piecemeal and without careful preparation, leading to disastrous results when the enemy's 'vulnerable' trucks turned out to be accompanied by towed guns, some of which turned out to be very dangerous indeed to attacking tanks.
>
> On Hafid Ridge this problem was made worse by the complexities of the terrain, which turned out to consist of three successive ridges rather than just one; the Axis forces lurking behind the second and

third caused all sorts of unexpected difficulties to the British armour that had successfully cleared the first.

This battle therefore stands as a classic early example of all those difficulties of reconnaissance, navigation and terrain analysis that proved such pitfalls for tacticians throughout the whole desert war.

The RAF had overflown Hafid Ridge but its photo-reconnaissance capacity was very limited and the enemy positions were never identified accurately. By day's end Battleaxe had ended with failure to take Halfaya Pass. There had been success in the centre but this was offset by 'a sharp check at the Hafid Ridge on the left'.[6] The 7th Armoured Division made three assaults on the ridge, at one point overrunning part of the German line but had only forty-eight battle-worthy tanks left of its original eighty-two. Ominously the RAF reported large numbers of vehicles moving east, a clear indication that Rommel was bringing forward reinforcements. The tank battle for Hafid Ridge on 15 June had been an expensive defeat. Wavell's misgivings were being borne out.

The second day of the battle started with a much-depleted British Force. The 7th Armoured Brigade could only muster twenty-eight Cruiser tanks in 2nd Royal Tank Regiment and twenty in 6th Royal Tank Regiment. The 4th Armoured Brigade had suffered a similar level of attrition and its original start strength of 100 Matildas had been reduced to thirty-seven, but with eleven repairable tanks expected to re-join in the future.

Beresford–Peirse recast his plans and determined to exploit the now isolated position of Bach's defenders at Halfaya Pass. He ordered 4th Indian Division to renew the attack on the pass and to consolidate its position at Capuzzo. The 4th Armoured Brigade was to join 7th Armoured Brigade and together they were to take Hafid Ridge. Rommel perceived the outline British plan after the astute analysis of wireless traffic that pointed to a regrouping and redistribution of the British Forces and this, coupled with other indications (such as increase of air activity and rail traffic), had proved convincing enough for General Rommel to expect to be attacked … in spite of the general impression that the British had not the necessary forces.[7]

The reality was that British signal discipline was singularly lax throughout the campaign in the Western Desert. Lapses in voice procedure were sufficiently frequent to allow the Germans regularly to evaluate British intentions.

In the event Bach held out at Halfaya – he had no option as he was surrounded and he had to fight or surrender. He chose the former option and again repelled all attempts to remove him. The Germans attacked Capuzzo with eighty tanks, organised into two columns, but an artillery concentration supplemented by fire from Matildas in entrenched positions was devastating. Fifty enemy tanks were destroyed and the attack failed. Meanwhile, 2nd

Battalion Scots Guards captured Sollum barracks on the escarpment and formed an effective block to any German attempt to reinforce Hauptmann Bach.

Out on the left flank the 7th Armoured Brigade and the Support Group were in contact with the 5th Light Division. It was a fluid battle that required commanders on both sides to have their wits about them and to be as flexible as if the battle was being fought at sea. The engagement veered away from Hafid Ridge and in a series of steps gravitated toward Sidi Omar.

Strafer was able to bring his artillery into play and it was a factor in thwarting an attempt by the Germans to outflank the brigade and to drive a wedge between 2nd Royal Tank Regiment and 6th Royal Tank Regiment. The fighting was protracted and intense – the measurement of that is that at day's end these two armoured regiments could only field twenty-one battle-worthy tanks between them. The 7th Armoured Brigade and the Support Group withdrew to the line of the frontier wire as night fell.

The third day of the battle started early. At 0430 hrs, 5th Light Division moved forward to contact 7th Armoured Brigade and succeeded in taking ground as far as Sidi Suleiman. Threatening moves by the 15th Panzer Division in the Capuzzo area were sufficient to alarm GOC 4th Indian Division and Messervy decided to ignore Beresford-Peirse's instructions to dispatch 4th Armoured Brigade to support 7th Armoured Brigade and consolidate his own position. O'Creagh, commanding 7th Armoured Division, asked Beresford-Peirse for support and by doing so sent a negative message that was picked up by General Wavell, who happened to be at Beresford-Peirse's headquarters.

Rommel intercepted the same message; he took heart from the evident British uncertainty and the situation worsened as a result. Rommel said later:

> It sounded suspiciously as though the British Commander no longer felt himself capable of handling the situation. It being obvious that, in their present bewildered state, the British would not start anything for the time.[8]

How right was Rommel's appreciation and, not for the first time, he had been able to exploit the capacity of the Germans to intercept British wireless traffic. In this particular case it had a significant effect on the outcome of Operation Battleaxe. Ultimately, it would change the face of the war in North Africa and the personalities who conducted it.

Wavell flew at once to O'Creagh's headquarters at Halfway House. The two German divisions continued to press forward from the west and reached a position within 10 miles of Halfaya Pass and the beleaguered Hauptmann Bach.

The 22nd Guards Brigade and 11th Indian Infantry Brigade withdrew and were protected by the combination of the 4th and 7th armoured brigades and

Support Group. The two soft-skinned formations made their escape although the delaying action lasted until well into the afternoon.

Messervy made contact with O'Creagh and told him[9] that he was withdrawing from Capuzzo and Halfaya at 1100 hrs. This order was being executed when Wavell and Beresford-Peirse arrived at Headquarters 7th Armoured Division. It was too late for change and Wavell had little option other than to rubberstamp the decision.

There was no way to camouflage the fact that Battleaxe was a failure, the British had been defeated and Tobruk remained besieged. The measure of defeat in the statistics and the imbalance in casualties and tank losses speak for themselves. British dead numbered 122, with 588 wounded and 259 missing. The Germans lost ninety-three, 350, and 253 respectively. The material losses were even starker: ninety-eight British tanks were destroyed against fifty – some of which were recoverable; thirty-six aircraft were lost against only ten from the Luftwaffe.[10]

Out of this sorry mess Strafer Gott was one of few to emerge with credit. He had, by now, established that he was a high-grade 'one-star' officer with a track record of innovative and determined leadership. Although he had the unqualified approbation of his seniors, it remained to be seen if he would be able to excel at a two-star level.

There was an immediate political backlash to Battleaxe because Churchill was furiously disappointed by the result. He blamed Wavell and determined to remove him from his command, although he had to proceed with caution. He decided that Wavell would swap appointments with General Claude Auchinleck.[11]

It did not all end there.

Beresford-Peirse[12] was sacked, as was O'Creagh.[13] Air Chief Marshal Sir Arthur Longmore, the RAF Commander, had preceded them, in May 1941, just before Battleaxe. They were the first of many senior British officers who would be dismissed/removed/retired over the following fifteen months as success eluded the forces of the crown. However, it's an ill wind … and one officer to emerge from Battleaxe with his reputation intact, indeed enhanced, was Brigadier William Gott DSO MC – and on 31 August it was announced that he had been selected to command 7th Armoured Division on promotion to major general.[14] It is worth noting that although Strafer was promoted to replace O'Creagh, the outgoing general, later said very generously of his one-time subordinate:

Strafer was a rock who gained everyone's confidence and affection. I can see him now when things were rough, cool, busy, and efficient. Happy pictures of him in his Mess [a tarpaulin], the father of a cheerful military family, and another picture of him when we bathed together and talked of things outside the range of the desert, when he was a delightful companion.

Lieutenant Colonel Jock Campbell DSO MC, who commanded one of Strafer's Jock columns, was promoted to brigadier and given command of the Support Group. The two men were close friends and shared a mutual admiration. It was a happy state of affairs that they would continue to campaign together.

Inevitably, there was a post-mortem after Battleaxe and the conclusions were undisputed. In summary and in brief, the principal causes of defeat were firstly the vulnerability of the Matilda, the most heavily armoured British tank, to the German 88mm gun and also to the guns mounted on the German PZKW[15] III and IV, which had a longer range that the British 2-pounder gun carried by Matildas. The Germans did not have many of these 88mm weapons but with their tank-killing ability they did not need many. There were estimated to be five 88s on Halfaya Pass, four on Hafid Ridge and four with the 8th Panzer Regiment. These guns could outrange the British tanks and effect a kill at 2,000 yards.

Secondly, the organisation of the armoured brigades was flawed. There was a mix of cruiser and 'I' tanks, which were incompatible. Their vastly different performances limited their ability to work together and:

> There was no time to practice the combined action of these two brigades [4th and 7th armoured brigades], which would be likely to resemble badly matched partners in a three-legged race.[16]

Finally, Wavell had realised at the commencement of the operation that his formations had had insufficient time to 'work up'. The lack of training was a serious issue and, in his defence, the overarching influence of Churchill has to be noted. Brilliant man though he was, Churchill was not a general and, when he interfered, he made difficult situations worse. His aspirations to generalship were by no means unique: Hitler and Stalin both shared the same trait. In a perfect world the political leader sets the objective and then lets the military get on with the job. In more recent times, Mrs Thatcher demonstrated the positive effects of well-judged, firm political direction of the military. However, in this case Churchill's haste was a factor in the defeat and it cost Wavell his job, although not his reputation. Cicero got it right when he said, most wisely, in *De Officiis*, 'An army is of little value in the field unless there are wise counsels at home.' That is particularly germane in this instance.

This is not the place to eulogise Wavell other than to say that his responsibilities in the summer of 1941 extended far beyond North Africa, and General Auchinleck, who replaced Wavell, said later:

In no sense do I wish to infer that I found an unsatisfactory situation on my arrival – far from it. Not only was I greatly impressed by the solid foundations laid by my predecessor, but I was also able the better to appreciate the vastness of the problems with which he had been confronted and the greatness of his achievements, in a command in which some forty different languages are spoken by British and Allied forces.[17]

These are generous words but Auchinleck was not to receive similar courtesy from the officer who followed him.

Thus it was that Gott moved up a rank in an army that had been badly beaten and knew it. He now took on far greater responsibility and had to lead what was probably the British Army's premier armoured formation – but one that had its tail down.

The Western Desert Force changed its title yet again and reverted to XIII Corps. Strafer's new boss was Lieutenant General AR Godwin-Austen.[18] This was the officer who had initially incurred Churchill's wrath and then his long-term antipathy over the loss of British Somaliland.

In that campaign Godwin-Austen withdrew, most skilfully, in the face of superior forces with minimal losses. Wavell, who was his superior, defended him and told Churchill that 'a bloody butcher's bill is not the sign of a good tactician'. This remark so infuriated Churchill that it contributed to his enduring ambivalence, bordering on hostility, towards Wavell.

Chapter notes
1.   Field Marshal FWE Paulus (1890-1957) surrendered his 6th Army after his defeat at Stalingrad on 31 January 1943; 270,000 of his men were taken prisoner and only 6,000 survived to return to Germany.
2.   German military messages, transmitted by means of an Enigma machine, were first deciphered as far back as 1932 by the Polish Cipher Bureau. On the outbreak of war British cryptologists working at Bletchley Park, with Alan Turing, wrestled with the problems posed by the introduction of a vastly more sophisticated version of Enigma. The Ultra (a grade above Top Secret) intelligence was an important factor in the Royal Navy's victory over the Italian navy in the Battle of Cape Matapan in March 1941.
      HMS *Bulldog* captured *U110* on 9 May 1941, complete with an undamaged Enigma machine. With this the German naval code was broken. It was the most import signal intelligence coup of the war. The Allies were defeated in the Battle of Crete in May 1941. However, the enhanced Ultra intelligence greatly affected the defence of the island and played a part in the heavy German losses. Barnett, C. *The Desert Generals*, p.25.
3   General Sir Alan Brooke (later Field Marshal Lord Alanbrooke KG GCB OM GCVO DSO* 1883-1963) was Churchill's senior military advisor. He wrote a voluminous diary that was published after the war. He was Chief of the Imperial General Staff from December 1941 until his retirement in 1946.
4.   Barnett, C., *The Desert Generals*, p.25.

5. Playfair, Major General ISO et al, The *Mediterranean and Middle East*, Vol II, p.167.
6. Ibid p.168.
7. Ibid.
8. Pitt, Barrie, *The Crucible of War: Western Desert 1941*, p.307.
9. It is alleged that Messervy spoke in Hindustani as a security measure. It was unfortunate he did not do so earlier!
10. Playfair, Major General ISO et al, *The Mediterranean and Middle East*, Vol II, p.171.
11. Later, Field Marshal Sir Claude Auchinleck GCB GCIE CSI DSO OBE (1884-1981).
12. Lieutenant General Sir Noel Beresford-Peirse KCB CB DSO (1887-1953) was sent to be GOC, Sudan 1941-42. He completed his service in India.
13. Major General Sir Michael O'Creagh KBE MC (1892-1970) returned to England and commanded Hampshire and Dorset District from 1942 until he retired in 1944 at the early age of fifty-two.
14. War Diary, 7th Armoured Division Support Group, 31 August 1941.
15. The abbreviation PZKW stands for *Panzerkampfwagen*. The generic term for all German tanks was *Panzer.*
16. Playfair, Major General ISO et al, The *Mediterranean and Middle East*, Vol II, p.172.
17. Auchinleck, Field Marshal Lord, *Despatch on Operations in the Middle East from 5 July 1941 to 31 October 1941, The London Gazette* supplement No. 37,695, p.4,215-30
18. Later, General Sir Alfred Godwin-Austen KCSI CB OBE MC (1889-1963) rose to the top of the Army, despite the constant opposition of Churchill. He ended his career in 1947 as Quarter Master General and Principal Administrative Officer in India.

Chapter 11

Operation Crusader
November-December 1941

*The objective is not the occupation of the geographical
position but the destruction of the enemy force.*

(General Piotr A Rumyantsev, 1725-96)

A new XXX Corps was being formed and Lieutenant General VV Pope was selected to command it. However, on 5 October, Pope and Brigadier Russell and Brigadier Unwin were all killed in an air accident. Major General CWM Norrie was picked to fill Pope's shoes and he set about forming his new command, which was to include Strafer's 7th Armoured Division.

Auchinleck found himself under the same pressure from the Prime Minister as his predecessor and he was pressed to start an aggressive campaign in Cyrenaica. In due course this would evolve into Operation Crusader. Meanwhile, Auchinleck had selected General Sir Alan Cunningham[1] to command the 8th Army, a man he never met and whom he knew only by reputation. It was an extraordinary decision - cavalier in fact.

This was to be the first of several appointments made by Auchinleck that time would show to be ill-judged. Cunningham was a charming, courteous man who had made his reputation in April/May 1941 by his skilful performance in the East African Campaign, in which he defeated the Italians in Somaliland where he took 50,000 prisoners at a loss of only 500 of his own men. On the face of it, and in Auchinleck's defence, he certainly seemed to be the horse for this particular course.

The grand strategy for the campaign in North Africa did not affect Strafer. He was fully involved in healing the wounds of 7th Armoured Division and integrating hundreds of battle casualty replacements. Gott was surrounded by some high-grade junior officers and not least of these was 26-year-old Lieutenant (acting major) Michael Carver RTR. Carver had been on the staff of

7th Armoured Division since early 1940 when Strafer Gott was GSO 1 (Chief of Staff) and Carver a staff captain (Q) with logistic responsibilities.

The two men knew each other well and Carver held his senior in the highest regard. Carver was mentioned in dispatches on 1 April 1941 and again on 8 July. It was evident that he was a rising star. He said of Gott:[2]

> I frequently visited the headquarters of the Support Group, which Strafer commanded. On return from the Staff College at Haifa in 1941 I became DAQMG (Deputy Assistant Quarter Master General)[3] of the Division and, when Strafer commanded the forward group – basically the Division without its tanks – I was attached to his staff. When he took over command of 7th Armoured Division, I succeeded 'Pip' Roberts[4] as GSO 2. ... Although I was a very young officer at the time Strafer would sometimes talk very frankly and openly to me about the problems we all faced. It would not be an exaggeration to say that I worshipped him as the ideal of all that I believed that a senior army officer should be.

These are very warm words from a man who could be austere and distant. He was certainly very demanding, did not suffer fools gladly and was direct and abrasive when necessary. Carver was alleged to have a pronounced romantic streak and he had moral as well as physical courage in abundance. He was also an objective judge of his fellow men. Carver did not praise lightly and his approbation is significant. There were many who, in due course, would be called upon to make a judgment of Strafer Gott and when that came to pass, the opinion of the future Field Marshal Carver would carry great authority.

The period July-November 1941 found both armies preparing for the battle that lay ahead. Air Marshal Tedder, who now commanded the Desert Air Force, supported Auchinleck in his aim of first building his forces and they won the agreement of the Defence Committee. This posture was anathema to Churchill, who wanted the rapidly growing British forces to engage the enemy continuously. He made note of his misgivings nine years later, in his history of the Second World War, and he wrote that 'General Auchinleck's four and an half months' delay in engaging the enemy was alike a mistake and a misfortune.'[5] A mild form of words given the events soon to unfold. Churchill clearly did not have a feel for the issues that commanders at all levels faced. The fact is:

> The many scattered campaigns that General Wavell had been obliged to fight with incomplete forces had greatly disorganised the Army. The repeated milking of units and formations to fit out one expedition after another had naturally had a widespread effect. Brigades and divisional units had become separated from their divisions and battalions from

brigades. The armoured formations had almost ceased to exist. To restore coherence and make proper training possible General Auchinleck was faced with the need for much reorganisation, which had of course to be carried out without relaxing vigilance on the western frontier or too far depleting the forces ready to defend Egypt.[6]

The priority was the reorganisation of the armoured forces and Strafer commanded one of those vital formations. This caused him to spend hours travelling around his units, meeting commanding officers, devilling out the problems that they could not, alone, deal with.

The historian Correlli Barnett wrote disparagingly about the management of Britain's armoured forces and in particular of its leadership and he only excluded from his all-embracing criticism Brigadier AH Gatehouse,[7] Commander 4th Armoured Brigade, on the basis that he was a 'tank officer'. He highlighted the wide scale ineptitude by focusing on Strafer Gott and saying:

> General Gott, General Officer Commanding 7th Armoured Division (by supreme British inconsequence, a light infantryman) himself summed up the state of British theory of armour on the eve of battle when he told his men, 'This will be a tank commander's battle. No tank commander will go far wrong if he places his gun within hitting range of an enemy'.[8]

* * *

It has to be said that this is simplistic philosophy and does nothing to enhance Gott's reputation as a military strategist. It certainly suited Barnett's argument that only 'tank officers were capable of commanding tanks'. Barnett obviously expected something deeper, subtler, perhaps less Nelsonian. At any rate, and for the purpose of his argument, he disregarded Strafer's previous practical performance and his successes.

Barnett's work divided military opinion at the time, not least because of his bleak assessment of Montgomery and his support of Auchinleck both of whom had passionate adherents. *The Desert Generals* is a valuable and authoritative source document, because the author interviewed the subjects of his book and his information was all obtained at first-hand. However, the work has no index and is sparsely referenced. Unfortunately, when the book was revised the footnotes were not revised and they do not now tie in with the new text – thus, for example, the quote by Gott above requires the reader to search for authentication.

* * *

Leaving Barnett to one side; Strafer and his staff officers worked hard as they sought to provide the materiel and manpower needed in the right place and at the right time. It was a comfort to Strafer to have the imperturbable Jock Campbell at Support Group – a safe pair of hands.

Time frames were short and there were no numbers on the clock face as Strafer pulled 7th Armoured Division into shape. Somehow he managed to accomplish his goal without ever losing his amiable exterior and his, almost diffident, personality charmed even the most cynical of old soldiers. No one, at any level, wanted to let Strafer down. Lieutenant General Sir Neil Ritchie [9] endorsed that view and opined:

> Strafer was the straightest of men. He always said what he felt, perfectly openly, and with no thought of personal repercussions. He hated 'yes-men' and had no use for those who were inclined to say what they felt their superiors would like to hear. Essentially he was a most human person and this was the secret of the happiness that was always present at his headquarters and with troops in contact with him. He had a fellow feeling for all men, great and small. More than almost anyone of my acquaintance he possessed the 'human touch'.

Auchinleck's policy was to rebuild Strafer's 7th Armoured Division by equipping 7th Armoured Brigade with British Cruiser tanks of various types and to send all the available American Stuart tanks to 4th Armoured Brigade. The available 'I' or infantry tanks were to be issued to two brigades designated 'Army tank brigades'.

The recovery and repair system for armour was hopelessly inadequate and unlike the Germans who could repair a tank and get it back into action in days, Auchinleck's best hope was three months or more. It was on this basis that he determined to hold about 50 per cent extra tanks as reserve.

By the end of October 1941, and to the frustration of Strafer, his 7th Armoured Brigade was still not fully equipped. The 22nd Armoured Brigade arrived from the UK on 4 October with its Crusader tanks. However, they had not been modified for desert warfare and each one had to pass through the base workshops; this took three weeks and, as they say, 'questions were asked', especially as ample prior notice had been given for the need for modification before the vehicles left the UK. It was almost incidental that, on 21 October 1941, Strafer was promoted to the substantive rank of Colonel.[10]

By the end of October only three armoured brigades were *almost fully equipped* but untrained. The training of tank crews as individuals was one thing, to work as a team, another, and to combine with other tanks in a troop or squadron, something else. It took time and patience. The training, in turn, caused wear and tear on the tanks.

General Cunningham had every right to feel confident in his new appointment. He had excelled in the re-conquest of British Somaliland in a brilliant campaign in April/May 1941 and as a result of this success he had found favour with Auchinleck. His 8th Army was composed of two corps, with a combined strength of 770 tanks, with 724 combat aircraft in support. The order of battle was:

XXX Corps – Lieutenant General W Norrie
7th Armoured Division (7 Armd Div) – Major General WHE Gott
1st South African Infantry Division (1 SA Inf Div) – Major General G Brink
22nd Independent Guards Brigade (22 Armd Bde)

XIII Corps – Lieutenant General R Godwin-Austen
4th Indian Infantry Division (4 Ind Inf Div) – Major General F Messervy
2nd New Zealand Division (2 NZ Inf Div) – Major General B Freyberg
1st Tank Brigade (1 Tk Bde)

Tobruk Garrison – Major General R Scobie
70th Infantry Division (70 Inf Div)
Polish Carpathian Brigade (Pol Carp Bde)
32nd Army Tank Brigade (32 A Tk Bde)

Reserve
2nd South African Infantry Division

The opposition was formidable and the German and Italian order of battle was:

Panzer Group Afrika – General E Rommel
15th Panzer Division (15 Pz Div)
21st Panzer Division (21 Pz Div)
90th Light Afrika Division (90 Lt Div)
55th Infantry Division (Savona Div)

XXI Italian Corps – General E Navarin
17th Infantry Division (Pavia Div)
102nd Motorised Division (Trento Div)
27th Infantry Division (Brescia Div)
25th Infantry Division (Bologna Div)

127

Under Italian High Command in Libya – XX Motorised Corps
132nd Armoured Division (Ariete Div)
101st Motorised Division (Trieste Div)

At this point it is appropriate to leave Cunningham planning his offensive and consider, albeit briefly, the intelligence scenario.

The British and Commonwealth forces had the benefits of Ultra intelligence from early in the war. It had been of inestimable value but, in September 1941, the scales tipped when the Axis forces secured regular access to Top Secret British plans.

The unwitting conduit of this priceless information was an American; Colonel Bonner Fellers.[11] He was a military attaché serving in Cairo assigned first to Wavell's, and then Auchinleck's, headquarters. His function was to act as a liaison between those headquarters and Washington.

In September 1941 the US was a friendly neutral but was supplying Britain with arms[12] (the Japanese had yet to attack Pearl Harbor). Politically it was desirable to keep the US up to date with British plans and accordingly Fellers was privy to highly sensitive material. He passed this on to his masters in Washington in radiogram messages after he had encoded them by means of the American 'Black Code'. He then passed the encoded message to the Egyptian Telegraph Company for transmission. This arrangement worked quite acceptably until September 1941.

In September 1941 the head of Italy's Servizio Informazioni Militare (SIM) was a General Cesare Amè and he approved a plan to break into the American Embassy in Rome.

Amè's organisation had obtained keys to the embassy and so a clandestine entry was easy to arrange. A team of four burglars simply walked in. Loris Gherardi, one of the team, was employed by the embassy and, quite incredibly, was able to open the military attaché's safe! The team emptied the safe and took the contents back to Amè's headquarters. All the documents were duly photographed and then returned. The safe was locked and the Americans were blissfully unaware that now the Italians had the Black Code and the cipher tables that went with it; they could read any messages sent using that embassy code.

Once the Italians started to intercept diplomatic messages they were in a strong negotiating position with their German allies, to whom they provided edited versions of the traffic. However, they did not pass on the Black Code.

Meanwhile, Fellers continued to communicate with the Military Intelligence Division in Washington and, inadvertently, with the Germans as well. To compound the problem Fellers was a committed Anglophobe and also ruthlessly ambitious. He saw that the high profile that his messages generated for him provided potential career opportunities in the future. Sadly, his messages were invariably negative and were designed to present Britain's activities in North Africa in the worst possible light. Within hours of transmission Rommel was reading in detail of his adversary's plans, enjoying his discomfort and then adapting his own plans accordingly.

This insight into Britain's strategy by Fellers' dispatches was so important that Rommel referred to him as *'Die gute quelle'* (the good source), as well as, allegedly, 'the little fellows', a joust with the American's name.

Inevitably, the British came to realise that sensitive information was leaking to the enemy. The Afrika Korps was still blitzkrieging the Cyrenaican coastline when security officers approached Fellers to, in his words, 'see my security measures for the [Black] code'. Fellers, however, apparently allayed any suspicions the British might have had about his being the source of the suspected leaks because they directed their investigation elsewhere. At least five suspicious-looking Axis signals had been picked up by Allied stations beginning on 25 January. One actually cited 'a source in Egypt'. It was not until 26 June 1942, that Rommel finally lost the services of his *'Gute Quelle'*.[13]

By that time, Fellers had already done dreadful damage to the Allied cause. However, all of that lay a long way ahead as Strafer readied his division for Crusader and Cunningham polished his plan of attack. In brief, it was Cunningham's intention to cross the undefended frontier between Sidi Omar and Fort Maddalena. The main body of his armoured force was to move north-west with the intention of engaging and defeating the enemy armour near Tobruk. When General Norrie, leading XXX Corps, had destroyed Rommel's armour, or at the least neutralised it, then the siege of Tobruk would be raised and the garrison would sally forth to join the battle. Meanwhile, another force would first contain and then envelop the enemy in the frontier area, moving on to clear the coast between Bardia and Tobruk.

The German line of communication ran between the two modest ridges of Sidi Rezegh and El Duda; these would be taken, XXX Corps would take the former and the recently released Tobruk defenders would then come under command of XXX Corps.

The role of 4th Indian Infantry Division (of XIII Corps) was to send two brigades to contain the enemy in the frontier area and to act as a guard for the forward bases and railhead. The third brigade of the Division was to move to Sidi Omar to cover the flank of the armour as it passed through the gap. When the enemy armour was fully engaged the 2nd NZ Infantry Division was required to head north around Sidi Omar and, by so doing, get behind the enemy's frontier positions and cut them off.

An enterprise on the scale of Crusader required high-grade administrative and logistic support. The battle would be fought over long distances in pitiless country. The re-supply of the Army, once it was committed, was critical to its success. The movement of vast amounts of ammunition, food, medical supplies and water called for careful coordination and it engaged some of Cunningham's most able officers. Strafer's Division and the soldiers in it could not survive on courage alone and, in due course, they would be grateful for the decision to establish the three Forward Bases (FB). These were near Sidi Barrani for the troops moving west along the line of the coast and another near Thalata. This second FB was close to the new railhead that had been built by two New Zealand railway construction companies (10th and 13th) and it would serve the needs of XXX Corps (7th Armoured Division included) and most of XIII Corps. A third FB was sited at Jarabub to service the Oasis Force.

The minimum quantity of stores for the first week of the operation was 32,000 tons, of which 25,000 were wanted at Thalata. It was hoped that at the end of the week Tobruk would be relieved and soon become usable as a sea-head.[14]

It seems to be evident, writing with 20/20 hindsight and seventy years later, that General Cunningham's plan was really little more than an aspiration – and an optimistic one at that. Any plan that includes an element of 'hope' does not inspire confidence.

Several Field Maintenance Centres (FMC) were to be fed from the three FBs; these were fully integrated organisations that included a field supply depot, field ammunition depot, a water issue section, and dumps of engineer, medical

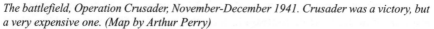

The battlefield, Operation Crusader, November-December 1941. Crusader was a victory, but a very expensive one. (Map by Arthur Perry)

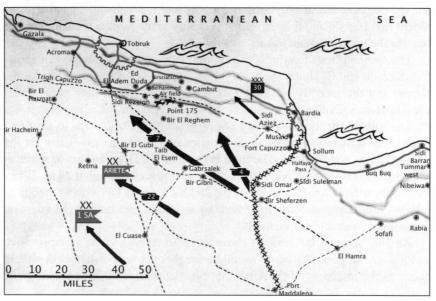

and ordnance stores, a field post office, and a drafting unit to deal with stragglers. In addition there were POW cages. The whole was dispersed, camouflaged and guarded. Four of these FMCs were provided to support XXX Corps.

Water and its provision was the ever-present issue. The Official History summed up the problem:

> The supply of water was, as usual, an immense problem. A detailed survey made in August 1941 of all drinkable sources west of the Matruh-Siwa road showed that not only was there nothing like enough water but also there was not enough transport to carry the balance forward from Matruh, which was the point to which the pipeline from Alexandria was being extended from El Daba. This meant that the piped supply had to be greatly increased and the pipeline extended as far west as possible, which entailed the laying of some 160 miles of piping and building of seven pumping stations and nine reservoirs. Many difficulties arose from competing demands for transport and machinery, and on 11 October a serious mishap occurred during an air attack at Fuka. The new pumps were damaged and nearly all the water, which had been accumulated to fill the pipes and reservoirs west of Fuka, was lost.[15]
>
> After this disaster every means of carrying water was engaged in the process of replenishment. Trains, trucks and the water carrier *Petrella* plied continuously between the water source in Alexandria and Matruh. It took four arduous weeks to return stocks of water to an acceptable level. The work on the pipeline was successful and by 13 November it had reached as far as Misheifa and water flowed along the 270 miles of pipe. This sufficiency of water did not cause any relaxation in the rationing of water set at ¾ gallon per man per day. To illustrate the immensity of the 'dumping programme' before the pipeline was completed the vehicles used 180,000 gallons of fuel a day.[16]

Tobruk was at the very centre of Crusader. The garrison of the 9th Australian Infantry Division, (9 Aust Inf Div) commanded by Major General LJ Morshead, had conducted a robust defence marked by aggressive patrolling since the Division was encircled on 11 April 1941. Since then it had been bombed and shelled on a daily basis but amply re-supplied from the sea. The Australian Government now insisted that the 9th Division be relieved, in order for all Australian troops to fight in the same formation.

It became a purely political issue and, against Auchinleck's better judgment but after specific instructions from the Chiefs-of-Staff Committee, he

131

conformed. Between 19 and 29 August, 6,116 troops and 1,297 tons of stores were landed and 5,040 troops evacuated. The rotation of troops was always a very hazardous affair for the mixed naval force, which had been supporting them since April. Nevertheless, the second tranche took place between 19 and 27 September, when 6,308 men were landed and 5,989 were shipped out. Later, between 12 and 25 October, the balance of the relieving force from 70 Division came ashore. Also in the fortress were 4th Royal Tank Regiment, HQ 32 Army Tank Brigade and the Polish Carpathian Infantry Brigade Group.

The whole exercise was costly; several ships were sunk and others badly damaged. Of particular importance was the loss of the fast minelayer HMS *Latona*, sunk by air attack. The 2nd Battalion 13th Australian Regiment (2/13 Aust Regt) and two companies of 2nd Battalion 15th Australian Regiment (2/15 Aust Regt) could not be evacuated and so they stayed, now under the command of Major General RM Scobie.

The statistics for the period April-October 1941 are:

Troops taken out (including wounded and prisoners)	47,280
Men carried in	34,113
Stores carried in	33,946
Warships and Merchant ships	
Lost	34
Damaged	33[17]

Strafer Gott was about to play his part in one of the great battles of the Second World War and in this biography his impact would not be appreciated unless it is in the context of the whole operation, vast and complicated as it was. However, in the interests of brevity and although both the Royal Air Force and Royal Navy were both engaged in Crusader, their roles have, for the most part, been excluded from this account as they had little direct, personal impact on Strafer Gott.

Major Carver had changed jobs and was now GSO 2 and serving on the staff of XXX Corps. Carver recorded:

In that capacity I saw a great deal of Strafer in the Crusader operation in November-December 1941. My commander, Willoughby Norrie, was a personal friend of his and seldom made a decision without first discussing it with Strafer, for whose judgment and experience he had a high regard.[18]

General Norrie generously confirmed Carver's observation and he said of his subordinate and contemporary:

One automatically went to Strafer and a guiding hand. He was like Solomon and his judgment uninfluenced by local events or reverses. His energy was unbounded and he never seemed to tire. When others were exhausted, Strafer was invariably cheerful and full of energy. His personal courage was astounding. He was always to be seen in the forefront of the battle and many were the tight corners from which he had to extricate himself.[19]

It was thus with the complete confidence of his boss that Strafer prepared for the next big battle. Like all generals, Cunningham hoped to surprise his opponent and to this end every effort was made to conceal the FBs and the FMCs. Despite the malign influence of Colonel Fellers, Rommel was unaware of any details of the forthcoming storm. He expected an attack but did not know when or quite where.

Operation Crusader was a major military event and it involved tens of thousands of men, many of whom would die in the course of the enterprise. Its success would ultimately depend on the private soldier and Victor (always known as 'Vic') Gregg, who was one of those, had a clear memory of the operation, at least of the smaller picture. He said the 'when' was 18 November 1941 and the 'where' was the Egyptian/Libya border that XXX Corps and specifically 7 Armd Div Support Group crossed. But before that:

Around 10 November the Company was mustered for a talk by our brigadier, one Jock Campbell, who was revered as a leader by all ranks of the brigade. He told us that Rommel was going to attack Tobruk, which was a thorn in his side. Australian forces had holed up in this small port and were resisting all attempts by the Germans to capture them.

We were told that our commanders had decided to forestall Rommel's grandiose ideas by mounting an offensive, which would end the German reign of terror and kill and capture the lot of them.

Jock Campbell wished us luck, rations were distributed and we were told to get as much rest as possible. ... On the night of 17 November the rains started. We didn't have the luxury of tents and it wasn't long before we were all soaking. By the morning of the 18th we were on our start line and I would say that there wasn't a truly happy man to be found anywhere. Our fight would be known as the Battle of Sidi Rezegh and it became the benchmark for future battles. The next ten to twelve days were to be the bloodiest and most frightening the Battalion (2 RB) had yet experienced both in length and sheer brutality. Other battles would be just as bloody but they were shorter and interrupted by periods of rest, moments when the battle went off the boil.[20]

Vic Gregg is incorrect in some of the detail but, nevertheless, he is a valuable surviving witness to an epic battle.

Rommel believed, on receiving first reports, that he was seeing 'a reconnaissance in force' and accordingly he did not alter his dispositions. In a curious way Rommel's non-response wrong-footed Cunningham and his generals, who had the initiative but now did not know what to do with it. 'Gott's orders to 7th Armoured Division early on 19 November reflect this state of mind.'[21]

Strafer was charged with securing Bir el Gubi and then Sidi Rezegh. His 4th Armoured Brigade was to protect the right flank of the Division and the left flank of XIII Corps. The 7th Armoured Brigade was sent off to reconnoitre the objective, Sidi Rezegh, and to establish a firm base on the escarpment if possible. Similarly, 22nd Armoured Brigade was to move toward Bir el Gubi and secure whatever ground was possible. Jock Campbell's Support Group (with 2 RB and 1 KRRC) was held back, ready to support either 7th or 22nd armoured brigades.

The 22nd Armoured Brigade consisted of three yeomanry regiments. These were 2nd Royal Gloucester Hussars (2 RGH) 3rd and 4th County of London Yeomanry (3 CLY) and supported by C Bty RHA and one troop of 102nd Northumberland Hussars Anti-tank Regt RHA (102 NH RHA). The Brigade made steady unopposed progress and its tanks were quite close to Bir el Gubi when, typically, Strafer Gott, already in the van of his division, came further forward and had a brief meeting with Brigadier J Scott-Cockburn, the Commander. Gott 'appreciated the situation' in the time-honoured way and, based on that, he was equipped to take a decision.

Facing 22nd Armoured Brigade, entrenched and well prepared, was the Italian Ariete Division. Strafer had several options at the time: he could have decided to stand fast and wait for the enemy to attack him (possible but unlikely), go round the position (a possibility) or withdraw (absurd). Alternatively, he could have conducted a deeper reconnaissance (possible) or called for major artillery support (desirable). He might have employed a combination of the above.

With the wisdom that hindsight brings, his best option was probably to wait for the enemy to attack him. However, after that conference, held by the side of a tank, Strafer took the initiative, as was his job, and made a strategic decision. He ordered 22nd Armoured Brigade to attack; this was no doubt with Scott-Cockburn's acquiescence.

The manner in which Gott's strategic decision was to be carried out was now a matter of tactics. That was the concern of the commander on the ground – Brigadier Scott-Cockburn. The Official History saw it like this:

> He [Gott] may have felt that it would be unwise to leave the Ariete Division unmolested on his left flank and may have thought that there was a chance of doing some damage to it at little cost. He may have wished to give the 22nd Armoured Brigade some battle experience before they [*sic*] met the Germans but without becoming heavily committed. Anyway, the Brigade attacked, perhaps rather impetuously, with the support of only one 25-pdr battery and after driving off the covering troops came under strong fire from Italian prepared positions.[22]

On the basis that Operation Crusader was an *offensive,* attacking does not seem to be an unreasonable course of action.

The approach march by 22nd Armoured Brigade had been 80 miles long and, over this distance, it had suffered any number of mechanical defects among its 136 Crusader tanks. Brigadier Scott-Cockburn made his plan and issued his orders to his three commanding officers. The attack was launched, 2nd Royal Gloucester Hussars in the centre of the brigade forged ahead and made inroads in the Ariete defence line. The 11th Hussars, who were providing a screen, sent a warning about anti-tank guns but 4th County of London Yeomanry ignored the warning and advanced at high speed on the left. One officer is alleged to have said: 'It was the nearest thing to a cavalry charge seen during the war.' Vic Gregg saw it too and commented:

> The fight started at fever pitch, and the mayhem and murder carried on until neither side had anything left to fight with; what remains most vividly in my mind is the sacrifice of our tank crews who were ordered to charge dug-in anti-tank guns. Most of them never got more than a hundred yards past the start line. We watched helpless while 22nd Armoured Brigade was blown to pieces attempting to advance over dead-flat terrain into the mouths of the waiting guns.[23]

Gregg rather overstated the case but certainly the attack was not a complete success in that the Brigade lost twenty-five of its 136 tanks – modest losses in comparison with what was to come in this bloody desert war of attrition. To counter that, thirty-four Italian tanks were destroyed and fifteen damaged. For the remainder of the day the brigade was involved in sustained fighting and by nightfall it had lost fifty tanks to enemy action and a further thirty to mechanical failure.

Some surviving participants would later lay the actions of 22nd Armoured Brigade and its losses on 19 November firmly at Strafer's door. He would have readily accepted that responsibility and although there is no evidence at all to support that categorical assertion by this biographer, it would have been wildly out of character for him to shift responsibility to others because the man exuded integrity. Alexander Clifford wrote of this period:

> We walked to the armoured command vehicle (ACV) – and sat down on the ground, talking with the officers. Inside, directing the battle was Strafer Gott, with whom I had traded biscuits down at Fort Mekili the winter before. Now he was a major general, commanding the 7th Armoured Division, but he still looked more like a bishop than a soldier with his silver hair and friendly blue eyes. Only the firmness of his mouth marked him down as a man of action.[24]

Elsewhere, 7th Armoured Brigade had made excellent progress on 18 November and that night leaguered 20 miles south of Sidi Rezegh. The next day, led by 4th South African Armoured Car Regiment (4 SAACR), they moved forward to their objective. A little after 1345 hrs, B Squadron reported that it had reached a position on the escarpment that enabled it to look down on the airfield of Sidi Rezegh – there were enemy aircraft parked there.

Gott did not hesitate and, with 6th Royal Tank Regiment and B Squadron leading, 7th Armoured Brigade swept down on the airfield, about 2 miles from Sidi Rezegh. The airfield was taken, along with nineteen aircraft. Irritatingly, three aircraft not only managed to take off and escape, but also rubbed salt into the wound by retaliating. The three aircraft strafed its earlier assailants, now the new tenants of Sidi Rezegh airfield. The nineteen Axis aircraft were then demolished – apparently by hand! Quite why this should be is unexplained.

Elements of 7th Armoured Brigade remained on the escarpment and overlooked Tobruk in the distance, but could go no further as the Germans had established a block on the only track down to the coastal plain.

The 4th Armoured Brigade had crossed the frontier wire without incident on 18 November, but was then engaged at Bir Sciafsciuf in a skirmish before it was able to move on. The following day it met much sterner opposition and was confronted at Taieb el Essem by 15th Panzer Division. Later in the day, 8th Hussars, pursuing a German reconnaissance unit, ran into a formidable and heavily armed element of 21st Panzer Division. The meeting cost 8th Hussars twenty tanks, not least because the Regiment was greatly outgunned by the German Mk III and Mk IVs. They could engage and destroy the British Stuart tanks from 1,500 yards – well out of the effective range of the Stuarts' lower calibre weaponry. There was a general retreat by the Brigade later on 19 November but fighting would resume the following morning.

During the night of 19/20 November, the Germans opened their counter-attack at Sidi Rezegh. The 2nd Royal Tank Regiment, up on the ridge behind the airfield, bore the brunt of the early exchanges and it was only the timely arrival of Jock Campbell's Support Group in mid-morning that stabilised the situation. A company of 1 KRRC had taken a position on the escarpment at the east of the airfield. A second company was seeking to dig in to the south.

Cunningham ordered 1st SA Infantry Division to move to Bir el Gubi, with one brigade ready to move at short notice to Sidi Rezegh. The enemy was clearly not going to surrender ownership of the airfield lightly and with 7th Armoured Division's three brigades now widely spread the dispositions were not ideal.

Strafer had moved his small headquarters to the escarpment very close to the front line and he concluded that the enemy to his front was weak. He suggested to General Norrie that his Support Group should be able to drive through and make contact with General Scobie's 70th Division as they broke out of Tobruk. Norrie, who was always much influenced by Gott, found the idea appealing, although it did run counter to the agreed plan of defeating the enemy armour as a priority.

The value of Ultra intelligence was to be seen on the morning of 20 November when German messages were intercepted and warning was sent to Strafer of the movement of both 15th and 21st Panzer Divisions towards 4th Armoured Brigade. The threat was enormous and imminent. Strafer ordered 22nd Armoured Brigade from its position at Bir el Gubi 25 miles away and where it was masking the Ariete Division, to close with 4th Armoured Brigade and support it. However, 22nd Armoured Brigade was delayed while refuelling and only 4th County of London Yeomanry and 3rd Regiment RHA got to the party – and then only late in the day. The 15th Panzer Division attacked with around 100 tanks. There was fierce fighting, which further reduced 4th Armoured Brigade's tank force to ninety-eight. Meanwhile, 1st SA Division had taken over the containment of the Ariete Division.

By last light on 20 November, 4th and 22nd brigades were spread widely across the desert and intermingled with enemy units. Re-fuelling and re-arming was difficult and confusing.

Norrie had passed on Gott's suggestion to Cunningham, who approved it and ordered the breakout for dawn on 21 November. The Official History saw events unfolding like this:

> [Just before 1700 hrs on 20 November] 5 SA Inf Bde, commanded by
> Brigadier BF Armstrong, began to move toward Sidi Rezegh. At dusk
> it halted, with General Gott's approval, because General Brink did not

consider the troops sufficiently desert-wise to make the move in the dark. At 2000 hrs, Gott gave his orders for the operation next day, which aimed at securing the airfield and making ground toward El Duda. He was not in signal touch with Tobruk, where General Scobie was preparing to carry out his well-rehearsed plan for capturing two main and several subsidiary positions between the south-east corner of the perimeter and El Duda, thus creating a defended 'corridor' leading into Tobruk. The principal attacks were to be made by tanks and infantry in close cooperation of the 32 Army Tank Brigade (32 A Tk Bde), 14 Inf Bde and 16 Inf Bde.[25]

On 21 November there began three days of some of the most ferocious fighting of the desert war. It was a confused savage situation. The battlefield was obscured by smoke and dust, with imprecise battle lines. Physical features on the ground were difficult to discern. Soldiers or tanks would emerge from any direction and had first to be identified, then either engaged and killed or waved on. This was a battle in which the junior non-commissioned officers (JNCOs) shouldered the responsibility for command. It was 'a soldier's battle'.

Strafer Gott and Brigadier Davy had previously agreed that 7th Armoured Brigade and the Support Group, both under Davy's command, were to attack northward from Sidi Rezegh to secure part of the ridge overlooking the Trigh Capuzzo.

At 0800 hrs on 21 November and just before the advance to the north, elements of 15th and 21st Panzer divisions were seen approaching from the south-east. This was an unwelcome complication but it was too late for Davy to abandon the original plan. However, he did divert 7th Hussars and 2nd RTR to engage the German armour. Then at 0830 hrs on 21 November, the Support Group advanced on the northern edge of the airfield. Leading the attack on the right was 1st Battalion, KRRC along with A Company, 2nd Battalion, The Rifle Brigade. They were supported by fire from 4th RHA and 60th Field Regiment RA, which shelled the enemy positions ahead. The vehicle-borne infantry created clouds of dust, which, although unpleasant, served to obscure the remainder who were on foot. But the dust did not deter the ever-present flies.

The 6th RTR was on the left and the plan was that, when the objective had been taken, 6th RTR was to move on with the aim of linking up with Scobie's forces as they burst from the confines of Tobruk. The attack was being made over 2,000 yards of open ground where there was not a vestige of cover and against a well-prepared and determined enemy. The carriers were prime targets for anti-tank guns and soon they were being picked off. Their passengers, those who were not disabled, continued on foot with great courage. A Company 1st Battalion, KRRC was dismounted but, moving over to its right, it carried its objective and took thirty prisoners. The position, together with 700 prisoners, was taken by noon. It was during the early phase of the attack that Rifleman John Beeley sacrificed himself and won a VC in the process. His citation said:

On 21 November 1941, during the attack at Sidi Rezegh, North Africa, against a strong enemy position, the company to which Rifleman Beeley belonged was pinned down by heavy fire at point-blank range from the front and flank on the flat, open ground of the aerodrome. All the officers but one of the Company and many of the Other Ranks had been either killed or wounded. On his own initiative, and when there was no sort of cover, Rifleman Beeley got to his feet carrying a Bren gun and ran forward towards a strong enemy post containing an anti-tank gun. The post was silenced and Rifleman Beeley's platoon was enabled to advance, but Rifleman Beeley fell dead across his gun, hit in at least four places.

Rifleman Beeley went to certain death in a gallant and successful attempt to carry the day. His courage and self-sacrifice were a glorious example to his comrades and inspired them to further efforts to reach their objective, which was eventually captured by them, together with 700 prisoners.[26]

Lieutenant Colonel Sydney de Salis, Beeley's commanding officer, would normally have initiated the award but he was captured the day after Beeley's action and Major C d'A P Consett KRRC, one of the few surviving officers of 1st Battalion, KRRC, prepared the citation. He had not been involved in the battle and so his draft citation must have been based on the accounts given by surviving eyewitnesses to Beeley's courage. Gott's signature appears on the original document and it must have given Strafer great pride and pleasure to support the citation for a member of his own regiment. It is unlikely that Strafer knew Beeley personally as the soldier was very young and the General had given up command of the 1st Battalion in late 1939, two years earlier.

The breakout of the 70th Division from Tobruk that morning was not easy but by afternoon, General Scobie had captured a salient nearly 4,000 yards deep and 4,000 yards wide. He had taken a mixed bag of more than 1,000 German and Italian prisoners. Then Scobie halted his thrust when he realised that he could not now expect any assistance from 7th Armoured Division.

The 6th RTR attacked across Trigh Capuzzo (this was a well-defined but unmade track running east-west) but encountered strong opposition and was severely mauled; only six tanks returned from this abortive thrust. Similarly, 7th Hussars had been crushed in an engagement with 21st Panzer Division. The CO was killed and the Regiment had only ten battle-worthy tanks remaining.

Meanwhile, the survivors of 1st Battalion, KRRC occupied Point 167, a prominent feature on the escarpment, and took over captured trenches. It was quite evident that control of the airfield, unusable by either side for the foreseeable future, and the ridge above it, was the key to the domination of the plain and approach to Tobruk.

The German tank force that had crushed 7th Hussars turned its unwelcome attention to the airfield and sent sixteen tanks forward to reconnoitre. The 60th Field Regiment, with some success, fired them upon them and four tanks were destroyed – the remainder withdrew, but only temporarily. The Rifle Brigade was in the forefront of the ensuing melee in which sixty tanks were backed up by dive-bombing Stuka aircraft. The German tanks were taken on by a troop of 3rd Regiment RHA and 60th Field Regiment RA. There had been limited success but superior firepower won the day.

* * *

There were many examples of great courage, none more so that that displayed by Second Lieutenant GW Gunn MC RHA of 3rd Regiment RHA. The citation for his VC sums up the nature of the desperate fight around the airfield:

On 21 November 1941, at Sidi Rezegh, Second-Lieutenant Gunn was in command of a troop of four anti-tank guns, which was part of a battery of twelve guns attached to the Rifle Brigade Column. At 1000 hrs, a covering force of enemy tanks was engaged and driven off but an hour later the main attack developed by about sixty enemy tanks. Second-Lieutenant Gunn drove from gun to gun during this period in an unarmoured vehicle, encouraging his men and reorganising his dispositions as first one gun and then another was knocked out. Finally, only two guns remained in action and were subjected to very heavy fire. Immediately afterwards one of these guns was destroyed and the portee of another was set on fire and all the crew killed or wounded except the Sergeant, though the gun itself remained undamaged. The Battery Commander then arrived and started to fight the flames. When he saw this, Second-Lieutenant Gunn ran to his aid through intense fire and immediately got the one remaining anti-tank gun into action on the burning portee, himself sighting it while the Sergeant acted as loader. He continued to fight the gun, firing between forty and fifty rounds regardless alike of the enemy fire that was by then concentrated on this one vehicle, and of the flames, which might at any moment have reached the ammunition with which the portee was loaded. In spite of this, Second-Lieutenant Gunn's shooting was so accurate at a range of about 800 yards that at least two enemy tanks were hit and set on fire and others were damaged before he fell dead, having been shot through the forehead.

Second-Lieutenant Gunn showed the most conspicuous courage in attacking this large number of enemy tanks with a single unarmoured gun, and his utter disregard for extreme danger was an example, which inspired all who saw it. He remained undismayed by intense fire and overwhelming odds, and his gallant resistance only ceased with his death. But for this very gallant action the enemy tanks would undoubtedly have overrun our position.[27]

By way of explanation: a portee is any vehicle that carries a gun as a burden but in a manner such that the gun is not secured permanently to the vehicle. The aim was to ensure that the gun could either be quickly unloaded, or could be fired from the truck.

* * *

The situation on the airfield was desperate but it was still in British possession, for what that was worth. Support Group was in positions both north and south and holding on. The 7th Armoured Brigade had taken heavy losses and by close of play on 21 November it was reduced to twenty battle-worthy tanks – a shadow of its former self. REME mechanics worked feverishly throughout the hours of darkness and, by dawn, eight more tanks could take their place in the gun line.

In the early light of a North African winter's day, on 22 November, Strafer was able to take stock. He had the Support Group on and around the airfield with a few tanks in the north, east and west. The 22nd Armoured Brigade was south of the airfield, about 2 miles away, armed with seventy-nine Crusader tanks. The 4th Armoured Brigade was to the south-east, not far from Bir el Reghem and armed with fifty Honey tanks. Gott's problem was 7th Armoured Brigade, which had only those twenty-eight tanks referred to above. The joining of hands with Scobie's 70th Division had not been achieved.

* * *

The reader who is confused at this stage should not be surprised. Putting the myriad actions taken by dozens of major units, over an almost featureless landscape, into a coherent timeframe is a recipe for mental constipation.

This was recognised by Major General ISO Playfair, the author/editor of the magisterial Official History. He, too, recognised the difficulty in understanding the complex situation, which even maps do little to clarify. He had this to say:

141

The situation was so extraordinary that a brief summary will not be out of place. Over the 20 or so miles of country from the front of the Tobruk sortie to the open desert south-east of Sidi Rezegh airfield, the forces of both sides were sandwiched like the layers of a Neapolitan ice.

In turn, starting from the north, there were (a) the troops of 70th Division who had broken out, opposed by (b) German and Italian troops facing north and west, (c) a layer of Axis troops facing south opposing (d) part of 7th Support Group north of Sidi Rezegh airfield, the rest of 7th Support Group and 7th Armoured Brigade facing south to oppose (e) the bulk of DAK (Deutsches Afrika Korps) heading south pursued by (f) the 4th and 22nd armoured brigades.

To complete the picture there were troops of the 361st Afrika Regiment on Point 175 to the east of Sidi Rezegh airfield and the whole of the 155th Regiment to the west. A complicated situation indeed, which, if suggested as the setting for a training exercise, must have been rejected for the reason that in real life these things simple could not happen.[28]

If it is difficult to absorb this complexity on the printed page how very much more difficult it was for commanders like Strafer Gott on the ground. He could not see or identify all of his opponents, nor could he be sure of the location and strength of friendly force. This was a situation that, not unreasonably, taxed the finest and most experienced of the desert generals.

* * *

As Strafer examined his assets and considered his options a significant force of enemy, including eighty tanks, was seen approaching the airfield from the north. Strafer was fortunate to have an officer of the calibre of Jock Campbell in command and he immediately called 60th Field Regiment into action with its 25-pounder guns. The German force dispersed and Campbell led an attack of twelve tanks from his staff car. It was a brave gesture, quickly abandoned, when the German tanks moved into line and opened fire.

The enemy attacked from the west in strength and infantry tackled the stiff climb up the escarpment. It is alleged that at one point Campbell was directing operations from atop a wrecked Italian aeroplane. He was an exemplary commander and was always to be found wherever the fighting was fiercest.

German tanks focused on the shallow trenches of 1st Battalion, KRRC and 2nd Battalion, The Rifle Brigade and enjoyed great success. A and C companies of 1 KRRC were overrun and only one platoon came through the attack.

Although tanks had accompanied D Company 1 KRRC, it found that in a tank engagement infantry are at a decided disadvantage. The Battalion was completely overrun and a second wave of armoured carriers and motorcyclists completed the job, although one or two small isolated parties continued to fight on until dusk. Then, too late, some British tanks appeared and from the melee that ensued, five officers and fifty soldiers with seventeen vehicles, managed to escape; a few more got away later. The Commanding Officer, Sydney de Salis, was among the prisoners. Thus, the bulk of this fine battalion was lost. Luckily, B Company was on detachment at this time and was available, together with the remnants from Sidi Rezegh, to start re-forming the Battalion at Mena camp just outside Cairo, where Major Consett assumed command.[29] It is not difficult to imagine the distress that the loss of so many of his old battalion caused Strafer.

Strafer and Sydney were never to see each other again.

The battle was by now very confused, with both sides milling about seeking an advantage. The 22nd Armoured Brigade was effective in aiding the Support Group but 7th Armoured Division's posture was now more defensive than aggressive. It had suffered serious losses in men and materiel and the confidence of a few days before had evaporated. That is not to say that Strafer's division had given up the fight – far from it, and certainly not the Support Group, where Brigadier Campbell was an inspiration to all who saw him.

The Germans had pulled back over the night of 21/22 November. They had been able to lick their wounds and then refuel, re-arm and reorganise. The gaps left by casualties were filled and new crews were made up. The men were fed and watered as well as was possible. There was no doubt that 21 November had been their day. The next morning was marked by sporadic skirmishing around the airfield and during this period of relative calm Gott called forward the 5th South African Infantry Brigade, which he had halted the previous evening. He directed it to capture part of the southern escarpment and, in particular, the high ground of Point 178. The attack went in at 1500 hrs but was repulsed with the leading battalion, 3rd Transvaal Scottish suffering 117 casualties. The Brigade then withdrew at dusk and took up defensive positions about 2 miles south-east of their earlier objective. A South African officer observed:

> When all control had vanished from our forces in the November/December campaign it was Gott's personal leadership and example that prevented a frightful disaster. The last I saw of him was the evening of the second day of the Battle of Sidi Rezegh. The Germans made several heavy and successful attacks with massed tanks. My own regiment had been reduced to seven tanks, and for the last hour we had no ammunition for them. Gott came up to our lines

in his Crusader, and I well remember him in his white sheepskin coat standing up in the turret just as the sun went down. Calm, purposeful and unflurried, making his plans for the night and morning. He was a great leader without a doubt.[30]

The German Commander decided to make yet another attempt to secure the airfield and, at the time 5th SA Infantry Brigade was being repulsed, 5th Panzer Regiment with fifty-seven tanks was to strike from the west while 104th Lorried Infantry Regiment came from the north. The 7th and 22nd armoured brigades met the attack assisted by a now very weak Support Group. Strafer sent a message to Gatehouse, commanding 4th Armoured Brigade about 5 miles to the east, and ordered him to move swiftly to the airfield. When 4th Armoured Brigade arrived it was to find that literally 'the fog of war' completely obscured the battlefield. Smoke and dust mixed and swirled to such an extent that the Brigade could not intervene.

The engagement went badly for 7th Armoured Division.

The Support Group was overrun; at one time Jock Campbell was seen serving a gun of 60th Field Regiment that was firing over open sights. He was indefatigable and an inspiration to all around him. Tank losses were high and as the light faded Strafer ordered his formations, or what remained of them, to fall back on 5th SA Brigade. He pushed 4th Armoured Brigade out to the west; it had been largely unscathed in the fighting at the airfield and it leaguered for the night. Then, by a stroke of the worst possible luck, 15th Panzer Division, which had been making its way to support the fighting on the airfield, blundered straight through the now completely unprepared, relaxing and eating 8th Hussars and Brigade Headquarters. The result was a shambles. The Brigade Headquarters dispersed in disarray and the Germans took 267 prisoners and about fifty tanks. The 8th Hussars ceased to be a viable force.

The 7th Armoured Division really had had a bad day, not least because Jock Campbell was eventually wounded and put out of action. In addition to the debacle at 4th Armoured Brigade, 7th Armoured Brigade could only muster ten tanks and 22 Armd Div merely thirty-four. On the other side of the coin the Germans had taken the vital ground and had an estimated 173 tanks. It is at times such as this that a leader shows his mettle and Strafer, as always, displayed the same urbane, equable and quietly confident mien.

* * *

Some things are best done on the spot and an example of that was the citation that Strafer wrote that night. It resulted in a much-deserved Victoria Cross for Brigadier Jock Campbell. The citation read:

On 21 November Brigadier Campbell was commanding the troops, including one regiment of tanks, in the area of Sidi Rezegh ridge and the aerodrome. His small force holding this important ground was repeatedly attacked by large numbers of tanks and infantry. Wherever the situation was most difficult and the fighting hardest he was to be seen with his forward troops, either on his feet or in his open car. In this car he carried out several reconnaissances for counter-attacks by his tanks, whose senior officers had all become casualties early in the day. Standing in his car with a blue flag, this officer personally formed up tanks under close and intense fire from all natures of enemy weapon.

On the following day the enemy attacks were intensified and again Brigadier Campbell was always in the forefront of the heaviest fighting, encouraging his troops, staging counter-attacks with his remaining tanks and personally controlling the fire of his guns. On two occasions he himself manned a gun to replace casualties. During the final enemy attack on 22 November he was wounded, but continued most actively in the foremost positions, controlling the fire of batteries, which inflicted heavy losses on enemy tanks at point-blank range, and finally acted as loader to one of the guns himself.

Throughout these two days his magnificent example and his utter disregard of personal danger were an inspiration to his men and to all who saw him. His brilliant leadership was the direct cause of the very heavy casualties inflicted on the enemy. In spite of his wound he refused to be evacuated and remained with his command, where his outstanding bravery and consistent determination had a marked effect in maintaining the splendid fighting spirit of those under him.[31]

There are not many generals who have the privilege of recommending someone for a VC and, even if they do, often the award is downgraded. Strafer had the good fortune to write, endorse or support three such awards, for Beeley, Gunn and Campbell – all members of his division. Later in the campaign he was to endorse the bar to Captain Charles Upham's VC. Each of the awards was granted and it says much for the quality of the men he had the good fortune to command. In Campbell's case it must have been a most agreeable task; although the two men were close, friendship had absolutely nothing to do with it, as there were countless independent witnesses to Campbell's sustained courage.

An interesting postscript to Jock Campbell's VC is an extract from a letter published in the *Daily Telegraph* in which the correspondent[32] stated that, in February 1942, General von Ravenstein, Commander of the 21st Panzer Division wrote to Major General Jock Campbell VC, saying:

Dear Major General Campbell,

I have read in the paper that you have been my brave adversary in the tank battle of Sidi Rezegh on November 21-22, 1941.

It was my 21st Panzer Division that has fought in these hot days with the 7th Armoured Division, for whom I have the greatest admiration. Your 7th Support Group of Royal Artillery, too, has made the fighting very hard for us and I remember all the many iron that flew near the aerodrome around our cars.

The German comrades congratulate you with warm heart on the award of the Victoria Cross.

During the war your enemy,
but with high respect – von Ravenstein.

* * *

Elsewhere, the battle had gone well; 70th Infantry Division had taken more ground but Scobie was aware of the confused state of play in and around Sidi Rezegh and at Norrie's urging he halted his advance – a rather unsatisfactory situation from Scobie's point of view as, to date, he had carried out his orders to break out with considerable success.

Capuzzo, little more than a ruin and some holes in the ground in an empty landscape, changed hands yet again and this time it was the 2nd NZ Infantry Division who triumphed. They also took Musaid and cut the water pipe from Bardia as well as all the enemy's telegraph and telephone lines. To cap this they put in a block across the coast road from Bardia to Tobruk.

Cunningham, who was distant from the fighting, did not have a detailed brief on the situation and he based some of his following decisions on false premises. He ordered the NZ Division to advance on Tobruk and XXX Corps to maintain the aim of destroying the Axis armour. Little did Cunningham realise that, in effect, his own armour was already on the edge of complete destruction. In the fluctuating fighting, on 24 November Gott's small Battle Headquarters was more or less encircled, but he personally led his staff to safety through the German lines and remained in complete control of the situation.[33]

The 15th Panzer Division made a swinging march, cutting through the remnants of 7th Armoured Division Support Group, and then it made contact with the 5th SA Brigade. The South Africans acquitted themselves well but suffered many casualties in the process. The 15th Panzer Division then linked up with the Italian Ariete Div and together they absorbed brutal artillery fire but, nevertheless, obliterated 5th SA Brigade. The Brigade had 3,394 losses –

most of them prisoners. The 22nd Armoured Brigade, who had been involved in this action, lost a further twelve of its thirty-four tanks. A contemporary account recorded:

> Both sides had literally fought each other to a standstill. Between the start of the battle and the end, an area of roughly 50 square miles became littered with the burning and the smashed-up remains of more than 800 armoured vehicles, hundreds of dead and rotting bodies and a dense pall of smoke thickened with the stench of rotting flesh.[34]

The bad news started to filter out of the maelstrom that was Sidi Rezegh and by 24 November 4th Armoured Brigade had four tanks – just a troop. The 22nd Armoured Brigade had fifty tanks but the whereabouts and fate of 7th Armoured Brigade was unknown.

It was unpalatable, but the fact had to be faced – 7th Armoured Division had been largely destroyed, albeit by two highly efficient enemy divisions. Nevertheless, Strafer's division was in shreds and his loss in tanks and brave men was enormous. That begs the question, 'to what extent was it his fault?'

Was it actually *the fault* of anyone?

General Ravenstein, one of the victors of Sidi Rezegh, certainly acknowledged the gallantry and performance of his adversary in that generous letter reproduced above. The 7th Armoured Division was part of a wider strategy and so it could not manoeuvre at will but was obliged to fit into the Corps and Army plan. Strafer's part in this plan was to 'destroy the enemy armour' and that was easier said than done.

He was facing two well-trained and experienced Panzer divisions. They were equipped with formidable tanks but they were no better than Gott's. 'The opposing tanks were not so very different in technical quality. The Matildas and Valentines, apart from their slow speed, were at a distinct advantage with their thick armour, which was immune to the enemy's tank guns at all but very short range.'[35]

The big difference was the German use and disposition of their vastly better anti-tank guns, which were deployed up front. Many British tank commanders thought that a German tank had knocked them out; in fact, it was usually a 88mm. A further factor was the failure to concentrate the armoured formations in mass and their fragmentation reduced the shock effect that was desired. The armoured battle was always going to be a close run thing and in this case Strafer Gott tasted failure. He had done very well but not well enough.

It is interesting to note that, hitherto, the pattern was for defeated, unsuccessful generals and even those with the wrong attitude to be summarily removed from command and reassigned to a military backwater. That pattern would be maintained throughout the desert war. However, any criticism voiced of Strafer Gott and his conduct of the Battle of Sidi Rezegh, such as it was, was muted. This is a matter discussed further in Chapter 18. Cunningham said, 'The main thing was to destroy Rommel's armour. One entered the battle with that object and then found one did not have the means.'[36]

By this Cunningham was alluding to his perceived disparity between the German and British/American tanks and the undoubted superiority of the German anti-tank guns, especially the 88mm. However, a number of historians, among them Correlli Barnett and Nigel Hamilton, believe the problem was the British class system. It is here that they lay the blame for the failure of the British armoured regiments, 'the cavalry', and their formations – indeed, on British generalship generally. It is alleged that the bravery and skill of individual officers was no compensation for an amateur, cavalier approach to their business by the majority who were the product of this class-ridden culture. Barnett describes the Army as 'a peasant levy led by the gentry and aristocracy'.[37] He goes on to opine:

> Most regular officers of the British Army were amateurs as well as gentlemen. Born into the gentry or the aristocracy, spending their lives in the last sanctuary of privilege in Europe their mental characteristics and morality were not surprisingly very different from those of managers, the scientists and technicians of industry.

The Army, any army, is a reflection of the society it serves and Britain in the 1940s, although far removed from the fascist dictatorships that it had so bloodily confronted, was a far from perfect society. Nevertheless, it was not all bad and was certainly a great deal better than some of the other models on offer. Barnett had a point but he overstated his case.

It is entirely true that Strafer Gott did come from a wealthy family, he had had an expensive public school education and he had joined an elite infantry regiment that only recruited young officers from his sort of background. He was, accordingly, the very personification of the sort of person that Barnett deprecated. He, and countless others, despite being products of this decadent class system, gave a great deal, and often their very lives, to allow Barnett the freedom to express his distaste for them. It could be argued that desk-bound, civilian 'class warriors' are ill-equipped to judge Gott and his peer group whilst according them scant acknowledgement for their commitment and courage.

It follows that the senior officers in the armed forces in 1940 were all born in late Victorian times and they were all brought up in a society that fostered a social order favouring the wealthy and well educated. It may not have been right and it may not have been fair, but it was the way of the world, and much the same all across Europe and the US. That state of affairs left the British Army to fight the Second World War with the cards it had been dealt.

One of those cards was Strafer Gott.

What is amazing is the extraordinary wealth of talent that emerged as the Army expanded and the opportunity it gave to many completely amateur soldiers, regardless of background, who took to soldiering with enthusiasm, alacrity and great success. Today, family background and affluence are no longer the criteria for HM's commission, but education still is – and rightfully so.

General Cunningham had decided to withdraw his army but, before he acted, he asked the Commander-in-Chief, Auchinleck, to visit. The great man flew up to HQ 8th Army and a very strained Cunningham outlined his plan, face to face. He got an unexpected and very robust response when Auchinleck rejected any thoughts of withdrawal/retreat. Instead, the C-in-C ordered that 'You will therefore continue to attack the enemy relentlessly using all your resources even to the last tank.'[38]

On 23 November 1941, with Cunningham in despair, 7th Armoured Brigade in ruins and with Auchinleck still present at HQ 8th Army, Rommel determined not to give the Allies the least respite and, accordingly, he had issued appropriate orders to General Crüwell. The latter was anxious to exploit his success at Sidi Rezegh and finish off the battered British armour. However, this did not suit Rommel, who had decided to move his entire Deutsches Afrika Korps (DAK) as soon as possible to Sidi Omar in order to relieve the pressure he *thought* was being applied to his frontier troops. He added to his DAK two Italian divisions, the Ariete and Trieste. This aggressive thrust came to be known as Rommel's 'dash to the wire', 'the wire' being the insubstantial lines of barbed wire that marked the border between Libya and Egypt.

Historians have dwelt at length on the wisdom of Rommel's decision not to exploit the situation at Sidi Rezegh. However, that debate has no relevance here other than to record that Rommel's change of direction was to Strafer's benefit. This was because Rommel, although accepting that the British armour could not be written off, 'it could be disregarded for the time being'.[39] Crüwell absolutely disagreed with the plan but Rommel would not countenance dissent; he rejected the advice of his subordinate and set off to lead his so-called 'dash'. Rommel's decision to lead from the front led to confusion as formations received conflicting orders not only from him but also from Crüwell.

Cunningham and Norrie met at Gott's HQ, which was now situated south-west of Gabr Saleh. A makeshift 'front' had been established from Point 175 just south of the Trigh Capuzzo to a position midway between Gabr Saleh and Bir el Gubi. These are little more than map references in an almost featureless landscape. The 4th and 22nd armoured brigades were at the northern end of this thinly held line.

It was 1000 hrs when 5th Panzer Regiment, leading 21st Panzer Division, moved out from Sidi Rezegh to the Trigh el Abd, intending to follow that track to the Egyptian frontier. At noon, 15th Panzer Division followed on. This procession, by chance, happened to pass out of snapping distance of most of 7th Armoured Division's remaining teeth, but it swept before it many units belonging to the British tail. The advanced and rear headquarters of XXX Corps were caught up in the flurry and some of the staff were captured, together with a quantity of water, petrol and other stores.[40]

The German Column did not enjoy an unopposed passage and while 4th and 22nd armoured brigades covered the flank of the 2nd NZ Division, 7th Armoured Brigade, weak as it was, along with the Support Group were able to take bites out of the moving column. These harassing activities did help to delay Rommel's progress but by 1600 hrs elements of 21st Panzer Division had reached the Egyptian frontier near Gasr el Abid, having advanced 60 miles in six hours.

Rommel had achieved his first aim of reaching the border; now it was his intention to surround the major forces he mistakenly thought were investing his Axis positions. He surmised that by this means he could bring about the defeat of the 8th Army, or at the very least cripple its capability. This was a serious miscalculation.

Rommel had not appreciated the situation and he had selected the wrong aim. He would have been better advised to focus on the 8th Army's logistic arrangements and its Field Maintenance Centres and along the way he could have picked off some of the airstrips that allowed the Desert Air Force (DAF) to operate so effectively. Rommel was well aware of the British supply system and had been fully briefed, but he chose to ignore the option because he was intent on relieving the besieged town of Bardia.

The Desert Air Force was a major player throughout the campaign and ultimately a key factor in the eventual British victory. For the sake of brevity its continuous operations and its success in debilitating the Axis forces does not figure in this text. The soldiers of the 8th Army held the DAF in very high regard. Jon obviously realised this when he produced the cartoon below.

Auchinleck was concerned at what he saw as Cunningham's lack of determination and this led to a loss of confidence in his recent appointee. Auchinleck, despite his austere and remote persona, was usually a compassionate and generous man and he agonised over Cunningham but eventually resolved to replace the General Officer Commanding-in-Chief (GOC-in-C) 8th Army.

Auchinleck looked around for a substitute but his options were limited, not least by the need to have the new man in place quickly. On that basis it had to be an officer already in the theatre. On 25 November he selected Major General

"DESERT AIR FORCE—we presume, old man"

Cartoon by Jon.

NM Ritchie[41] and the following day Ritchie flew to HQ 8th Army with General Sir Arthur Smith, the Chief of the General Staff, Middle East Command. Smith was Auchinleck's right-hand man. Ritchie was Smith's deputy and a contemporary and personal friend of Strafer Gott. However, unlike Gott, he had not held a command appointment in the desert campaign. His most recent active command had been 51st Highland Division between October 1940 and June 1941.

There was a view that, by appointing a member of his personal staff to command 8th Army, Auchinleck would have a firmer grip on events. Certainly it would have been more logical to appoint either of the corps commanders, Norrie or Godwin–Austen. Indeed, in terms merely of experience Gott would have probably been a better choice. Very fortunately for Strafer his hat was not in the ring. As it was, Ritchie leapfrogged over both corps commanders. He had been handed a poisoned chalice.

Auchinleck appointed Ritchie and the latter gave Auchinleck unqualified loyalty. Despite this, Ritchie received the basest treatment at the conclusion of the war when Auchinleck's biography appeared. Field Marshal Lord Carver, who knew both men and was an eyewitness to the events, was sufficiently incensed that he wrote a book to redress the balance.[42]

Ritchie was a popular and capable officer who was commissioned in 1914 into The Black Watch, with whom he won the DSO and MC before he was twenty-one. He was an unabashed admirer of Strafer Gott and spoke of his friend, and now unexpected subordinate, with affection. Ritchie was of the opinion that:

> His outlook was great in the widest sense. He never approached any problem without viewing it from the broadest outlook, and his first concern was not how best he might fulfil a particular role for himself but rather what action of his would most directly contribute toward the whole issue. To him anything small or petty was hateful, and one can understand how the great open space of the desert attracted him. He disliked being hemmed in; he loved the feeling of being able to move in any direction. He looked upon the desert as a friend, a place where he could always find security in manoeuvre, and he never spared the opportunity of impressing this point of view on others who, lacking his breadth of vision, were inclined to lay too much store by the imaginary terrors of the desert.[43]

Cunningham was, predictably, very distressed at his premature removal from command but accepted the situation with grace and courtesy. The return air journey with General Smith was difficult for both men. There then followed a charade that, while Ritchie adapted to his new command, Auchinleck sought to explain Cunningham's replacement as necessary because he had had a mental breakdown. This was not the case and, having been urged to go into hospital for 'treatment', Cunningham complied. Later, his doctors pronounced that he was 'suffering from severe over-strain'; although this diagnosis is now open to question.[44]

Strafer's scattered division south of Sidi Rezegh now made use of a lull in the battle. The 4th and 22nd armoured brigades scavenged the desert for repairable tanks. They absorbed hastily mustered battle casualty replacements and, not least important, caught up on sleep after five days of the most intensive fighting.

Rommel's thrust was halted by the artillery of 4th Indian Infantry Division (Messervy).[45] The Division had been positioned along the frontier around Sidi Omar and had had time to prepare defensive positions. The unexpected and vigorous defence made it clear to Rommel that he could not linger at Sidi Omar because he had outrun his own line of communications and recognised that he was now vulnerable. Rommel's supply dumps were located on the coast between Bardia and Tobruk and convoys, carrying food, water and ammunition, were obliged to circumvent two New Zealand brigades (4th and 6th) who were inconveniently placed to intercept them. Thus, on 26 November, 15th Panzer Division bypassed Sidi Azeiz and entered Bardia to be resupplied from the garrison's stocks. At a stroke this reduced the survival capacity of the besieged garrison.

The area bounded by Bardia, Halfaya, Sidi Omar and Sidi Azeiz was a confused melange of armoured and infantry units of both sides, who feinted, thrust and dodged. Heavy losses were taken on both sides in order to secure temporary occupation of a few square miles of worthless scrub. In practice, geographical gains were less important than the destruction of enemy assets.

In Bardia, in the darkness of the early hours of 27 November, Rommel called a conference with General Neumann-Silkow (15th Panzer Division) and General von Ravenstein (21st Panzer Division). He expressed concern that, on the Tobruk front, about 75 miles to the west, 70th Division and the NZ Division were making progress and there was the possibility that the Tobruk breakout would be completed.

In order to thwart this, 21st Panzer Division, by now much depleted, was ordered to move west to the Tobruk front. Notwithstanding the supply difficulties, 15th Panzer Division was ordered to attack British forces in Sidi Omar and Fort Capuzzo. Neumann-Silkow decided that to do this he would first need to take Sidi Azeiz, around which the 5th NZ Infantry Brigade was deployed. The 15th Panzer Division succeeded and, after fierce exchanges, the position and 700 prisoners, including the Brigade Commander, were taken. Thereafter, 15th Panzer Division abandoned its ambitions for Sidi Omar and Fort Capuzzo and turned its tanks westward towards Tobruk and the deepening crisis on that front.

The 21st Panzer Division, en route for Tobruk, ran into 5th NZ Brigade's 22nd Infantry Battalion and the Kiwis forced the Panzer Division to detour and lose time. Radio intercepts at 8th Army made it clear that the eastward movement of the Axis forces had ceased and the 'dash to the wire' had failed to achieve its objectives.

By noon on 27 November Strafer and his 7th Armoured Division were back in action against its old opponent, 15th Panzer Division. The 22nd Armoured Brigade, with only fifty tanks, took the initial pressure but 4th Armoured Brigade, with seventy tanks, arrived from the southwest to impact on the German left flank and its rear echelons. RAF bombers inflicted further heavy casualties.

On 28 November there was no let-up in the fighting but there had been progress. The 70th Infantry Division and the 4th NZ infantry Brigade had now joined hands at El Duda, on the road that skirts Tobruk, and opened a slim corridor into the garrison. The 6th NZ Infantry Brigade had cleared the Sidi Rezegh escarpment of enemy and, briefly, the sun shone for the Allies. However, the pendulum swung, as it always does, and a New Zealand Field Hospital was overrun. About 1,000 patients and 700 medical staff were captured. The events that followed, although they are a story worth telling, are not relevant here.

Three further Italian divisions (Trieste, Bologna and Pavia) moved west and engaged the 2nd NZ Division soon after that the 21st NZ Infantry Battalion was overrun by Ariete Division around Point 175. In quick succession afterwards, 24th and 26th battalions suffered the same fate. The 20th NZ Infantry Battalion was destroyed at Belhamed on 1 December.[46] New Zealand losses were huge: 880 dead, more than 2,000 captured and 1,699 wounded. The contribution made by New Zealand to the Allied cause, measured against the size of its population, was remarkable; 880 dead was a national disaster.

General Ritchie was proving to be a very aggressive commander and he was just what Auchinleck had ordered. Radio intercepts convinced him that 21st Panzer Division and the Ariete Division were vulnerably weak and he called on Gott to assist the New Zealanders in retaking Point 175. 'Stick to them like hell,' was his unvarnished command.[47] On the morning of 1 December Strafer swung his armour toward Belhamed in direct support of the New Zealand Division. The 4th Armoured Brigade on arrival there, probably had the opportunity to savage 15th Panzer Division, which they actually outnumbered in tank strength as 15th Panzer Division was down to just forty tanks. However, the Commander of 4th Armoured Brigade believed that his orders from Strafer gave priority to covering the withdrawal of the 6th NZ Infantry Brigade. The chance was missed. Is that an error to be laid at Strafer Gott's door?

The severely battered NZ Division moved off to the east. Freyburg, the GOC, having failed to consult Godwin-Austen about his intentions, gained the comparative safety of XXX Corps lines but was by now reduced to 3,500 men with 700 vehicles.[48] This withdrawal cut the fragile link with the 70th Division, now re-incarcerated in the Fortress of Tobruk. To be fair, Freyburg 'may not have been able to make radio contact with Godwin–Austen but he did consult Norrie, who agreed but did not [in turn] consult Ritchie, perhaps for the same reason. The latter had no alternative but to agree.'[49]

Rommel's logistic support had been depleted by the combined actions of the Royal Air Force operating from Maltese fields and the Royal Navy. He had been told not to expect any Italian reinforcement and his situation was parlous. Despite this, he boldly decided upon another thrust towards the wire. Crüwell was more concerned about the salient that Scobie had created outside Tobruk and the two generals, after discussion, reached a compromise. Afrika Korps (15th Panzer Division and Ariete) set off for Bardia and Capuzzo while a reinforced 21st Panzer Division attacked Scobie.

Ritchie had Auchinleck sitting on his shoulder and the latter approved when Ritchie opted to send Norrie to move on El Adem, first bringing forward the

2nd SA Division to relieve the 4th Indian Division on the frontier. Ritchie assumed that if he (Norrie) could meet Rommel in the open it would negate his use of anti-tank guns, which Ritchie presumed to be dug in on the escarpment. The skilled use and manner of the deployment of anti-tank weapons by the Germans had still really not dawned upon the British.

Under Norrie, XXX Corps duly made its advance and his 11th Indian Brigade was halted at El Gubi by an isolated Italian battalion that inflicted severe casualties and held up his entire corps. Ritchie, who was now concerned about Tobruk, about 30 miles from El Gubi, signalled Norrie and reminded him that it was his job to destroy enemy armour regardless of boundaries. Norrie bridled and, in effect, said, 'Make up your mind, I thought you said take El Adem?'

The Italians bravely held out in El Gubi and the 136 tanks under the command of Gatehouse were not employed to eliminate this pocket. This is difficult to justify or explain because successive infantry attacks were repulsed.

Rommel responded to the presence of Norrie's XXX Corps around El Gubi and he saw it as a further threat to Tobruk. Accordingly he abandoned his eastward advance to the wire.

Until 7 December both sides jousted without any conclusive result and then the logistic reality struck Rommel, who realised just how vulnerable he was. He gave orders for a withdrawal; his Italian allies and superiors were unable to see the necessity and they argued the toss for almost a week – a period in which the RAF had become increasingly dominant.

Godwin-Austen's XIII Corps was designated as the pursuit corps and this was probably because the GOC-in-C was thought to be the more aggressive and one whose performance had been more effective than Norrie's.

On 7 December, famously designated by President Roosevelt as 'a day in infamy', the Japanese attacked Pearl Harbor and by so doing expanded the scope of the Second World War not entirely to their advantage. Three days later and thousands of miles away in a different theatre, Japanese aircraft sank HMS *Prince of Wales* and HMS *Repulse*. The effect both nationally and internationally was dire.

This was the backdrop against which Strafer's 7th Armoured Division and 4th Indian Division were moved back under command of XIII Corps. This realignment took time to put into effect and in the resulting lull Rommel was able to reposition himself defensively on a line from Gazala (37 miles west of Tobruk) to Alam Hamza (20 miles south of Gazala).

The Axis outposts at Bardia and Sollum were abandoned and they quickly fell to the attentions of XXX Corps. It was on 13 December that the first assault on Rommel's new defensive line was made and the main player was the 4th Indian Division (Messervy), which was without 11th Indian Brigade, which was recovering from the ignominy of the El Gubi battle. The 4th Indian Division was to move around the southern flank and focus on Tmimi (on the coast 62 miles west of Tobruk). Strafer's division was to protect the northern flank of 4th Indian Division and 'raid Rommel's supply lines'.[50] By now 7th Armoured Division's tank strength was ninety, all under the command of Brigadier Gatehouse.

On 14 December, in the midst of all of this, Strafer got a message from home to say that his father-in-law, Brigadier Walpole Kays CMG, had died. Pamela was, of course, upset, but there was no question of Strafer going home. The old soldier was eighty-three and Strafer lost a good friend from the 60th with his passing.

British units had been inadvertently aiding Rommel by very loose wireless discipline and throughout Operation Crusader the garrulous exchanges had been subject to expert analysis. The results of this, in conjunction with the steady stream of first-rate intelligence from Colonel Fellers, enabled Rommel to meet most of his threats with a degree of confidence. To balance Rommel's advantage Ritchie was the recipient of Ultra intelligence and so, perhaps, it was swings and roundabouts on the intelligence front.

Godwin-Austen's grand plan did not succeed because both of Messervy's brigades were drawn into battle unexpectedly. One bumped into elements of the Italian XX Corps, was outgunned and unsupported, because at the same time the Africa Korps engaged the other brigade. To compound the problem, unfortunately Gott's tanks were too far away to assist either brigade.

Godwin-Austen reacted to this situation by ordering Gott to outflank the enemy, who were delaying the 4th Indian Division. Although the tactic was sound Gott could not conform until 15 December as he was suffering breakdowns and logistic shortages. When these issues were resolved the 70-mile outflanking movement commenced. This wide sweep would involve re-fuelling twice and although the spirit was willing, the broken nature of the desert made for very hard going and fuel consumption was even higher than anticipated.

The upshot was that Gott could not bring his tanks into action in support of Messervy's brigades, which were committed to frontal attacks. They took heavy casualties and made no progress. However, Gott finally succeeded in his flanking move and engaged the Africa Korps on Rommel's right flank. The arrival of 7th Armoured Division unsettled Rommel and he told Cavallero, the Italian Chief of Staff that 'he had no alternative but withdraw to Mechili and Tmimi as the enemy had enveloped the whole of his front.'[51]

Gott's forward troops witnessed the withdrawal and air reconnaissance endorsed the reports. On 17 December Strafer pressed on to Mechili and Rommel accelerated his move westward, denying Godwin-Austen the chance to replay a Beda Fomm manoeuvre. Crüwell was pulled all the way back to

Agedabia and the Italians passed through to Benghazi on their way to Tripolitania.

It was a 'Happy Christmas' for Strafer Gott and 7th Armoured Division when his advance guard entered Benghazi on Christmas Eve 1941.

Operation Crusader had achieved its aims. Crusader was a victory but an expensive one. British losses were numerically greater than those of the Axis forces with 2,900 killed and 7,300 wounded. The Germans, however, lost far more men as prisoners: 29,000 to 7,500 British. Field Marshal Lord Carver analysed the operation in 1986. In his book *Dilemmas of the Desert War*, he asked:

> Why, in spite of this victory, was there a feeling of failure? It was that, with few exceptions, the enemy had consistently appeared to have had the better of the tactical battle. At the time this was attributed to the superiority of his equipment, particularly of the German tanks over the British. Tank 'experts' like Hobart, particularly those who were not in the Middle East, blamed failure on the fact that senior commands were held by officers who did not understand how to 'handle' armour.

Carver then goes on to refute the equipment superiority argument in respect of tank versus tank but readily conceded that in anti-tank guns, artillery and armoured personnel carriers the Germans did have a distinct advantage. He also identified the forward presence of anti-tank guns with both armour and infantry as significant. This meant that German infantry was quite capable of looking after itself when facing an armoured attack.

On 24 December 1941 Churchill had complicated Auchinleck's position by 'addressing a "hard request" [tantamount to an order] that he relinquish at least 100 American tanks and accept that a consignment of Hurricanes were to be diverted'.[52] This was to counter the rapidly worsening situation in the Far East that would soon culminate in the surrender of Singapore. Auchinleck complied and offered up 7th Armoured Brigade, complete with all of its support units.

The 7th Armoured Division was now withdrawn and Gott was ordered to take it 400 miles or so back to Egypt to refit, but before he went, and on the retreat of the Axis forces, Strafer was one of the first into Benghazi after its capture on 24 December and 'remembering his own feelings as a prisoner of war, one of his first actions was, in company with Jock Campbell, to visit the hospital where many of the British wounded had been left by the Germans.'[53]

That seems to be a typically Strafer thing to do and, after his death, Mrs Daphne de Salis, who was serving as a nursing sister in a different military hospital, wrote to Pamela Gott. She had this to say:

157

I will tell you a true story; it happened at the Reception Station Ward where I was in charge. I was standing by a troop's [soldier's] bed – he was Corps of Military Police, not 60th. I heard the sick parade called to attention outside. I said to the man, 'Whoever is going by?' He answered, 'Just an officer.' I laughed and said, 'From the way the parade was called to attention I thought it was at least a general.' The man replied, 'Generals need much more fuss and attention than that. I don't hold with it all, *but* there is one general for whom I would stand at attention all day – just to see him go by.' I asked him who he was. He said, 'Sister, you wouldn't know him – he's always in the desert with his men up in the front line. He's the finest and most wonderful man we have in the Army – he is called General Gott, Strafer Gott.'[54]

Alan Moorehead, the war correspondent and author of *African Trilogy*,[55] was a close observer of Strafer Gott and the operations in Libya that had temporarily been concluded. He lunched with Gott and Norrie at the Gezira Club after Crusader and noted that neither man 'seemed to be particularly confident'. This is an interesting statement considering that they had just won a famous victory. After this lunch, and at Strafer's Divisional Headquarters in Cairo, Gott gave his maps and notes on the campaign to Moorehead. He told him that he wanted him to make use of them in the writing of *African Trilogy*. Moorehead, when writing that book in 1945, commented on Gott's capacity as an instructor:

His lecture to the officers was especially brilliant. He emphasised the necessity for good supply, the necessity for always keeping your supply line at a right-angle to your front so that it would present the smallest possible target and ensure the quickest delivery.
All of Gott's theories on supply were being ignored at that very moment. This was not because the men in command were ignorant or pig-headed. It was happening because Eighth Army was simply incapable of overcoming the physical difficulties of distance and time. It was too far away from its base.[56]

Moorehead had been present in the military hospital in Benghazi just after the town fell to the Allies and he observed after meeting the wounded prisoners that, despite their privations, there was no cynicism in the ranks about their generals and that 'Gott, in particular, was loved.' Moorehead's first-hand account of the events of 24 December bears repeating in full. Speaking of Gott, he said:

I had seen him in Benghazi, just a few days previously. He had come in from the front, dirty, unwashed and tired. He drove through the shattered streets to the hospital, which was still intact and full of British wounded who had been left there by the retreating enemy. As I stood in the doorway I heard a whisper go around the ward – a filthy, evil-smelling place – that Gott was coming in. And with him was Jock Campbell. Gott and Campbell together were a remarkable sight, both of them very tall and heavily built, both soldiers who fought at the front alongside their men, both as far as one could guess indifferent to any form of high explosive.

The sick men heaved themselves up on their elbows and grinned as the two leaders went down the ward. It was, in some ways, a pathetic little thing, that current of enthusiasm that swept through the hospital and I do not know why I remember it so clearly. Still, there it was – the men still had their leaders and they were willing to fight on to Tripoli, if they could get there.[57]

It would be a mistake to attribute more to Gott's hospital visit than it merits. Certainly it was the act of a compassionate, Christian soldier who cared deeply about his men. His actions should be no more than normal for any commander. Unfortunately, it probably was not the norm and that is why it has been so well chronicled.

Chapter notes

1. Lieutenant General (later General) Sir Alan Cunningham GCMG KCB DSO MC (1887-1983), brother of Admiral of the Fleet Lord Cunningham of Hyndhope. General Cunningham was the first of several commanders of the 8th Army who would falter and then be removed.
2. Vernon, Brigadier HRW, *Strafer Gott*, p.18.
3. DAQMG is a major's post with responsibility for the management of the logistics required to support the Division. He reported to a lieutenant colonel – the AQMG.
4. Later, Major General GPB Roberts CB DSO MC (1906-97), General Officer Commanding 7th Armoured Division 1947-49.
5. Churchill, WS, *The Second World War* Vol. III, p.357-8 and 364.
6. Playfair, Major General ISO et al, *The Mediterranean and Middle East* Vol. III, p.3.
7. Brigadier (later Major General) AH Gatehouse DSO* MC (1895-1964) was commissioned into the Royal Northumberland Fusiliers and transferred to the Royal Tank Regiment in 1931. He commanded 4th Armoured Brigade from May 1941 until June 1942, when he was promoted to command 10th Armoured Division. He fought at Alam Halfa and Second Alamein. Montgomery sacked him after the Battle of Alamein. Gatehouse retired from the Army in 1947.
8. Barnett, C, *The Desert Generals,* p.108. This book was first published in 1960 and revised in a second edition in 1983. The book was very successful and hugely controversial at the time when this 33-year-old historian wrote in judgment on a group of much respected, living household names. The original source is Davy, GMO, *Seventh and Three Enemies*, p.144.
9. Later, General Sir Neil Ritchie GBE KCB DSO MC KStJ (1897-1983). He was a

contemporary and friend of Gott and his commander for the six months January-June 1942.

10. *The London Gazette* supplement 35,396, p.7,332, 21 Oct 1941.
11. Bonner, Frank Fellers (1896-1973) was a protégé of Gen. Douglas McArthur and rose to the rank of brigadier general. He wielded great influence and played a part in ensuring that, at war's end, Emperor Hirohito was not prosecuted. Eisenhower made it his business to discharge Fellers from the Army in the rank of colonel.

    This was an indication of his personal dislike of Fellers, which stemmed from their service in the Philippines in 1936-37, and his animosity towards McArthur and those associated with him. In civilian life Fellers devoted himself to extreme right-wing causes.
12. Britain paid for the equipment supplied by the Americans. The war debt was not finally paid off until 2006 – more than sixty years after the cessation of hostilities, by which time the debt had doubled from the initial £2.2 billion at 1945 prices.
13. Deac, W, *World War II* magazine.
14. Playfair, Major General ISO et al, *The Mediterranean and Middle East* Vol. III, p.10.
15. Ibid, p.11.
16. Ibid.
17. Ibid, p.26.
18. Vernon, Brigadier HRW, *Strafer Gott*, p.18.
19. Ibid, p.45.
20. Gregg, V, *Rifleman: A Front Line Life*, p.68.
21. Playfair, Major General ISO et al, *The Mediterranean and Middle East* Vol. III, p.39.
22. Ibid, p.40.
23. Gregg, V, *Rifleman: A Front Line Life*, p.69.
24. Clifford, A, *Three Against Rommel*, p.141.
25. Playfair, Major General ISO et al, *The Mediterranean and Middle East* Vol. III, p.43.
26. *The London Gazette* supplement 35,530, 17 April 1942.
27. *The London Gazette* supplement 35,530, 17 April 1942.
28. Playfair, Major General ISO et al, *The Mediterranean and Middle East* Vol. III, p.46.
29. KRRC Association website.
30. Major RJ Crisp DSO MC (1911-94), quoted in Vernon, Brigadier HRW, *Strafer Gott*, p.8. Major Crisp was a South African Test cricketer and adventurer. He was later recommended for a second DSO but it is alleged that he annoyed authority to such degree that Montgomery intervened and the DSO was downgraded to an MC.
31. *The London Gazette* supplement No. 35,442, p.545, 30 January 1942.
32. The writer was Mr Peter Burnand from Hungerford, Berkshire. His letter was dated 12 June 2007.
33. Vernon, Brigadier HRW, *Strafer Gott*, p.14.
34. Gregg, V., *Rifleman: A Front Line Life*, p.69.
35. Carver, Field Marshal Lord, *Dilemmas of the Desert War*, p.51.
36. Barnett, C, *The Desert Generals*, unsupported quotation, p.103.
37. Ibid.
38. Playfair, Major General ISO et al, *The Mediterranean and Middle East* Vol. III, p.52.
39. Ibid.
40. Ibid, p.54.
41. Later, General Sir Neil Ritchie GBE KCB DSO MC KStJ (1897-1983).
42. Carver, Field Marshal Lord, *Dilemmas of the Desert War*.
43. Vernon, Brigadier HRW, *Strafer Gott*, p.41.

44. Hamilton, N, *Monty – The Making of a General*, p.485. After the war, Montgomery, now Chief of the Imperial General Staff, sent for the War Office file that included Auchinleck's letter of dismissal to Cunningham. This was dated 27 November 1941. Attached to the official communication was a personal letter. In this letter Auchinleck thanked Cunningham for agreeing to go to hospital 'in the public interest' and, he continued, 'for the way you accepted my decision and for your great loyalty and public spirit in agreeing to go into hospital secretly and against your will. I ask your forgiveness in having inflicted this indignity on you and I know very well how you disliked having to pretend that you are sick when you are not.'

45. Later, General Sir Frank Messervy KCSI KBE CB DSO* (1893-1974).

46. Mason, Captain WW, *The Second Libyan Campaign and After (November 1941- June 1942)*, p105.

47. Murphy, WE, *The Relief of Tobruk* (1961), the official history of New Zealand in the Second World War, p.411.

48. Ibid, p.458-64.

49. Carver, Field Marshal Lord, *Dilemmas of the Desert War*, p.47.

50. Ibid, p.49.

51. Ibid, p.50.

52. Playfair, Major General ISO et al, *The Mediterranean and Middle East* Vol. III, p.125.

53. Vernon, Brigadier HRW, *Strafer Gott*, p.14.

54. Ibid, p.67.

55. Alan McCrea Moorehead OBE (1910-83).

56. Moorehead, AM, *African Trilogy*, p.248.

57. Ibid.

Chapter 12

The Battle of Gazala and the Fall of Tobruk January-June 1942

If your officer's dead and the sergeants look white,
Remember it's ruin to run from a fight;
So take open order, lie down, and sit tight
An' wait for supports like a soldier.

(Rudyard Kipling, *The Young British Soldier*)

In the New Year of 1942 Churchill's military ambitions were given full rein. He had long planned that, immediately following the success of Crusader, the 8th Army should follow up with a further advance to Tripoli, and this was to be termed Operation Acrobat. Similarly, Churchill hoped that the Americans would apply pressure on the Free French forces of General Weygand to the degree that they would invite British forces to join him in French North Africa. This exercise was codenamed Operation Gymnast. As it happened Weygand was not to be a player because, while Churchill and Roosevelt were actively planning Gymnast, Petain dismissed Weygand.

Churchill's strategic ambitions were not matched by Auchinleck's logistic capability. The General, despite being willing, could not possibly put an army into the field until he had re-armed and resupplied his force. Churchill had little sympathy for inaction, regardless of the reason.

Nevertheless, XIII Corps, spearheaded by 22nd Armoured Brigade, moved on Agedabia on 28/29 December. This coastal town is south of Beda Fomm, 93 miles south of Benghazi, and here 22nd Armoured Brigade faced Crüwell's Afrika Korps. Brigadier Scott-Cockburn (the recent recipient of the DSO) had ninety tanks and he faced a force of sixty. Despite numerical superiority the engagement went badly and 22nd Armoured Brigade was reduced to thirty-nine tanks. The Germans lost only seven vehicles. This did not augur well for Operation Acrobat if it were to be launched.

Strafer played no part in this operation as he was back in Cairo. His 7th Armoured Division had been replaced in XIII Corps by Lumsden's[1] 1st Armoured Division. The other formation was Messervy's 4th Indian Division. However, the line of communications was so extended that only one brigade of the 1st Armoured Division could be kept as far forward as Benghazi.

The short-term plan was to harass Rommel and keep him in defensive mode until a full-out offensive could be launched. Auchinleck planned to make his move in February 1942 and he was confident that Rommel was so depleted by Crusader that he could not, and would not, venture out. This was a poor appreciation of the situation because it made no allowance for the supplies delivered to Rommel via Tripoli and he was actually much stronger than Auchinleck realised.

The British General was also completely unaware that the insecure British signals system complemented by the intercepted messages of the American military attaché – Rommel's *'Die gute quelle'* – allowed the German General to assess, accurately, the strength and disposition of the 8th Army. On 21 January, well knowing that he had armoured superiority in the front line, the German General launched a violent, well-judged and devastating offensive.

This assault was the precursor to a change in the fortunes of the 8th Army and the euphoria of December 1941, post-Crusader, evaporated over the next six disastrous months as the Army retreated, step-by-step, to a position near an obscure little railway halt called El Alamein. The 8th Army was to be completely defeated – 'routed' is the word that springs to mind, and it would not be overstating the case.

Every British general shared in the blame for the debacle and Strafer, who was commanding a major element of 8th Army, is obliged to accept his share of the criticism. However, it was General Neil Ritchie upon whose shoulders the bulk of the ordure fell. Ritchie was a gallant, capable, charming and engaging personality but quite lacking in command and desert experience. The forthcoming Battle of Gazala laid bare his deficiencies and this reflected upon Auchinleck, who had mistakenly appointed him to command 8th Army.

Under Godwin-Austen, XIII Corps fell back in the face of the German assault and as Godwin-Austen made preparations to vacate Benghazi he ordered 4th Indian Division to demolish all the installations in the port and withdraw. Churchill got wind of this via Royal Navy channels and promptly fired off a furious telegram to Auchinleck, who got Ritchie to order Godwin-Austen to cancel his orders.

This was the start of a breakdown in the relationship between Godwin-Austen and his commander, Ritchie. The situation was exacerbated when Ritchie started to communicate directly with the GOC 4th Indian Division; now Major General FIS Tuker.[2] Soon after this Ritchie took the Division under his own direct command. There were local difficulties of communication that made this a reasonable decision but it did not find favour with Godwin-Austen. There were further disagreements on tactics and the end product was that Godwin-Austen, who had had a 'good war' to date, felt undervalued and bypassed. He believed that Ritchie had demonstrated a lack of confidence in him and Godwin-Austen was very seriously aggrieved.

It is easy with the advantage of hindsight to see that Godwin-Austen's tactical advice was realistic and practical. It was certainly preferable to the unsupported and unrealistic optimism of Auchinleck, who dominated Neil Ritchie. 'The Auk' spent a week from 25 January until 1 February in Ritchie's headquarters watching his every move. It was an impossible position for Ritchie but, to his credit, he stuck loyally to his task. Behind both Auchinleck and Ritchie was the hot breath of Churchill, whose ill-judged pressure for Acrobat was the real problem. Nevertheless, it was reasonable to assume that Rommel would be unable to sustain a major offensive as his logistic problems expanded with every mile he advanced.

By 23 January Rommel had taken Agedabia and a week later Benghazi capitulated. This was ignominious as it was expected that the better-armed 1st Armoured Division (Messervy) would have easily repulsed the modest force Rommel employed. By 4 February, Ritchie had re-established a front line between Gazala and Bir Hacheim. The latter is an isolated oasis about 30 miles south of Gazala. There was a rudimentary fort there but today the setting is every bit as bleak as it was in 1942.

Suddenly, and quite unexpectedly, on 2 February Lieutenant General Reade Godwin-Austen resigned from his command of XIII Corps. For a general in command and on active service in the face of the enemy, to resign was a step almost without precedent in the British service. It was an extraordinary situation.

Some historians, among them Barrie Pitt[3] and Michael Carver, believe instead of accepting Godwin-Austen's resignation, Auchinleck should have removed Ritchie and replaced him with the battle-proved Godwin-Austen. That would have been an entirely rational decision but Auchinleck was in a difficult position. He had selected Ritchie and had then supervised his every move. To remove Ritchie would have been to tacitly admit that any errors made had been his and that he was making Ritchie his scapegoat.

Godwin-Austen had to go and his resignation was accepted.[4]

Gen Tuker, who had been unwillingly at the centre of the matter, made his position clear and said, 'His going was the latest of many misjudgements that had started to shake confidence in the leadership. We had lost the wrong man.'[5]

An army is a hierarchical, structured organisation, which not unreasonably selects for senior appointments only individuals of appropriate seniority and experience from a small pool of similarly suitably qualified candidates.

Auchinleck had to find a new corps commander and no doubt the 8th Army held its breath as, hitherto, he had established a track record in picking the wrong man. He was, of necessity, going to pick a divisional commander with extensive desert battle experience and the obvious choice was Strafer Gott.

In truth, it was a shortlist of one.

Thus, on 7 February 1942, Colonel (acting Major General) WHE Gott became Temporary Lieutenant General. In forty-two months he had advanced five ranks from major to lieutenant general. There are very few who have enjoyed such a meteoric rise.

Had Godwin-Austen *not* resigned, Gott would have soldiered on as a divisional commander and *might* have commanded a corps later in the campaign. As it was, Gott was propelled, purely by circumstances, involuntarily, further up the command chain. There was a large element of chance in all of this. Gott was the right man in the right place at an opportune moment. In addition, there was an element of patronage in the mix. He needed the support of the man at the top. In this case that man was Auchinleck, who saw Gott as something of a protégé and he swiftly and inevitably selected him for the command of XIII Corps.

This may have been an opportunity, but it was a promotion that Gott did not seek or expect. Nevertheless, he happily and willingly accepted the appointment, a perfectly reasonable response. The appointment raised his public profile and exposed him to close scrutiny – not least by the Germans, who already had a healthy respect for his ability.

Ritchie had won Crusader, but only by dint of Auchinleck's hand upon the tiller. In February 1942, and after the withdrawal to the Gazala line, Auchinleck embarked on a singularly unworthy exercise. He sent his Deputy Chief of Staff, Major General Eric 'Chink' Dorman-Smith,[6] to speak to Ritchie's subordinates to gauge the level of support the GOC-in-C 8th Army enjoyed … (or did not enjoy?). This was an unforgivable act of disloyalty and those who dished the dirt on Ritchie behaved little better. Auchinleck was minded to remove Ritchie from command but he realised that to do so would reflect badly on himself and his judgment in picking Ritchie in the first place – he thought he needed some high-calibre ammunition.

Ritchie was painfully aware that he was far less experienced and junior to both corps commanders and, on that basis, since his appointment he had consulted them at every turn. This had the practical effect of reducing command of the 8th Army, during Crusader and afterwards, to management by a committee of three. Gott, then a divisional commander and another level down, was certainly more able than Ritchie – and the GOC-in-C knew it. Now, on his promotion, Gott was the same rank, and so he joined the 'committee'.

Dorman-Smith was thought by many to be too clever by half, but there is no doubt that his quick mind, sharp wit and acid tongue served Auchinleck well. Dorman-Smith had been the brains behind O'Connor's early success at Sidi Barrani but his unfortunate manner was so abrasive that he had been moved sideways to teach at the Staff College in Haifa. Now he was restored to a place in the first team (as Colonel, Acting Major General) and was sent on a two-week expedition around Ritchie's 8th Army.

It is not surprising that Dorman-Smith discovered the consensus was that Ritchie was overly confident and that his limited ability and command experience was apparent to all. He was, clearly, not the man for the job. Among those officers consulted was Strafer Gott. He did not join in the derision heaped on Ritchie by vociferous opponents. His comments were characteristically muted although he went as far as expressing 'reservations' about Ritchie, 'which is about as far as he ever went in saying a bad word about anyone.'[7]

Dorman-Smith reported back to Auchinleck and, in a typically clever phrase, summed up his findings as an *'embarras de Ritchies'*.

Auchinleck, having the ammunition to hand, did not use it. Ritchie, probably unaware of what had been done and said behind his back, soldiered on although in practical terms his position was untenable. Auchinleck had irreparably damaged a weak commander by his own deplorable conduct and then vacillation. This irresolution on Auchinleck's part was because he realised that, if Ritchie was dismissed, the most likely new GOC-in-C was Montgomery, an officer he held in the very lowest regard. They did not like each other and that antipathy would last until the death of Montgomery in 1976.

The bad feeling stemmed from the time Montgomery replaced Auchinleck as GOC-in-C V Corps in July 1940. Then, and immediately on taking up his appointment, Montgomery promptly and publically reversed most of Auchinleck's arrangements and he missed no opportunity to ridicule his predecessor. Auchinleck would walk on broken glass to avoid serving anywhere near Bernard Montgomery. Better an ineffective Ritchie than a pushy, bombastic Montgomery.

Strafer's unexpected advancement was popular within the 8th Army. His reputation had spread far beyond the confines of 7th Armoured Division and great things were expected of him when he arrived in HQ XIII Corps on the Gazala line. His promotion left a gap and it seemed to be obvious that the only man to take command of 7th Armoured Division in his place was Brigadier Jock Campbell VC. The elevation of both men was roundly applauded. Only three weeks later, on 26 February, Campbell visited Gott in his new HQ. After the meeting he was returning to 7th Armoured Division and was being driven by his 21-year-old ADC – a flamboyant and courageous young man called Roy Farran. The car skidded on a newly laid clay road surface. It overturned and Campbell was killed outright. Farran was so distraught that he contemplated suicide.[8]

The death of Campbell devastated Gott. They had shared so much and Campbell had seemed indestructible. He had been Strafer's supporter and confidant. *Crusader*, the newspaper of the 8th Army, asked Strafer to provide a few words about Campbell and he wrote of his friend:

> He and his renown are secure for all time and the memory of his character, so loyal, so brave and so unselfish, will remain a constant source of strength to his comrades. For those of us who now stand in the desert facing the same enemy but without his presence, his loss may seem irreplaceable. Now, when in a tight corner, when our dangers and difficulties seem insurmountable, we can take courage by remembering what he would have done. One thing is certain; he would never have thought about himself.[9]

These words might have been just as well applied to Gott himself only a few months later. Campbell was a very deeply regretted casualty but in context he was only the most recent on a long list because British Army casualties, between 21 January and 6 February, amounted to 1,390 killed, wounded or missing, forty-two tanks destroyed and thirty damaged. In addition, forty field guns were lost. This unwelcome sequel to Crusader seemed to have turned success into failure and spelt the ruin of Acrobat. The 1st Armoured Division, commanded briefly by Messervy (between January and March 1942), was often outfought by a better-trained, better-disciplined enemy who also employed more effective tactics. The inexperienced and largely untrained 1st Armoured Division had simply not been up to the task. This defeat of the British armour was particularly disturbing.[10]

Rommel commented on the tactical issue when he reported back to Berlin on his success and said, among other things, 'Never anywhere at any time during the fighting in Libya did the British High Command concentrate all its available forces at the decisive point. This fundamental tactical mistake was one of the reasons the British offensive failed to achieve final success.'

Those remarks about concentration of force are particularly germane and more is the pity that the British armoured commanders seemed to be unaware of their deficiency in this regard.

Ritchie issued his orders and they catered for the eventuality of a further withdrawal to the east. The next defence line would be Sollum-Maddalena. Strafer had as his Brigadier, General Staff Bobby Erskine of the 60th. Erskine was an avowed Strafer fan and as they were close friends, it was a happy arrangement.

Erskine said that this alternate defence line was very much in Gott's mind when he assumed command but as the logistic build-up continued and the 8th

Army gathered strength, so the possibility of further withdrawal became less and less likely.

The date for the launch of Acrobat was the continuing subject of contention. Churchill wanted action *now*. Auchinleck declined until he had a significant numerical advantage in tanks and 3:2 was his stated aim. He opined it was unlikely that the circumstances would be right until June. It seemed that there was little that Auchinleck and Churchill could agree upon.

To be fair to Churchill he was dealing with a bigger global picture and one of the factors he had to consider was the defence of Malta and its retention as a major base. The island had been under siege since June 1940 and its role was critical to the Allied cause. Acrobat would help to relieve the pressure on Malta if only Auchinleck could kick-start the operation.

Churchill's burden was vastly increased when, on 15 February 1942, the rampant Japanese captured Singapore. This was, indisputably, the greatest defeat in British military history. The impact on British prestige was cataclysmic and it was not the only bad news. It had been preceded only four days earlier, on 11 February, by the debacle of the escape of *Scharnhorst, Gneisenau* and *Prinz Eugen* through the Straits of Dover. These events in combination added to the general air of despair. This was close to being the nadir of British fortunes although there were further defeats to come – not least in the Western Desert.

The period from late January until late May 1942 has been described as 'the lull'. Both armies established themselves in defensive positions, re-stocked, serviced their vehicles, gave soldiers leave from the front, trained replacements, waved away the ever-present flies … and waited. Strafer wrote a report on 7th Armoured Division's activity during Crusader. He commented to Auchinleck:

> Tanks require the support of field artillery, anti-tank guns and motor infantry. The higher proportion of these supporting arms to actual tanks in their Panzer divisions gave the Germans a distinct advantage. To our own tanks, the value of good support from 25pdrs was demonstrated time and time again – therefore it would appear that, in future, the Armoured Brigade Group should take the place of the Armoured Brigade.[11]

Auchinleck was persuaded by Gott's ideas and at once set about reorganising the order of battle for the 8th Army. Auchinleck said later, 'It seemed to me that our pre-war divisional organisation was too rigid and lacking in flexibility to be really adaptable to the conditions of modern quick-moving warfare in the desert or even elsewhere.'

It was rather late in the day, after eighteen months of desert war, to come to this conclusion and then only when faced with the view of one of his

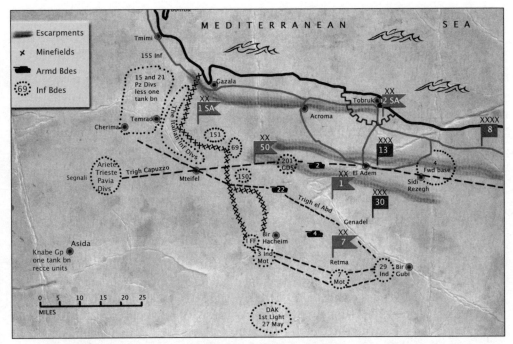

The Battle of Gazala, disposition of forces, May 1942. (Map by Arthur Perry)

experienced desert soldiers. This is a further illustration of the influence Gott exercised outside the confines of his own command, although neither Auchinleck nor the Official Military History gave Strafer any credit.

The organisation of XIII Corps standing on the Gazala line in early May 1942 was:

Headquarters XIII Corps (Lieutenant General WHE Gott)
1st and 32nd Army Tank Brigades (1 & 32 Army Tank Brigade)

50th Division (Major General WHC Ramsden)
29th, 150th and 151st Infantry Brigade Groups (Brigade Group)

1st South African Division (Major General DH Pienaar)
1st, 2nd,and 3rd South African Infantry Brigade Groups (SA Brigade Group)

2nd South African Division (Major General HB Klopper)
4th and 6th South African Infantry Brigade Groups and 9th Indian Infantry Brigade Group (Ind Brigade Group)

Gott's command was multi-national and as a consequence there were quasi-diplomatic issues that he had to be aware of. National sensitivities had to be recognised. Strafer Gott, with his relaxed and amiable style, was probably the British officer best able to deal with them.

In the 8th Army, British officers in the main led Indian troops and British units were integrated into Indian divisions. However, the forces of Australia, New Zealand and South Africa were composed entirely of troops from that country and the 8th Army had no powers of discipline over the officers and men from those 'dominions'. The commanders of the Australian and New Zealand contingents had the right to appeal any orders issued to them by the 8th Army to their own governments. The South African situation was a little different but they were, nevertheless, able to take an independent line on discipline, training and administration. Thus it was that Strafer Gott had responsibility for two divisions that he could encourage, chide and co-ordinate but not 'command' in the accepted sense.

Major General Dan Pienaar was a particularly difficult and recalcitrant officer. He was one of the few who did not fall under Gott's spell. Indeed, he actively disliked his commander, though what led to this animosity has never been explained. Pienaar played the diplomatic card throughout the campaign, entirely to his advantage. He did not accept orders and viewed them as no more than the opening position in a debate. The consequence of his very public, negative and uncooperative attitude was that Auchinleck readily appreciated that Gott was not entirely master of his divisions and he tried to ensure that, if possible, the 1st SA Division was not entrusted with any vital operation.

Klopper, in command of the 2nd SA Division, was inexperienced and, as future events were to show, perhaps over-promoted, although he had commanded a brigade earlier in the campaign and had won the DSO in the process. For Gott and his staff there was a wide range of extra issues arising from the composition of XIII Corps.

* * *

Strafer and his 7th Armoured Division had been at the very heart of Crusader and having suffered grievous losses at Sidi Rezegh his position might well have been in doubt. If that were the case, then the usual penalty was removal from command. He was not found to be wanting and, of course, had been promoted to Lieutenant General at the first available opportunity. During 'the lull' his performance and that of his division was the subject of further careful consideration by the command chain above him. Gott was not blamed for the defeat suffered by 7th Armoured Division.

Godwin-Austen, who had gone to pastures new, was almost certainly not consulted although Auchinleck was and then Ritchie drafted a citation that read:

> *General Gott was GOC 7th Armoured Division during the major part of the campaign, has shown himself as a commander of armoured forces of the highest class. Owing to his cool and sound judgment, wide experience of desert warfare and knowledge of the enemy's methods his division fought with such bravery, skill and determination that it defeated the enemy armour and largely made possible the advance into Cyrenaica.*
>
> *The magnificent qualities displayed by all ranks in the 7th Armoured Division and the success it achieved were in great part the outcome of the thoroughness of their training by Gen Gott, and of the confidence that they felt in him, as their leader. He is imperturbable in action and on many occasions he showed the qualities of great courage in the decisions made by him during the battle.*
>
> *During the last two months Gen Gott has been in command of XIII Corps and throughout this period has been untiring in his efforts to strengthen the defensive positions now held by his corps and is instilling the offensive spirit into all troops under his command.*

The British Army does not award corporate decorations other than battle honours and these are awarded to units and not formations. Nevertheless, many senior decorations from DSO upwards do sometimes recognise corporate performance. For example, the VC awarded to Colonel Carne after the Battle of the Imjin River recognised not only his leadership and personal courage but also the exemplary performance of his 1st Battalion, The Gloucestershire Regiment.

The citation above is not of the same magnitude nor is it a direct comparison because the text does focus on Gott's judgment and leadership; but every member of 7th Armoured Division could take pride in the award and feel that, although defeated at Sidi Rezegh, their bravery had been noted. The citation was for the appointment as a Companion of the Most Honourable Order of the Bath (CB) and his was duly promulgated on 9 September 1942.[12] Although this was a month after Gott's death he probably knew of the impending award – although strictly speaking it should have remained Honours-in-Confidence until promulgated.

This decoration indicated quite clearly that the defeat of 7th Armoured Division at Sidi Rezegh had not adversely affected Gott's reputation and its award underscored the standing and esteem in which he was now held in military and political circles.

* * *

Ritchie was planning an offensive and to this effect he had established his storage dumps well forward at Belhamed (26,000 tons), Tobruk (10,000 tons) and Jarabub (1,000 tons). The rapidly extending desert railway had reached as far as Capuzzo and then it was hurried on to Belhamed. Logistically, the 8th Army was well placed for an offensive. However, these vital logistic assets were not mobile and their presence inhibited Ritchie's room to manoeuvre when it became apparent that, instead of fighting an offensive battle, Rommel was going to beat him to the punch and the 8th Army was going to be obliged to defend itself.

Ritchie's plan was to establish a line from just west of Gazala on the coast to Bir Hacheim, about 40 miles to the south and slightly east, but Bir Hacheim was not at the edge of a natural barrier. It was merely the southern end of the longest defendable line. Along this line infantry brigade groups were to be positioned, each in a defensive box. The major fault in this plan was that the defensive boxes were miles apart.

The 1st Free French Brigade was allocated the very isolated locality of Bir Hacheim to defend. The 50th Division was distributed over a wide area; for example, its 150th Brigade Group was 13 miles away to the north of Bir Hacheim, and from there to its 69th Brigade Group was a further 6 miles. There were extensive minefields between the boxes but they were really a second-best solution because they were not all covered by fire. The boxes were not mutually supporting and each box, by the nature of its static role, became a logistical problem. Little wonder that Gott thought the whole idea impractical and Norrie, predictably, agreed with him.

To defend each of the boxes it was necessary to dig in – cruel back-breaking toil, as the desert surface was unyielding. Although it was early in the year the sun was hot, the nights were cold and the flies unrelenting. Those soldiers able to get to the sea to bathe found the water to be very cold; it is a myth that the Mediterranean is always warm. The infantry slowly got below ground level, laid out their wire – and then dug latrines. The soldiers sheltered from the sandstorms and waited … and while the 8th Army waited, Jon continued to amuse with work such as the cartoon on the following page.

Thus, Strafer's XIII Corps, with most of the infantry, held the right of the line with 1st SA Division (Pienaar) on the coast and 32 Army Tank Brigade in close support. The 50th Division (Ramsden) held the centre with 1st Army Tank Brigade in support. Strafer established his HQ on the ridge just south of El Adem.

In the south XXX Corps held the flank and had most of the armour under command. The arrangement was not to Strafer's liking and Major General Dorman-Smith was well aware of that, observing:

172

"...and if it isn't a mirage, I'll bet it's full of booby traps!"

Cartoon by Jon.

> He was ill at ease on the northern flank, immobile and away from his open desert. He was at his best on his own with plenty of room and the desert as a weapon. Herein he resembled Lawrence. He understood modern military space and time.[13]

Ultra intelligence had established that Rommel was planning to attack sometime after 22 May but unfortunately the direction of the attack could not be established. Meanwhile, Colonel Fellers was leaking information to the Germans like a running tap. Auchinleck and Ritchie corresponded frequently on the topic of Rommel's options – there were only three. He could attack along the coast and strike at 1st SA Division, in the middle of the line at 50th Division or outflank the line to the south, around Bir Hacheim.

Auchinleck and Ritchie's debate was, later, the subject of forensic examination but it is sufficient to say that Ritchie anticipated an outflanking move to the south. Despite this, the principal weakness of his disposition was that there remained ample room for Rommel to outflank Bir Hacheim. Auchinleck saw this weakness and so the southern line was beefed up by the addition of 3rd and 7th Motor Infantry brigades (3 Mot Bde) and further east, 29th Indian Infantry Brigade. See map on page 169.

The British Gazala line was purely defensive and there was no ambition to use it as the baseline for an attack. Consequently the stage was now set for a battle to be initiated by Rommel. The Desert Fox needed no urging and the

173

subsequent events are known as the Battle of Gazala – it lasted until 15 June, when the battle for Tobruk began. The battle was fought in three phases; the first was of three days duration (26-29 May) when Rommel attacked the British position from the south to strike at its rear.

Robert Lee, a member of the Royal Artillery, described his experience of a box on the Gazala line at the end of May 1942:

> Boxes were originally to protect the Infantry. ... When you're in an established position, they're like a camp. A huge area. Barbed wire all the way round the outside, then minefields with a gap, similar to a drawbridge. The tracks that go out from the box and then through the minefield are planted with mines each night. At dawn stand-to it's the infantry's job to go out and take up those mines and bring them back inside, all carefully accounted for. Then the OP Officer can ride out to his position. One morning they did a miscount. Left one on the track. Killed a troop commander. He drove into it.
>
> The men are arranged inside. The most vulnerable units are in the middle. ... Our system of boxes was essentially a defensive thing. It was too rigid. The boxes couldn't help one another. The Afrika Korps methods were more flexible. They could take each of our boxes in turn and have a battle with it. ... [As the situation deteriorated.] We held them off a long time. Getting on for four days and nights. Our guns were in action on 28th and 29th, plus the infantry – machine guns and mortar fire. Coming at us we had artillery shells, airburst rapid fire, machine-gun fire. On 30th and 31st, German armour and German vehicles got right up on us. They were in full view – to our south, mind. One vast football field. Vehicles and Valentines burning all around us, palls of that acrid smoke, the smell of human flesh roasting, burning. The first taste of hell. But not the last. ... I remember listening in to a bombardier specialist, and he was talking to a sergeant out at the OP. This sergeant was one of my old B Troop blokes. I knew the voice. He was obviously getting disturbed. The Germans were right there in front of him. He could see them clearly. Out at the OP they were just in a dug trench. Just telephones with them, wires running back. Nothing else at all. There's this sergeant saying, 'I'm afraid it's getting impossible now. There's nothing much we can do. They're getting so close.' He says, 'I hope you'll explain to my wife what happened.' He was talking to someone who knew him well. He was in a state. That's how it was at the end.[14]

Crüwell, in command of four Italian divisions (Sabratha, Trento, Brescia and Pavia), advanced on Strafer's XIII Corps on the coastal flank and 1st SA

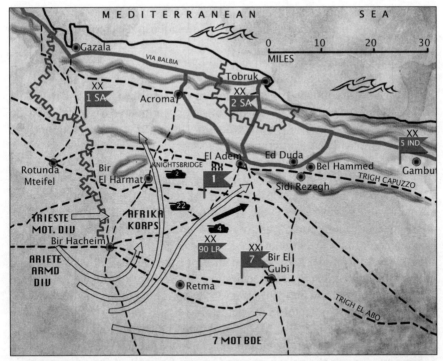

Battle of Gazala, the German flank attack, 26 May-21 June 1942. (Map by Arthur Perry)

Division and 50th Division perceived this to be the main axis but, as it transpired, it was just a feint.

Rommel's main thrust, and just as Ritchie had anticipated, was made with the Italian Ariete, 21st Panzer Division, 15th Panzer Division and 90th Light Division. He went round the southern flank of 8th Army and then planned to cut up into its heart. The Ariete Division was sent to tackle 1st Free French Brigade at Bir Hacheim and quickly discovered it had chosen a very tough nut to crack.

The French had something to prove and they inflicted grievous casualties on their Italian attackers who could, quite easily, have bypassed Bir Hacheim. It was probably a battle that did not need to be fought. Initially, reports of German tanks to the south had been disbelieved, but very soon the painful reality dawned as Rommel created mayhem among the widely dispersed 8th Army, most of which was facing the wrong way. Auchinleck had previously emphasised to Ritchie that the British armour must:

> Not fight in bits and pieces. They have been trained to fight as divisions and fight as divisions they should. Norrie must handle them

as a corps commander, and thus be able to take advantage of the flexibility that the fact of having two formations gives him.

Ritchie paid lip service to this advice and by failing to consolidate his armour it would be destroyed in detail. Matters were not helped when General Messervy, now in command of 7th Armoured Division, his GSO 1 and two other staff officers were captured by fast-moving enemy armoured cars. The Division had no effective leadership until Messervy escaped from his captors and resumed command on the afternoon of 29 May.

To the east of Bir Hacheim the Axis forces swept through the British line and 15th Panzer Division was faced by the armour of XXX Corps – to be more accurate, 4th Armoured Brigade, because 22nd and 2nd Armoured brigades were 12 and 15 miles away respectively. Hitherto, the view was that if attacked from the south the armour could rapidly be concentrated to meet the threat. As it happens, 'the threat' was stationary for lack of petrol, in a highly vulnerable situation, and Rommel knew it. The speed of the German night attack had, initially, prevented that vital concentration of force that should have delivered a British hammer blow but had failed to do so. This failure was perhaps the single most important factor in the defeat that was to follow.

Australian journalist Alan Moorehead came up to the front on 1 June and on his way he was passed by eastbound convoys carrying Axis prisoners and equipment. Among the prisoners was General Crüwell, Rommel's erstwhile deputy. Moorehead found Strafer Gott, who seemed to be in confident mood. 'There are only two places where I want to fight the Nazis,' he said, 'either on our minefields or here.' Moorehead expanded by recording that 'here' was an undulating patch of desert sown thickly with the saltbush that sweeps up from the sea not far from the old Italian fort at Acroma.[15]

It was arid, flat, inhospitable, featureless country and well populated by flies. 'Here' was 'Knightsbridge'. It was nothing more than a point on the map – Gott would soon get his wish because it was to be the scene of a major engagement.

The next phase of the Battle of Gazala is known now as The Cauldron (see map on page 179). Early in this phase, at 0830 hrs on 1 June, Ritchie went to see Gott to discuss their options. They were armed with the Ultra intelligence, which revealed that Rommel was short of petrol, water and ammunition and he intended to hold off the British with an anti-tank screen before he was re-supplied and able to renew his armoured thrust north and east. The German offensive had stalled and it was pinned against the minefields on its now left flank (west). The Ultra information should have triggered a major attack on the stationary Axis force. Had it done so the campaign could have been won there and then.

The Axis force was left undisturbed and the chance was lost.

Not one to sit on his hands, Rommel personally led a supply convoy to his immobile tanks. The Axis armour, when fully sustained, renewed its efforts. Rommel, in an original measure, decided to break through the minefield to the north of the stubborn 1st Free French Brigade, at Bir Hacheim, cut the Gazala line and, by so doing, reduce the length of his supply chain. Once this was achieved he could form a safe bridgehead with secure lines of communication through the left centre of the British line. Only the Yorkshiremen of 150th Infantry Brigade stood in his way.

At this stage honours were about even; with the French still holding Bir Hacheim with enormous resolve. Later on 1 June, and after Gott had left his meeting with Ritchie:

> Returning from a visit to his divisional commanders Pienaar [1st SA Infantry Division] and Ramsden [50th Infantry Division] – he had to pass close to two German armoured laagers, where his car received fifteen bullet holes and he himself was slightly wounded. His driver got the Military Medal [MM] for this episode. On another occasion (but not the same day) he was dive-bombed by a Stuka while standing on a tank with two other commanders. The bomb hit his car standing alongside; both commanders and his ADC were wounded, the latter so severely that he lost a leg. Strafer escaped with only a scratch.[16]

Throughout the German counter-offensive, which resulted eventually in the Allied withdrawal to the Alamein position, Strafer Gott was in the thick of the fighting around Knightsbridge and Tobruk. He could have been killed half a dozen times but although he courted danger he appeared to have a charmed life. His high visibility to his soldiers is oft remarked upon.

The British counter to Rommel's initiatives was to hold conferences and Ritchie, charming man though he was, exuded completely unrealistic optimism. Messervy commented to that effect, adding that he was always saying, 'Ah, now we've got him,' when it was quite clear we hadn't.[17]

Ritchie had always leaned heavily upon Gott for advice since he took up his role as the Army Commander and they agreed that they should relieve the pressure currently being shouldered by Strafer's 150th Infantry Brigade. Rommel sought to eliminate this brigade in order to open up a wider passage to the west but 150th Brigade was a serious obstacle and its artillery had effectively closed Rommel's route through the minefields.

The brigade was composed of Territorial battalions from Yorkshire (two battalions of Green Howards and one of East Yorks) and they all fought tenaciously and bravely defending a 5-mile front while surrounded and outnumbered. Eventually, the Brigade position was overwhelmed and the formation was destroyed on 1 June. Their adversary said afterwards, 'The defence was conducted with considerable skill.' Rommel added, 'and as usual the British fought to the last round.'[18]

The loss of the 150th Brigade was a savage blow but, meanwhile, the talking continued – all to little effect. General Ramsden reported that Strafer returned from yet another interminable conference and saying, 'I *think* Ritchie is going to do this or that.'[19] (Author's italics.)

It transpired that the attack on 150th Brigade had exhausted the Germans and Ritchie had another opportunity to launch a determined assault that evening, as he had originally planned. Success was in his grasp. The German situation was grim; they were short of water, ammunition, food and fuel but they hung on and when the 150th Brigade was cleared out of the way German resupply was quickly established.

Ritchie's optimism and charm were no substitute for 'grip' and this he completely lacked. He remarked to Air Commodore Tommy Elmhirst, 'I have sent my orders for tomorrow, but I know my corps commanders will hold a tea party on them and whether they will comply with my exact intentions is questionable.'[20] This sad and revealing remark reflects badly on Norrie and Gott, who by now seemed to have forgotten the precepts of discipline fundamental to any army.

The reluctance to accept an order as an order had spread further down the command chain. Lumsden and Messervy made life difficult for Norrie, and Pienaar challenged every order from Gott as a matter of routine. This breakdown in discipline was symptomatic of the malaise now infecting the 8th Army.

The organisation of the Army started to break down and this was manifest in the bizarre command structure that was agreed for an assault on the German bridgehead; this was designated 'Operation Aberdeen'.

Rommel now had a firm base that had been left unmolested for four days, during which time it had consolidated resupplied and rested. Major General Briggs (5th Indian Division) and General Messervy (7th Armoured Division) were to be in joint command of Operation Aberdeen. In reality, this was a task for a corps commander because command by consensus or by committee just does not work. Soldiers understand and accept willingly and gratefully the autocratic nature of military command. In this case that autocracy was missing and the command arrangement was the height of absurdity.

Strafer Gott shrewdly disassociated himself from the arrangements and, rather as he expected, Operation Aberdeen was a disaster. The operation was poorly planned and inadequately coordinated. Barnett summed up the debacle:

> The infantry went in first at 0300 hrs on 5 June under cover of darkness. They made an encouraging advance. After daylight, 22nd

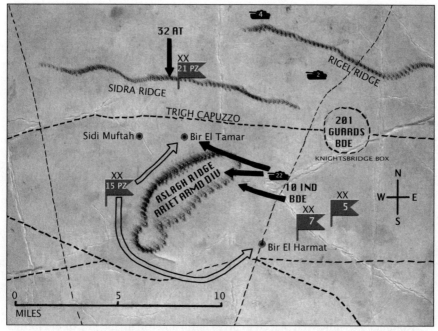

The Cauldron, 1-13 June 1942. (Map by Arthur Perry)

Armoured Brigade not having come up, the infantry were furiously counter-attacked. Then the 156 Stuarts (the lightest of 8th Army tanks) of 22nd Armoured Brigade advanced 3 miles beyond the British infantry and were fired upon by Rommel's concentrated artillery. They fell back behind the infantry, who were attacked by German combined groups of all arms and massacred.

It had taken 8th Army four days to think up Aberdeen; it took Rommel half a day to plan and launch a counterstroke against Aberdeen's left flank, which rested on an uncovered minefield.

The German counter-attack had won the day and, along the way, captured Messervy and HQ 7th Armoured Division for the second time. The 8th Army had lost 110 tanks. Nevertheless, and with heroic understatement, it signalled to Auchinleck at GHQ that, 'while the operation had not been entirely successful there were signs that the enemy was not entirely happy.'[21]

Messervy escaped, yet again, and did what he could to restore stability and rescue British assets stranded in The Cauldron. These rescue efforts were marked by indecision, order and counter-order. The final bill that had to be paid was 168 Crusaders, fifty 'I' tanks, four regiments of artillery, an Indian brigade, and 7th Armoured Division Support Group.

Gott tried to persuade Pienaar to attack to his south but Pienaar flatly refused on the basis that he was not going to hazard his division against a superior force. Pienaar was appeased and was invited to make a raid at brigade group strength but the South African responded by saying that he had insufficient time to organise it. Graciously, he did agree to lay on a few company-sized forays around 7 June. These achieved nothing but caused the loss of 280 men. Patently, Pienaar was in the wrong job and in the wrong army. He and his division were becoming a liability.

Ritchie realised that he was now in damage limitation mode and he ordered General Koenig, who was commanding 1st Free French Brigade, to break out of Bir Hacheim on the night of 10/11 June. Koenig complied, unwillingly, and brought out 2,400 very angry, gallant survivors (of his original 3,700), most of whom wanted to continue the fight. Bir Hacheim had been the pivot in the elbow of the British position and the southernmost point. By vacating it Ritchie had abandoned the Gazala defensive line. Ritchie pulled, what remained of his left flank back to a line parallel with the Trigh Capuzzo line and running east-west, in line with the Mediterranean.

Rommel was now well placed to drive north and roll up the line of the former British positions towards the coast, take the Knightsbridge box and cut off part or all of Strafer's XIII Corps, which occupied a salient with Ist SA Division (Pienaar) holding the right of the line and anchored on the coast and his 50th Division (Ramsden) just to the south. The 2nd SA Division (Klopper) was further east and now in residence behind the much depleted and derelict defences of Tobruk.

The boxes at El Adem and Knightsbridge were the only bastions that obstructed Rommel's march to the sea. In XXX Corps there was a scene of complete confusion, with Messervy (7th Armoured Division) and Norrie, his corps commander, each issuing plans that were not complementary. Messervy wanted to get his armour out of the defensive line of the Trigh Capuzzo and into the open desert where he could be more flexible and so he issued orders to that effect. Norrie, his boss, had decided to drive south and confront 15th Panzer Division. The only commonality in these orders was that both completely ignored the 8th Army instructions on the management of armoured forces.

The lax radio discipline that had for too long been a feature of British communications in the desert again played into Rommel's hands, as he knew Messervy's intentions. The German Commander put in place arrangements to counter them. Historian Correlli Barnett observed succinctly:

At noon [on 12 June] Norrie placed 7th Armoured Division under the command of General Lumsden [1st Armoured Division] – because once more Messervy had disappeared – and instructed him to attack 15th Panzer Division immediately. Almost simultaneously Rommel ordered the 21st Panzer Division to drive into the rear of 7th Armoured Division. This division, caught waiting for orders and unprepared for battle, melted into a confused mass of vehicles ringed by German anti-tank guns and tanks.

Lumsden arrived on the scene, made an appreciation of the situation and he told Norrie that this was not the time to advance south. Norrie rejected Lumsden's advice and insisted that the two armoured divisions must break through the lines of 15th Panzer Division and not fall back to the allegedly safe haven of the Knightsbridge box. The Battle of Knightsbridge that followed was the greatest defeat of British armour in history.

Typically, the battlefield was wreathed in smoke and swirling dust, the savagely hot summer sun was a further cruel element but despite countless acts of gallantry by anonymous British soldiers and, incidentally, a VC won by Lieutenant Colonel Henry Foote. Royal Tank Regiment,[22] Rommel obliterated his British opposition. At the end of the day Rommel had swept all before him, cut the Trigh Capuzzo line between Knightsbridge and El Adem and established a strong position on the escarpment north of the 'road'. He had also cut the bypass road around Tobruk. The implication of this was that the only viable route between those troops still manning a useless Gazala line and the sanctuary of the Egyptian border was the Via Balbia. Gott's two divisions were highly vulnerable and he determined to take corrective action.

In the chaos, communications had been disrupted and Lumsden, who could get no orders or guidance from XXX Corps HQ, finally got a message that told him he was now under command of Gott's XIII Corps. Much good that did, because for twelve hours he could not get in touch with Gott either. The losses of British armour was staggering – 200 Cruisers and sixty 'I' tanks.

The following day matters went from bad to worse when Knightsbridge was cut off and overrun with appalling losses; the few survivors slipped away after dark leaving a battlefield carpeted with British dead. A German soldier, Rolf-Werner Völker, was shocked by the sights he saw and observed, 'It was like a naughty child had had a tantrum and thrown his toys all over the room, there were upturned guns, trucks and tanks everywhere – a lot of them burning.' Another witness said, 'I have never seen so many dead Englishmen before.'[23]

Auchinleck had, up until this point, offered Ritchie advice but the tone of the advice altered and Ritchie's attempts to run his own command could be seen to wane. Auchinleck was now giving the orders. The possibility that the 8th Army could be cut off and destroyed piecemeal was now more and more likely. The political interference coupled with poor communications and compounded by imprecise objectives led to the next great debacle as the bulk of the 8th Army was scrambling to get out of the path of the German juggernaut.

The 50th Division (now less 150th Brigade) broke out to the west and then outflanked the German force by rounding it to the south. By taking this route The Cauldron was avoided. All credit to Ramsden for salvaging as much as possible of his 50th Division. This move to the east by the 8th Army was to become known as the Gazala Gallop.

On 14 June, Ritchie signalled Auchinleck telling him that he proposed to evacuate the Gazala line and regroup west of the Egyptian border. What he did not tell the Commander-in-Chief was that Strafer Gott had already taken the initiative. His 50th Division (Ramsden) was already moving east and 1st SA Division (Pienaar) was taking the shorter coastal route as XIII Corps withdrew to safety and avoided being cut off. Pienaar, very typically, argued the toss with Gott about withdrawing in daylight and was allowed to delay until dark accommodated him. This delay could have been fatal and nearly was, but good fortune favoured Pienaar and two brigades of 1st SA Division moved out in good order. The 2nd SA Infantry Brigade (Brigadier WHE Poole) was the rear guard; it left its position in stygian darkness and spent an exciting night trying to find its route to safety. All was well and the Division extricated itself from the salient and was available to fight another day – Pienaar permitting.

Tobruk, east of the Gazala line, was a military issue and a political football. It had been agreed earlier in the year by both the military high command and the British Government in London that Tobruk would not be defended as an isolated Fortress. Churchill now applied great pressure on his generals to hold and defend Tobruk come what may. This volte-face by Churchill was because he had committed himself to the retention of Tobruk in his negotiations with Roosevelt. By so doing had hung an 'emblematic albatross'[24] around his neck as well as the necks of his generals.

Gott's opinion was outlined on 8 October 1949 when Erskine wrote to Brigadier Latham of the Historical Section of the Cabinet Office. In his letter he said:

> Gott always urged that Tobruk should only be garrisoned at all if we were going to fight on the Gazala line in earnest. The first conception of the Gazala position was that it was an outpost on which we would delay the enemy as long as we could and then fall back to the frontier … the frontier was not an ideal place for defence, but it was a good deal better than Gazala, provided we had a strong armoured force to protect the southern flank.

However, Gott was not the decision maker and, when it became apparent that his views were in a minority, he loyally played his part in defending the Fortress.

Despite the wholesale withdrawal from the Gazala line the retention of Tobruk was still desirable because its port facilities reduced the 8th Army's lines of communication. However, Auchinleck's policy in respect of Tobruk was:

> Full of obfuscation, evasion and downright dissembling. When Churchill was about to leave London to see Roosevelt, he sought guarantees, not for the first time, that Ritchie's withdrawal from the Gazala line would not mean abandoning Tobruk. ... Auchinleck replied that he 'did not intend that the 8th Army should be besieged in Tobruk ... he had no intention whatever of giving up Tobruk.'[25]

This firm commitment to Tobruk was all very well but the General Officer Commanding-in-Chief realised that, if it were to be invested, Tobruk could be an anvil upon which Rommel would hammer the 8th Army. Churchill's political aspirations once more did not match the military reality. Nevertheless, Churchill was in constant contact with Auchinleck during the middle of June and left no doubt as to his desire to hold Tobruk, which somehow had to be accommodated. On 15 June Auchinleck took a deep breath and signalled Churchill, saying:

> Although I do *not* intend the 8th Army should be besieged in Tobruk I have no intention whatever of giving up Tobruk. My orders to General Ritchie are: (a) to deny the enemy the general line Acroma – El Adem – Bir Gubi; (b) *not* allow his forces to be invested there; (c) to attack and harass the enemy whenever the occasion offers. Meanwhile, I propose to build up as strong as possible reserves in Sollum-Maddalena with the object of launching a counteroffensive as soon as possible.'[26]

Later that day Ritchie and Lieutenant General Corbett, Auchinleck's Chief of the General Staff, met and a blazing row erupted, the crux of which was that Ritchie rejected his detailed orders, declining to reinforce the area between Tobruk and El Gubi 'with static infantry nor would he guarantee that he could prevent Rommel from moving further east.' Corbett flew back to GHQ to report to his master.[27]

The following day Auchinleck did concede, in a signal to Ritchie, that although Tobruk was not to be invested he realised that 'it might well be isolated for short periods until our counteroffensive can be launched.' He told Ritchie to organise the garrison as he thought fit.

The fog had cleared and Ritchie now knew that the 2nd SA Division (Klopper) was to remain in place and on that basis there was no requirement for wholesale destruction of stores or of port facilities.

In Tobruk Klopper was unrealistically optimistic about his capacity to resist a possible German siege, no matter how short. Klopper had only very recently been promoted and his command experience was limited. His staff did not include a single professional soldier and so the fortunes of the vast Tobruk cantonment were in the hands of amateurs. Klopper was willing, but the task he had been given was far and away beyond his capacity and that of his untrained staff officers. Numerically he had far more men under command than Morshead the year before but Klopper's soldiers were not of the calibre of Morshead's Australians who had fought so bravely in the earlier siege.

Ritchie now reinforced Tobruk and its garrison to include four brigade groups. There were in addition 8,000 support troops and about 2,000 uniformed, but non-combatant, labourers employed to service the port. Klopper had to defend a perimeter 35 miles long and a coastline of 20 miles. It was a vast piece of country with inadequate defences. The anti-tank ditches had filled with wind-blown sand; the minefields had been scavenged to secure the Gazala line, leaving significant gaps. The defensive plan was uncoordinated.

However, despite all this, Churchill was content, Klopper was confident, Ritchie was mollified and Auchinleck hopeful.

Gott, who had moved his headquarters from El Adem as it became a focus of Rommel's attention, visited Tobruk on 16 June, saw the defensive arrangement and pronounced that they were 'a tidy show'. He indicated to Ritchie that, although he thought Klopper was capable of defending the Fortress for several months, he was prepared to take command in Tobruk himself, if necessary.

His very poor assessment was accepted but his offer was declined.

It was now important that Rommel be kept at bay while Klopper consolidated his defences, and the position of El Adem was critical to this end. The 29th Indian Infantry Brigade (Brigadier DW Reid) was in place but under great pressure. The Brigade repulsed an attack by 90th Light Division. However, 21st Panzer Division overran an isolated battalion position, covering the pass where the bypass crossed the escarpment, 3 miles to the north-west.

The 29th Indian Infantry Brigade and 20th Indian Infantry Brigade were under command of 7th Armoured Division (Messervy). The GOC was trying to put together an effective force from the remnants of 1st and 7th Armoured Divisions and he was increasingly concerned about the vulnerability of the two Indian brigades and his ability to support them. On 16 June Messervy told Norrie, his corps commander, that El Adem could 'only be held for another twenty-four hours at most.'[28] He asked permission to withdraw and Norrie referred the request to Ritchie who point-blank refused and said that El Adem must be held at all costs.

Gott's influence on Ritchie was evident when, at 1630 hrs on 16 June, the

General Officer Commanding-in-Chief signalled the Commander-in-Chief, saying that he had:

> discussed the matter with Gott and we can accept investment for short periods with every prospect of success if we go all-out to build up strength in the south … am trying with accordance with your wish to reinforce El Adem box with additional artillery but this has not yet been possible due to tactical situation here.

The situation on the ground did not improve and Messervy finally obtained, from Norrie, permission to withdraw from El Adem that evening. However, Reid (29th Indian Infantry Brigade), said, 'Thank you, but no thank you' and opted to wait a further twenty-four hours as he alleged that his soldiers were all keyed up to fight a battle and a rushed withdrawal at night would be confusing. In due course the brigade moved out, in good order and without any losses.

The 20th Indian Infantry Brigade had re-established itself at Belhamed (about 10 miles east of Tobruk) but did not stay there for long. The 4th Armoured Brigade (Richards) with about ninety tanks, not all of which were in good order, had orders to dominate the Sidi Rezegh area (about 4 miles south of Belhamed) and provide support for the Indian Brigade. Later in the day, 15th and 21st Panzer Divisions engaged, and by 2135 hrs Norrie had no option but to withdraw the 20th Indian Infantry Brigade. Unfortunately, just after the order to withdraw had been given, Rommel cut the coast road at Gambut and a large number of 20th Indian Infantry Brigade personnel fell into his hands as they streamed to the east.

Auchinleck flew to see Ritchie on 18 June and the latter, although by now accepting that Tobruk would be besieged, was optimistic that that would only be a temporary state of affairs. The result of the meeting was that Strafer Gott was called to the fore. He was given responsibility for all the forces in the forward area, except Tobruk, which was to come directly under Ritchie's command.

Strafer's mobile element would be 7th Armoured Division (Renton) with command of 4th Armoured Brigade (sixty-six tanks), 7th and 3rd Indian Motor Brigades: 1st SA Division and 50th Division were each to provide three columns. Much less mobile, he had 10th Indian Division (Rees). These infantry formations were to position themselves in a series of widely separated brigade boxes. Gott had command of a formidable, but widely dispersed, force and his task was to halt the German advance on Tobruk.

Norrie's XXX Corps was moved back to Mersa Matruh, 'to form and train a striking force with which, in due course, to resume the offensive.'[29] On 19 June Rommel was polishing his plan for the attack on Tobruk and Ritchie was issuing complicated orders to Klopper that were designed to cover all exigencies. The South African was told: (a) if Rommel attacked the frontier he was to destroy the enemy investing Tobruk; and (b) his objectives in the first place were 2 miles west and secondly 6 miles south-west of the perimeter.

Laying on the hard-pressed Klopper responsibility for action outside his perimeter was unreasonable and beyond the ability of his staff. To add to the confusion these orders came hard on the heels of Gott's orders to Klopper when he had seen him on 16 June. At that meeting Gott told Klopper that he should prepare three plans: (a) for defence; (b) for evacuation; and (c) for counter-attack if Belhamed were to be lost.

Klopper's assets were considerable but the geography was daunting, his infantry battalions each having a frontage of 3 miles to defend. There were sixty-nine anti-tank guns very thinly spread over the perimeter, arithmetically about one every 750 yards, although of course they were not deployed like that. Klopper had aggravated the situation by placing a disproportionate percentage of his force facing the sea – he obviously perceived a threat from that direction.

The initial threat did not come from the sea; instead, early in the morning of 20 June, it fell upon 11th Indian Infantry Brigade (Anderson) in the south-east of the perimeter. By 0700 hrs, the Indian defences had been breached. It was the crack in the dam.

Anderson called for support and Klopper responded by ordering Willison, who commanded his armoured element, to send tanks to support Anderson. In practice, what should have been a straightforward task was beset by lethargy and muddle. It took more than two hours for any tanks to arrive at the 11th Brigade position and by then it was too late. By noon, Rommel had 113 tanks through the perimeter defences and heading for key objectives in the port.

Significant and damaging German advances and imprecise intelligence being passed between Tobruk and 8th Army, and vice versa, marked the remainder of the day. By late afternoon, Klopper's headquarters was being shelled and he decamped to HQ 6th Indian Brigade, which was in the north-west corner of the garrison. The Commander of 4th Indian Infantry Brigade also moved his headquarters at about the same time and 'from that moment all command arrangements broke down.'[30]

Auchinleck and Ritchie were quite unaware of the gravity of the situation. Auchinleck had the benefit of Ultra intelligence but as late as 1756 hrs on 20 June he was signalling Ritchie to say, 'I repeat that the enemy must not be allowed to launch an unimpeded attack on Tobruk.'[31] That was a bit late in the day because by 1756 hrs German troops were in sight of the Senior Naval Officer of the Inshore Squadron, who reported 'enemy tanks supported by a small party of infantry approaching the town ... may be ordered to blow demolitions any time. If so, intend to withdraw naval personnel and craft.'

The situation at nightfall was that Rommel's troops had driven a narrow wedge into the Fortress, with its apex at the harbour, and in doing so had knocked out all of Willison's tanks and put out of action two battalions of 11th Indian Brigade and one of the Guards Brigade and also the latter's headquarters. Neither of the South African brigades (of 2nd SA Division) nor the Gurkha battalion on the coast north of the thrust had been seriously involved and the majority of the artillery, including one medium regiment, was intact. But Klopper, in spite of what he reported, took no steps to organise a counter-attack by night, to which the Afrika Korps, short of infantry, would have been very vulnerable.[32]

Klopper decided that his only realistic option was to break out. Accordingly, at 2008 hrs, about fourteen hours into the first day of the battle, he signalled the 8th Army to say that there would be a mass breakout at 2200 hrs. Brigadier Whiteley, the Brigadier, General Staff 8th Army, responded by saying, 'Come out tomorrow night preferably, if not tonight.' Whiteley gave instructions as to the axis of the breakout, of which the centre line was to be Medauar; this was the corner of the perimeter just east of Acroma. A gap was to be left between Harmat and El Adem. Whiteley then emphasised the importance of destroying the 1.5 million gallons of petrol stockpiled in Tobruk.

Klopper took advice from his South African subordinates and found that there were divided opinions. Some were entirely at ease with a breakout and others wanted to fight on. Klopper came up with a soggy compromise. He decided that his mobile troops would leave the Fortress at once and the remainder 'would fight to the last round.' This resolve only lasted until 0600 hrs on 21 June, when after more thought he concluded that fighting on would not further the cause of the 8th Army.

The next step was to negotiate surrender but Klopper had very few cards to play. He joined in captivity 33,000 of his men (Carver), or 35,000 (Bierman and Smith), of which well over half were British. As many as 2,000 vehicles changed ownership, as did 5,000 tons of food. The assurance that the petrol had been destroyed was not true and 1,400 tons – countless hundreds of thousands of gallons – were taken by the Germans. A handful of men escaped in a convoy of trucks, including 199 members of the Coldstream Guards and 188 others from assorted units. For several weeks other survivors trickled into British lines.

The last unit to surrender was the Queen's Own Cameron Highlanders, who resisted until early on 22 June. The Battalion marched into captivity led by their commanding officer and their pipes. The 'Fortress of Tobruk' had been no more than a military myth.

A temporary POW cage was established at Derna and, charitably, Rommel permitted Klopper to speak to his men. It was a large audience and Klopper had to employ amplifying equipment and speak through a microphone. It must have come as a nasty shock to him when he was jeered and booed by his discontented fellow prisoners, who believed that he had let them down. He had failed miserably and was party to a British defeat only eclipsed by the loss of Singapore.

Churchill was in Washington conferring with Roosevelt when an aide passed a message to the American President. The pink slip of paper was passed on to Churchill, who winced as he read the news it contained. It was one of the most bitter memories in that man's long and varied life. Later, he said, 'Defeat is one thing, disgrace is another.'[33]

Klopper's performance had been dire but a court of inquiry held after the war exonerated him. This begs the question that if he, the Commander, was not responsible, then who was?[34]

Chapter notes

1. Later, Lieutenant General Herbert Lumsden CB DSO* MC (1897-1945). Lumsden was a strong personality and a brave man. He famously disagreed with and clashed with Montgomery during the Battle of Alamein and was sacked for his trouble. He was killed in action by a kamikaze attack on the bridge of USS *New Mexico* while acting as Churchill's personal envoy to General McArthur in the closing months of the war.
2. Later, Lieutenant General Sir Francis Tuker KCIE CB DSO OBE (1894-1967).
3. Pitt, B, *The Crucible of War*, p.478.
4. Later, General Sir Alfred Godwin-Austen KCSI CB OBE MC (1889-1963). Churchill held a very negative view of Godwin-Austen (G-A) and despite the support of General Sir Alan Brooke, the Chief of the Imperial General Staff, and Sir James Grigg, Secretary of State for War, Churchill was adamant that G-A not be re-employed. It was not until Field Marshal Smuts intervened in November 1942 that Churchill changed his position. Thereafter, G-A was fully employed and rose to be Quartermaster General and then Principal Administrative Officer in India, reporting to none other than … Field Marshal Lord Auchinleck!
5. Tuker, General F, *Approach to Battle*, p.81.
6. Major General (Later Colonel) EE 'Chink' Dorman Smith MC* (1895-1969). He was Chief of Staff to Auchinleck until August 1942. He was thought to have an excessive and malign influence over Auchinleck and was accordingly viewed with suspicion by Churchill and Alanbrooke. He was reduced to his permanent rank and retired from the Army in 1944. In later life he allied himself with the IRA.
7. Bierman, J and Smith, C, *Alamein: War without Hate*, p.157.
8. Major RA Farran DSO MC** Croix de Guerre, Legion of Merit (1921-2006) died in his bed after a life packed full of incident and adventure.
9. Vernon, Brigadier HRW, *Strafer Gott*, p.13.
10. Playfair, Major General ISO et al, *The Mediterranean and Middle East*, Vol. III, p.152.
11. Barnett, C, *The Desert Generals*, p.136.
12. *The London Gazette* 9 September 1942, p.3,945. Generals Norrie, Messervy and Scobie were all appointed CB at the same time.
13. Vernon, Brigadier HRW, *Strafer Gott*, p.79.

14. The Second World War Experience Centre.
15. *Daily Express*, 2 June 1942.
16. Vernon, Brigadier HRW, *Strafer Gott*, p.15.
17. Letter to Barnett, C, quoted in *The Desert Generals*, p.150.
18. Liddell Hart (ed), *Rommel Papers*, p.212.
19. Letter to Barnett, C, quoted in *The Desert Generals*, p.150.
20. Holland, J, *Together We Stand*, p.97, original source, *The Elmhirst Papers*.
21. Ibid.
22. Lieutenant Colonel HB Foote RTR (later, Major General) VC CB DSO (1904 -1993). He was commanding 7 Royal Tank Regiment when he won his VC.
23. Bierman, J and Smith, C, *Alamein: War without Hate*, p.177.
24. Dimbleby, J, *Churchill's Desert War*, BBC 2, 5 November 2012.
25. Bierman, J and Smith, C, *Alamein: War without Hate*, p.178.
26. Connell, J, *Auchinleck*, p.574.
27. Ibid, p.576.
28. Carver, Field Marshal Lord, *Dilemmas of the Desert War*, p.114.
29. Playfair, Major General ISO et al, *The Mediterranean and Middle East* Vol. III, p.259.
30. Carver, Field Marshal Lord, *Dilemmas of the Desert War*, p.122.
31. Ibid.
32. Ibid.
33. Bierman, J and Smith, C, *Alamein: War without Hate*, p.185.
34. General HB Klopper DSO (1902-78), captured at Tobruk but escaped in 1943. It is significant that he was not decorated. After the war he rose to become the head of the South African Army 1951-53.

Chapter 13

The Retreat to El Alamein, Operations Bacon, Splendour and Manhood July 1942

While the three-day debacle of Tobruk was being enacted, Gott's mixed force was establishing itself east of the Fortress. This was not without its difficulties; Pienaar (1st SA Division) had refused to occupy his allotted area 35 miles south of the Sollum-Sidi Omar defences held by 10th Indian Division (Rees). Pienaar was a noted pessimist but now he plumbed new depths and added outright insubordination to his portfolio.

The sequence of events is unclear but Pete Rees represented to Gott an objection to the disposition of his battered division, saying that he did not think he could delay the enemy for long – even if the Germans did not outflank him. Whatever the form of words used and the setting in which they were employed, they were sufficient to provoke Strafer and, uncharacteristically, he sacked Rees on the spot for being negative. It may well have been that Strafer's meeting with Rees[1] followed on from a disagreeable joust with Pienaar and for once his equable front had slipped. Whatever it was, Rees went.

Ritchie's plan was that Gott should screen the 8th Army and delay any German advance for as long as possible. Gott was not expected to fight and win any major battles and the preservation of his force for action with a reinvigorated army was important.

XXX Corps (Norrie) had been dispatched back to El Alamein to establish a defensive position blocking access to the Nile. He had taken with him the 1st SA Division and Gott was probably relieved to see the back of the mutinous Pienaar.

Ritchie decided not to defend the Egyptian border because it was in effect no more than a line on the map and had no attractive and defendable features.

190

He focused his initial defence on the coastal town of Mersa Matruh, about 100 miles inside Egypt.

He disposed his forces by placing 10th Indian Division and 50th Division under command of the newly arrived X Corps (Holmes), which had come from Syria. The X Corps was centred on Gerawla, about 15 miles further down the coast.

Rommel could muster only forty-four tanks but he was undaunted and planned to assault the eastern end of the escarpment directly south of Mersa Matruh. He planned to create a gap between the 2nd NZ Division and 1st Armoured Division and through this he would pour 15th Panzer Division and two Italian divisions, sufficient force to overwhelm the garrison. Ritchie was complacent but recognised that a night attack was a strong possibility. On 23 June he reported to GHQ that Gott was 'fully alive to the fact that offensive action, especially after dark, against the southern flank … may have great effect'.[2]

The British and Commonwealth forces braced themselves for Rommel's next assault, having been reorganised and redeployed. Formations had changed in shape and content and were 'shaking down' as quickly as they could. Then, on 25 June, the most important change of all – Auchinleck told Ritchie that he was taking command of the 8th Army himself. So Ritchie was sacked and he became the latest in a long line of generals removed from command.[3]

Ritchie had struggled manfully to please Auchinleck but he never dominated either his subordinates or the battlefield. He was an honourable man, picked to do the wrong job, at the wrong time and probably for the wrong reasons. He had been unfailingly loyal to Auchinleck, who had repaid him in a different coin. After the war Auchinleck ruthlessly savaged Ritchie's reputation in order to salvage his own.

Auchinleck's declared intention now was 'to keep all troops fluid and mobile', but shortly after he assumed direct command circumstances worked against him. 10th Indian Division was positioned in the unkempt, poorly maintained and un-mined defences of Matruh. 50th Division, with only two under-strength brigades, was sitting outside the wire, to the east. Both divisions were under command of X Corps.

Strafer Gott commanded two divisions; the first was 1st Armoured Division, comprising 4th and 22nd armoured brigades. The Division occupied a great space 25 miles south-west of Matruh and 15 miles further to the east covering the southern flank. Secondly, Gott had the 2nd NZ Division, whose two brigades faced the sea up on the escarpment at Minqar Qaim. The 5th Indian Division (now of X Corps) provided several mobile columns in the country between Gott's two divisions. This arrangement, with 5th Indian Division operating in the XIII Corps area, was untidy. It proved to be a mistake.

Auchinleck realised that Mersa Matruh was not the setting for a decisive battle as it had a vast exposed flank to the south guarded only by 1st Armoured Division. Auchinleck opted to eventually withdraw a further 100 miles to the east and base himself on and around El Alamein. The advantage of this position was that its left or southern flank was inviolate, guarded by the impassable Quattra Depression, and it would reduce the width of his front. At Mersa Matruh the desire to inflict damage on enemy forces was balanced by the aim of not being trapped by the coast and cut off. This early period of Auchinleck's command was one of confusion between X and XIII Corps; the efforts of Gott and Holmes were poorly coordinated and that contributed to the losses that inevitably followed.

Rommel, despite his numerical inferiority (he had only 2,500 infantry and in armour only sixty tanks), pressed his moral advantage and acted outrageously. His audacious plan should have brought disaster and cataclysmic defeat. It did not and he won a battle that marked him out as *the* great general of the Desert War.

The 26-27 June were days of bloodshed, with fierce fighting at Mersa Matruh. The 90th Light Division and 21st Panzer Division negotiated a way through Auchinleck's minefields in the south, although early on 27 June the effective artillery of Ramsden's 50th Division did temporarily halt the progress of 90th Light Division.

Meanwhile, 15th and 21st Panzer Divisions moved east above and below the escarpment. Although 4th Armoured Brigade and 7th Motor Brigade blocked the passage of 15th Panzer Division, they could not impede 21st Panzer Division (which charged toward Minqar Qaim) and the 2nd NZ Division, which it surrounded.

Auchinleck's policy of 'flexibility and mobility' had led to a presumption that an early withdrawal was likely and that mind set caused some to jump the gun. Auchinleck intended that initially the 8th Army should regroup at Fuka, 31 miles east of Matruh, to establish another delaying position. He issued orders to that effect at 2120 hrs on 27 June, but poor communication generated confusion and the two corps commanders had no idea what the other was doing.

Freyberg led his 2nd NZ Division out of their encirclement on the night of 27 June but the charismatic and gallant Divisional Commander knew nothing about the Fuka arrangement and withdrew all the way to El Alamein, having misinterpreted a radio message from Gott.[4] The Kiwis had taken a further 800 casualties. Strafer then ordered the remainder of his corps to withdraw, a decision that Holmes (X Corps), to the north, knew nothing about.

X Corps was out of communication with Army HQ from 1930 hrs until 0430 hrs on 28 June. Consequently, it did not receive the message to withdraw and was left isolated and very vulnerable when Gott withdrew his XIII Corps as ordered. By now 90th Light Division had succeeded in cutting the coast road 27 miles east of Matruh and was well established between X Corps and safety. This was a disaster in the making and the only route for X Corps was to drive south and outflank the coast road. Gott was told to provide support but he was in no position to do so.

At 2100 hrs on 28 June, X Corps broke out by brigades. It was an untidy business and the darkness added to the confusion. In the path of the British force were enemy units laagered for the night. The 5th Indian Division suffered heavy casualties and its 29th Indian Infantry Brigade was destroyed at Fuka. Holmes later estimated that he lost 60 per cent of his corps in this operation.[5]

It could be argued that if the 8th Army had mounted a properly coordinated counter-attack on 27 or 28 June, the campaign would have had a different shape and the later events around El Alamein would not have taken place. This is certainly the view of Michael Carver. He concluded:

> Both Auchinleck and Gott must bear a heavy load of blame for the that precipitate and ill-organised withdrawal and Lumsden and Inglis who took command [of 2nd NZ Infantry Division] when Freyberg was wounded must share some of it for being so anxious to withdraw quickly.[6]

The early light of 29 June revealed the clouds of dust being kicked up by a defeated army in full retreat; this was now no well-ordered 'withdrawal', it was a frantic rush to safety. In Cairo Lieutenant General Corbett (Auchinleck's Chief of Staff) ordered that confidential papers should be burned and an air of panic was abroad. The resultant clouds of smoke and burning embers of paper floating on the wind gave the day the title 'Ash Wednesday'. Many of those who could fled the city and the local population happily prepared to receive Rommel, who would free them from 'the brutal yoke of the British'. They had no idea what life under the Nazis was likely to be like.

It was on 26 June that a German radio drama programme revealed the part being played by the American Military Attaché in Cairo. This was presumably intended to be a fictitious setting but the plot was absolutely in line with what was actually taking place. The messages to Washington of Colonel Fellers, the American Military Attaché, had revealed all British plans and since September 1941 these had been routinely intercepted by the enemy. There was consternation in Berlin and even more in Cairo. Abruptly, on 29 June, the plug was pulled on Fellers' and Rommel's 'Gute Quelle' fell silent, but not before he had done incalculable damage to the Allied cause.

Only a month had passed since the British 8th Army had been holding a strong defensive position with significant superiority in manpower and materiel.

Since then, it had been out-fought, forced to retreat 300 miles and had suffered massive losses – not least in prestige as the rapidly changed attitude of the Egyptians clearly showed.

Rommel estimated that he would be in Alexandria by 6 July, and who was to gainsay him?

On 30 June the remnants of Auchinleck's Army was distributed across the El Alamein front and outline plans were being drawn up for possible further withdrawals to Alexandria, Cairo and the Suez Canal.

Given the events of the previous month the laying of such plans seemed to be prudent and the senior command group was in broad agreement. Gott passed on this news to Brigadier Kippenberger,[7] the temporary Commander of 2nd NZ Division, who 'protested that we were perfectly fit to fight and that it was criminal to give up Egypt to 25,000 Germans and 100 tanks' (disregarding the Italians). Gott replied, 'Sadly, the NZ Division was battle-worthy but very few other people were'. He went on to say that 'he feared the worst'.[8] Kippenberger thought that Gott was quite openly defeatist and that his attitude, even in defeat, was unacceptable in a corps commander.

Auchinleck had selected El Alamein and it was here that he laid out his stall.

El Alamein was a nondescript little station – no more than a halt on the coastal railway, 2 miles from the Mediterranean. It was of no consequence whatsoever but geography would make it world famous. July 1942 was to see the pendulum of war swing slightly back in favour of the British and Auchinleck's adherents assert that it was during July that he laid all the foundations for the subsequent destruction of Rommel, his Afrika Korps and his Italian cohorts.

The Allied position at El Alamein was based on a series of natural features that are to be seen on the map on page 195. About 800 yards north of the railway station the coast road ran along an escarpment that was not of itself a major feature but in the land of the blind, the one-eyed man is king and in this landscape any raised ground that gave line of sight and line of fire was important. From this unnamed escarpment the view west and south extended for miles. The desert was not nearly as flat as it appeared and the subtle folds in the ground afforded some concealment, even from a vantage point such as this. About 7 miles south-west of the station was Miteiriya Ridge. This was about 400 yards wide and it ran roughly east-west. Miteiriya was just a large outcrop of rock and digging here was difficult, bordering impossible. The map shows the juxtaposition of the other key features, which were Ruweisat Ridge and the much more significant Alam Halfa Ridge. The Qattara Depression just shows its face at the bottom of the map.

Ruweisat Ridge ran through the middle of the Alamein position and as such it constituted vital ground. 'The ridge had to be held at all costs for its loss would

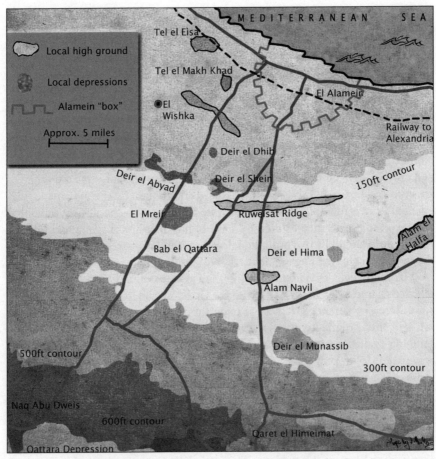

El Alamein area of operations, July 1942. (Map by Arthur Perry)

give the enemy observation and a springboard onto the area through which ran the whole communications of the 8th Army.'[9]

Throughout history this modest ridge, a mere lump of rock, had attracted no attention and it was apparently of no importance to anyone. However, in the next few weeks thousands of men would die in the dispute over its possession.

Auchinleck did not have a front line as such. He formed and manned a series of boxes '*à la* Gazala line'. The first of these boxes was around the halt at El Alamein, a second was at Bab el Qattara and, in the south, a third at Naqb Abu Dweis. These boxes had all the deficiencies experienced at Gazala. They were about 15 miles apart and the assumption was that the gaps in between would be filled – somehow and by someone. Norrie recognised the problem only too well

195

and he set up a fourth box at Deir el Shein, halfway between El Alamein and Bab el Qattara. This latter box was occupied by 18th Indian Infantry Brigade.

Meanwhile, stragglers were arriving and being directed from a series of control points that Norrie had established for the purpose. Pienaar on the coast was persuaded to organise strong mobile columns to operate outside his defences around 18th Indian Infantry Brigade, which was to the Division's south-western front.

The Arabic word *'deir'* translates as 'depression', or 'low-lying ground'. The value of Deir el Shein was that its defenders were concealed from all except aircraft and that it provided excellent fields of fire. Artillery was out of sight and only vulnerable to speculative counter-fire. Deir el Shein was the scene of an epic battle on 1 July, in which the 18th Indian Infantry Brigade was eventually overrun and destroyed, despite fighting with the utmost gallantry. However, the resistance offered by 18th Indian Infantry Brigade had blunted the edge of Rommel's two armoured divisions and later assessments recognised the importance of the engagement.

The 90th Light Division moved in the darkness of early morning 1 July to take the Alamein box, defended by 1st SA Division, and it bumped into Pienaar's south-western defences. It was at once the recipient of heavy and effective artillery fire. So effective was the response that the German Division went to ground and then started to crack; panic broke out and it took energetic action by senior staff to prevent a complete rout. Unfortunately, no one realised just how close to breaking point 90th Light Division was as it withdrew to think again.

The extraordinary thing is that the philosophy of defended boxes had been jettisoned after the Gazala battle, yet now it was two similar boxes that had bought the 8th Army valuable time and put Rommel onto the back foot.

After these first exchanges Auchinleck prepared to fight a series of battles that were to become 'First Alamein'. Gott's XIII Corps positioned in the south made a series of attacks on the exhausted Germans, who were now 1,400 miles away from their logistic base in Tripoli. The attacks were poorly coordinated and, as a result, did not have the success that they might have expected. Strafer Gott and his staff bear the responsibility for that.

Nevertheless, on 3 July, the 2nd NZ Division won an engagement with the Ariete Division south of Ruweisat Ridge. After the New Zealand gunners had registered on the Italians' soft-skinned vehicles they switched targets and, with the enemy cowed under their firepower, the 19th Battalion of 4th NZ Infantry Brigade attacked with the bayonet. A total of 350 prisoners were taken, as well as thirty-six guns, six tanks and 100 trucks. It was a tremendous fillip to morale.

Gott had been out of touch with Auchinleck for some time and after this particular battle the C-in-C received a hand-written note from Strafer, which said:

Unless I stay near my divs I have the same difficulties of coms as from you to me + they have not the means to overcome them. I explained this on the air to your HQ today, + I was told 'OK for present', so I am not moving. I do consider it essential to remain in close contact with the div HQs, especially NZ.

This last sentence is probably an indication of the sensitivity of 2nd NZ Division. It appears that circumstance required Gott to conduct his own campaign and he made it clear that his corps was attacking and had been since the previous day. He repeated that communications were an issue but that he knew Auchinleck's intentions and his efforts were to that end. He added that he was NOT (Gott's capitals) concentrating on withdrawal.[10]

On 8 July, Norrie was removed from command of XXX Corps. His departure is something of a mystery and whether he jumped or was pushed has not been established. He was replaced by William Ramsden, previously the GOC 50th Division. Ramsden was described as 'pedestrian',[11] and his appointment was much to the irritation of the Australian Morshead, who considered himself far more suitable to command XXX Corps than Ramsden, and he said so – loudly.

On 10 July, 9th Australian Division (Morshead) joined 1st SA Division in an attack on Tel el Eisa. There was sustained fighting over the next seven days, but it was a successful operation and the enemy lost about 2,000 killed and 3,700 prisoners. A very significant coup was the capture of the German Signals Intercept Company 621. This unit had hitherto provided Rommel with most of his signals intelligence (SIGINT).

Later, Morshead followed Pienaar's poor example by challenging the disposition of his division – warning that unless he had his way he would appeal, over Auchinleck's head, to his government. Similarly, Pienaar's attitude and inability to accept direction was becoming an issue that had to be managed on a day-to-day basis.[12]

On 14 July, Auchinleck sought to make a thrust along the Ruweisat Ridge and attack the Italian Pavia and Brescia divisions. This initiative was christened Operation Bacon. It fell to Strafer to coordinate the tanks of, 2nd NZ Division and 5th Indian Infantry Brigade. Cooperation between armour and infantry was poor. The operation, which lasted until 17 July, was a failure and the New Zealand infantrymen were aggrieved by the inability of the armour to support them when needed. Trust between the upper echelons of command (all British) and the forces of the Empire were getting increasingly strained because the 'unsupportive' armour was British but most of the infantry was not.

The Kiwis lost 1,405 men[13] but did take 2,000 Axis (mostly Italian) prisoners. The operation had, however, further weakened Rommel. He had a total ninety-two battle-worthy tanks and he faced 172 in 1st Armoured Division.

The odds against Rommel worsened when, on 17 July, 23rd Armoured Brigade reached the forward area.

Auchinleck was well aware of Rommel's difficulties, as he was a recipient of Ultra intelligence. On the other hand, Rommel's intelligence source in Fellers had long since dried up, although careless and ill disciplined wireless procedure by British radio operators continued to provide valuable, if random, information.

It became apparent on 16 July that Rommel was concentrating his entire strength on the two flank divisions 5th Indian Division and 1st Armoured Division. The 5th Indian Infantry Brigade was especially vulnerable, occupying Point 64 on Reweisat Ridge. The 9th Australian Division (Morshead) was asked to detach a brigade to support the Indians, but this provoked a furious row between Morshead and Auchinleck – by no means the first or last of these spats, the former accusing the latter of going back on a promise not to detach any units of 9th Australian Division. The military situation, it seemed, came a poor second to national and personal pride. Later Morshead relented but the incident had further damaged Auchinleck's relations with Morshead and sapped the former's authority.

Operation Splendour was planned and in part it was to be a replay of XIII Corp's recent unsuccessful Operation Bacon along the Ruweisat Ridge. The operation was to start on 20 July and Gott's corps was to retain its position while gaining ground on Ruweisat Ridge 'as opportunity offers'. The operation was then subject to delay and amendment. The aim was changed and once more confusion came to the party, bringing his friend chaos to keep him company.

On the eve of battle, Strafer wrote to the wounded Freyberg and, in his upbeat message, he was optimistic about success in the next operation and complimentary about the NZ Div, saying, 'Your chaps are always cheerful and in good heart and I feel confident with them in the Corps.'

On the basis that Rommel was weakened, Auchinleck decided that he must strike while the omens were good and despite 23rd Armoured Brigade being completely unprepared, having had no time to acclimatise, he determined to commit it to battle.

Lumsden (1st Armoured Division) and Briggs (5th Indian Division) were both wounded and Gatehouse, who was busy forming 10th Armoured Division in the Nile Delta, was brought in to take command of all of Auchinleck's armour, that is to say, 2nd, 22nd and 23rd armoured brigades.

Gott was not alone in sensing that Rommel was weak and that a crushing victory was just around the next ridge. That was, in actuality, precisely the situation. Strafer held a coordinating conference on 20 July but Alec Gatehouse, the new GOC 1st Armoured Division, did not arrive until the evening of 20 July. Brigadier AF Fisher, the temporary Divisional Commander and the officer whose brigade was responsible for supporting the New Zealanders, had represented Gatehouse at the conference.

Unfortunately, Inglis (GOC 2nd NZ Division) thought that Fisher was GOC 1st Armoured Division and this led to a series of misunderstandings. Strafer had made his wishes 'perfectly clear' to Fisher at the conference in respect of the deployment of his armour, but not to the absent Gatehouse. Thus, when the attack began, Gatehouse was not fully aware of what was expected of his division – not least, very close support of 6th NZ Infantry Brigade. He was briefed that evening and their meeting concentrated upon the role of 23rd Armoured Brigade, about which Gott was far from happy. Gatehouse recorded:

> Straffer [*sic*] told me he did not care about the plan much, and when I heard it, I did not think much of it either, and said so. Straffer (sic) gave me a promise that (a) if pt 63 was not captured by the Ind Bde and (b) if the minefield was not lifted, that the attack of 23 Armd Bde was off.[14]

Meanwhile, Morshead (9th Australian Division) and Ramsden (XXX Corps) were at loggerheads over the employment of the Australian Division. There was talk about references to the Australian government and once again the 'command' of Dominion forces was revealed as little more than a myth. Ramsden passed the buck upwards to the Commander-in-Chief.

Morshead was quite right to object if he thought that the plan was flawed but the situation had escalated when Auchinleck arrived on the scene. There had been strong words and misunderstandings on both sides but matters were resolved ... over a cup of tea! It was all very British. Nevertheless, it had been unfortunate that Auchinleck and one of his most effective divisional commanders were in disagreement.

It was against a backcloth of confused planning and disagreement that 23rd Armoured Brigade prepared to go into action for the first time under the direction of Strafer Gott. The Brigade was a Territorial formation and it was commanded by Brigadier L Misa. Neither the Brigadier nor his officers and men were remotely prepared for the battle ahead. In short, the men were not ready, nor were the tanks. The radios were not adapted to desert conditions and the few that worked were not 'netted in'. The level of competence is illustrated by the ignorance of all ranks of how to take a 'hull-down' position using the natural contours of the desert to conceal the bulk of the tank but leaving its gun with line of sight to a target. Similarly there was no awareness that the Germans had anti-tank guns that could penetrate a Valentine tank.

The attack on El Mreir was launched during the night 21/22 July and 6th NZ Infantry Brigade, taking the lead, marched into the lion's den and suffered 200 casualties, but occupied the eastern side of the El Mreir depression. They did not receive the close support of 1st Armoured Division that they had been promised because the armour would not move at night. Major General Inglis (2nd NZ Division) was beside himself with anger.

The 6th NZ Infantry Brigade was in serious trouble; Gott realised he had to get them armoured support and 23rd Armoured Brigade was his only available asset to achieve this. The Brigade was composed of three regiments of the Royal Tank Regiment (40th, 46th and 50th), 11th Battalion, KRRC and a battery of RHA. The 23rd Armoured Brigade had to advance 6 miles into the face of an entrenched enemy bristling with anti-tank weapons. Providing that its northern flank was secure and the minefield to its front had had gaps cleared for its passage, all *might* just have been well. Both Gatehouse and Gott fully realised the limitations of 23rd Armoured Brigade.

General Nehring stormed El Mreir and swamped it, using 15th and 21st Panzer divisions. The 6th NZ Infantry Brigade was outnumbered and had no defence against the enemy armour. As many as 700 men were killed, wounded or captured and twenty-three guns were lost.

Point 63 had not been taken by 161 Indian Infantry Brigade and gaps had not been fully created in the minefield. Gott realised that he had to support 2nd NZ Division and he had to do it soon. Gatehouse reminded his corps commander of his promise not to commit 23rd Armoured Brigade until conditions were right. Notwithstanding, Gott realising that he no other options decided to attack with 23rd Armoured Brigade, *but a mile to the south of the previously selected axis through the minefield*. The aim now was to outflank the hazard. The order was issued, but because of the Brigade's faulty radios, it was not received and Brigadier Misa stuck to his original axis, which was through the centre of the un-cleared minefield. It was a fatal decision.

* * *

The engagement fought by 23rd Armoured Brigade on 22 July 1942 was a disaster. Understanding the degree of the disaster depends upon the source one reads. The losses in this engagement are difficult to ascertain accurately as different sources provide different figures for the strength and composition of the Brigade at the start of the engagement. The losses are subject to similar variation.

For example, Playfair asserts, 'It consisted of three regiments, each of about fifty tanks and the losses were 203 casualties, forty tanks destroyed and forty-seven tanks badly damaged.'[15]

Barr reports that tank strength was 106, of which only seven survived.[16]

Hughes, Ryan and Rothwell claim that the start strength was 140 tanks, of which 116 were lost.[17] Hughes also asserts that 44 per cent of its tank crews had been either killed or wounded.

* * *

At 0800 hrs on 22 July, the tanks of the Brigade lined up in column – the formation normal for breaching a gap in a minefield. They set off and achieved early success but the combination of inadequate training, lack of experience, poor communications and a resolute enemy caused the Brigade's destruction. Strafer Gott was blamed for the destruction of 23rd Armoured Brigade and as the Commander it is quite correct that he should be. However, it was not quite as simple as that – there were several factors that Gott could not have influenced. The Brigade's late arrival in the theatre and its complete lack of readiness prevented the imposition of any sort of training programme, and the faulty radios, even if they had worked, were not 'netted in'. These two elements alone would have guaranteed failure. Captain Tom Witherby, one of the officers to survive the nonsense, was the wireless officer of 23rd Armoured Brigade and, as such, he might well have looked closer to home when he sought a scapegoat for the debacle. (See page 237/8.)

Elsewhere, Point 63 was taken by 1st Battalion 2nd Punjab Regiment, lost, retaken and lost again. Gott was determined to take and hold Point 63 and he ordered 9th Indian Infantry Brigade to take on the task. This endeavour also failed and the casualties suffered were disproportionate to the importance of the objective.

Operation Splendour was anything but. It limped on for a few more hours until it was clear that despite personal gallantry and persistence, it had failed in all of its objectives.

Gott withdrew, badly blooded.

A week later, Brigadier Misa, who had carried out his orders to the letter, was sacked and was replaced by Brigadier GW Richards, a very experienced tank officer.

Operation Splendour had damaged the Axis but not sufficiently to balance the loss of about 116 tanks and 1,000 prisoners. The indifferent planning and doubtful tactics of their generals had not matched the courage of the Allied soldiers. Relations between the 2nd NZ Infantry Division and Ist Armoured Division were fraught and the mistrust was evident. Strafer Gott was one of the two corps commanders in the field and to him must be attributed a portion of the blame for the failure of Splendour.

Auchinleck realised that XIII Corps was not ready for another set piece operation and so his final throw of the dice was down to XXX Corps. This was Operation Manhood, which started on 27 July. It was another crashing failure. Gott was a spectator to the end of Auchinleck's offensive ambitions in the Western Desert.

A conference was held on 28 July as Manhood wound to its unhappy end. Auchinleck, Gott and Ramsden discussed the 8th Army's defensive plan in detail and looked towards renewing the offensive in September. They met again on

30 July, when tasks were allocated. Auchinleck now embarked on a plan to completely reorganise his army. As a first step he replaced Whiteley (the Brigadier, General Staff) with Brigadier Freddie de Guingand and then turned his mind to restructuring his divisions in an attempt to resolve the lack of cohesion between armour and infantry.

By 1 August, both armies were exhausted. The month of July had cost many lives but the 8th Army was still intact and in defence. It awaited massive reinforcement of the men and materiel in transit to Suez. In the meantime planning for fighting a defensive battle was taking shape. The Axis forces were at the end of a very long logistic chain that was under constant air attack from an increasingly assertive Desert Air Force. Rommel's infantry numbers were very low and he too was unable to contemplate a large-scale offensive.

On 27 July, Dorman-Smith drafted an 'appreciation' for Auchinleck's approval. This document is key to the argument surrounding Auchinleck's preparations for a 'Second Alamein'. The appreciation, it is said, laid out the future of the 8th Army and disproves completely Montgomery's claim to have thrown out the legacy left to him by Auchinleck. The 'Auk' endorsed Dorman-Smith's work and then burst into print himself on 1 August. He laid out his plan for a very active defence by the 8th Army in which it would seek to disrupt, harass and damage the enemy 'by every means in its power'.[18]

This was not the attitude of a man preparing to retreat to the Suez Canal. Strafer Gott was told by Auchinleck to prepare his corps to face an offensive and to this end his staff also prepared an appreciation. Gott was at one with Bobby Erskine, his Brigadier, General Staff, and Major Freddy de Butts, one of his Grade 2 staff officers. They drafted the document, having ascertained their General's view. Gott left behind little evidence of his thinking but this document, which he signed, is instructive. Gott had had time to study the ground over which the next battle was to be fought and he recognised that Alam el Halfa Ridge was vital ground. In itself this is not particularly noteworthy because any prominent feature on the desert landscape was important and most soldiers would have preferred to defend a feature such as this rather than attack it.

Gott had no illusions as to the capability of XIII Corps, which was currently composed of an under-strength infantry division and an armoured division made up of 4th and 22nd Armoured Brigade and 7th Motor Brigade. He commented wryly, 'These forces are barely sufficient to hold the present corps front. No opportunity to train or prepare these forces for offensive operations.' He estimated that facing him were 30,000 men and 250 tanks, and he calculated that this force could be ready to attack XIII Corps by 15 August – just two weeks away. Strafer concluded that Rommel would almost certainly:

> attack with Alam el Halfa as his first objective, going round anywhere
> south of Alam Nyal Ridge [also spelt Alam Nayil, about 4 miles south

of Alam el Halfa] and thrusting straight for Alexandria. A raid down the Barrel track towards the delta might be combined with this. This is much the most likely course and the most difficult to meet.

He also concluded that any attack north of Alam Nyal in the gap between it and Alam El Halfa was unlikely as the enemy would have to cope with British minefields and well-prepared positions. The ground was broken and that would add to the difficulty but he mused that 'there are many possible variations in the details of such a plan, but it is the only one that he could carry out with his present shortage of infantry if he is making Alexandria his objective.'

Although Ramsden had been given the task of planning a future offensive by the 8th Army, Strafer Gott recommended in his appreciation 'an attack between Qattara and Abu Dweis, with a view to gaining a footing on the Fuka escarpment'.

Ramsden recognised that the succession of failed operations in the past month –Bacon, Splendour and Manhood – all shared one common feature. It was the dearth of infantry and armour cooperation. The infantry had fought successfully but, at the critical time, the armour had not been on hand either to drive home success or provide protection. It should not have taken so long for the penny to drop but Ramsden now grasped the nettle. In his appreciation he made it clear that before any offensive could be mounted there was some serious training to be undertaken. Among these were 'night operations' (British armour was loath to move at night), the 'passage of minefields' (23rd Armoured Brigade's destruction was still fresh in everyone's minds), and the 'use of smoke'.

Auchinleck gratefully incorporated the thinking of his two corps commanders into his own appreciation and it showed 'that he was thinking in a fertile and imaginative way.'[19] Similarly, Gott, although deeply involved in operations for months and probably tired, nevertheless demonstrated 'the high quality of his military thinking'.[20]

In combination, Auchinleck, Gott, Ramsden and Dorman-Smith devised the plan for the major offensive that would become known as Second Alamein. In short, 8th Army would attack in the north having made overt preparations to attack in the south.

A number of historians have poured scorn on Montgomery for his behaviour after the Battle of Alamein, in which he claimed omnificence. Among these are Barnett, Carver and, more recently (2004), Niall Barr, who spoke for all by saying:

Every single element of Auchinleck's plan was later followed by the 8th Army under Montgomery's leadership. The complete text of the appreciation provides final and conclusive proof that Montgomery's much-vaunted 'master plan' for 'his' battle of Alamein actually originated with Auchinleck and his corps commanders.[21]

Gott and his staff realised that ere long they would be required to fight the 'modern defensive battle' at Alam el Halfa – the vital ground in the 8th Army defences. In the north the Chief Engineer, Brigadier Frederick Kisch, and Dorman-Smith devised two defensive zones that were designed to provide defence in depth. At the same time they advertised that the south was less well defended in order to encourage Rommel to once again carry out a right hook – employed so effectively at Gazala and Tobruk.

XIII Corps was to hold Alam el Halfa and Gott gave that task to 2nd NZ Division (Inglis); there was some horse trading over the detailed disposition of the Division but issues were resolved after Strafer personally visited all positions. As a result of his close attention to the detail, minefields were realigned. The 22nd Armoured Brigade (Roberts) was ordered to give the New

"Don't think we'll have much of a leave here, old man"

Cartoon by Jon.

Zealanders close support and Gott ensured that both commanders met to discuss the forthcoming operation. There were to be no misunderstandings this time.

It was while energetically engaged on his defensive plan on 5 August 1942 that Strafer received an urgent message to report to GHQ, at 1030 hrs, with his divisional commanders. Clearly something was up.

Life in the line at El Alamein did not offer much in the way of creature comforts and leave opportunities were sparse. Jon took a jaundiced view and the cartoon, on the previous page, will have struck a responsive chord with Strafer's officers and soldiers.

Chapter notes
1. Major General TW Rees CB CIE DSO* MC DL (1898-1959). The 'sacking' did him no lasting damage and he went on to command a division in Slim's XIV Army in Burma. He was a much respected and successful commander.
2. Agar-Hamilton, JAI, and Turner, LCF, *Crisis in the Desert*, p.235.
3. General Sir Neil Ritchie GBE KCB DSO MC (1897–1983). After his abrupt dismissal he went to Palestine to rest and then returned to UK, where Churchill received him warmly. He was appointed to command 52nd Lowland Division in the rank of Major General. In 1944 he was again promoted to Lieutenant General and commanded XII Corps in Dempsey's 2nd Army, part of 21st Army Group. He retired in 1951 and moved to Canada, where he was a great commercial success.
4. It was during this phase that Captain Charles Upham won a bar to his VC, an award that Gott will have supported.
5. Holland, J, *Together We Stand*, p.179.
6. Carver, Field Marshal Lord, *Dilemmas of the Desert War*, p.131.
7. Later, Major General Sir Howard Kippenberger KBE CB DSO ED (1897-1957).
8. Kippenberger, HK, *Infantry Brigadier*, p.139
9. Tuker, Major General F, *The Pattern of War*, p.53.
10. Gott to Auchinleck, 1000 hrs, 3 July 1942, MUL966 Auchinleck MSS, John Rylands Library, Manchester.
11. Carver, Field Marshal Lord, *Dilemmas of the Desert War*, p.133.
12. Barr, N, *Pendulum of War*, p.89.
13. Playfair, Major General ISO et al, *The Mediterranean and Middle East*.Vol. III, p.351.
14. Gatehouse, Major General AH, *Notes on Operation on Reweisat Ridge*, on July 22 1942. 9/28/42 Liddell Hart, MSS LHCMA.
15. Playfair, Major General ISO et al, *The Mediterranean and Middle East* Vol. III, p.353-6.
16. Barr, N, *Pendulum of War*, p.169.
17. Hughes, D, Ryan, D and Rothwell, S, *British Tank and Armoured Brigades: 79th Armoured Division and Armoured Car Regiments*, p.37.
18. Appreciation by C-in-C Middle East 1 August 1942, WO201/556, The National Archives.
19. Barr, N, *Pendulum of War*, p.191.
20. Ibid.
21. Ibid.

Chapter 14

Succession
5-7 August 1942

T he 'something' that was most definitely 'up' was that Churchill had decided to accompany the Chief of the Imperial General Staff, General Alan Brooke, on a visit to HQ Middle East and, what is more, he was on his way.

Churchill was always an impatient man and his discontent with the complete lack of progress by the 8th Army in the preceding six weeks was no secret in Whitehall, where he criticised Auchinleck publically and frequently. Brooke had done his level best to keep the situation under control and had at least persuaded Churchill not to rush out to the Middle East.

On 27 July Churchill had sent a signal to Auchinleck in which he had mentioned a planned visit by the CIGS and warned of 'our plans, which are considerable'.[1]

Auchinleck was somewhat naïve and seemed not to appreciate the impact that the failures of Operations Bacon and Splendour had had on Churchill. When the signal of 27 July was sent Churchill was waiting for good news about Operation Manhood. There was no good news and accordingly an already irritated Churchill decided to accompany Brooke. Brooke, who had hitherto been a constant supporter of The Auk, was now also starting to question his ability as he was the recipient of Auchinleck's somewhat negative and unenthusiastic letters.

Politically, Churchill was under pressure because the Americans and British had now come to an agreement to mount an operation to be known as Torch. This was much along the lines of the abandoned Gymnast, to take Morocco and Tunisia. Originally, the great plan was for the 8th Army to destroy Axis forces in Egypt and Libya as part of the wider Allied strategy, but its defeats at Gazala and Tobruk not only failed to further the strategy but, in addition, had damaged British prestige. Churchill was deeply unhappy but Auchinleck did not seem to detect this.

Brooke arrived in Cairo before the Prime Minister and took the chance to interview Lieutenant General Corbett, Auchinleck's Chief of General Staff (CGS). Brooke was highly unimpressed and recorded in his diary:

> One interview with him was enough to size him up. He was a very, very small man. Unfit for his job of CGS and totally unsuited for command of the 8th Army, an appointment that The Auk had suggested. Consequently, Corbett's selection reflected very unfavourably on The Auk's ability to select men and confirmed my fears in that respect.[2]

Churchill arrived via the airstrip at Berg el Arab[3] on 5 August and was met by Auchinleck, Tedder[4] and Coningham,[5] the two senior airmen. It was clear from the start that it was not going to be an easy meeting and it was perhaps significant that Churchill did not share a car with the general he had come to see.

The procession drove to El Alamein and Churchill and Brooke met both Pienaar (1st SA Division) and Morshead (9th Australian Division). Some Australian soldiers, all in high good humour, barracked Churchill but he affected not to notice and sat down to breakfast in Auchinleck's Mess. The arrangements for this simple meal were poor. The setting was bleak and Spartan, the flies had free rein around the 'dining room' and the fried breakfast was unappealing. Brooke generously described it as 'light'. It was evident that Auchinleck had given no thought to the hosting of his political and military superiors – and they noticed!

The visit had got off to a bad start and it became worse when the party moved over to the operations caravan; its walls were covered in maps, each of which was under a plastic sheet of 'talc', upon which a grease pencil could inscribe the arrows to show successful advances – or withdrawals. The inept and negative briefing he was now given by Auchinleck and Dorman-Smith further discommoded an already very discontented Churchill. He did not seem to be paying attention and Dorman-Smith later recorded that Churchill:

> quickly began to demand that the 8th Army should attack afresh. He thrust stubby fingers against the talc; 'Here,' he said, 'or here.'
>
> We were alone with him, for the CIGS had gone forward up the line. It was a little like being caged with a gorilla. Eventually Auchinleck said, quietly and finally, 'No, Sir, we cannot attack again yet.'
>
> The Prime Minister swung round to Dorman-Smith: 'Do you say that too; why don't you use the 44th Division?'
>
> 'Because, Sir, that division isn't ready and anyhow a one-division attack would not get us anywhere.'
>
> Churchill, rose, grunted, stumped down from the caravan and stood alone in the sand, back turned to us. The chill was now icy.[6]

This meeting spelled the sack for both the soldiers concerned. Churchill did not want excuses and he did not want to be told what could not be done. He had come to Egypt with a shuffling of senior officers in mind and now his shuffling would be rather more robust.

A poor breakfast, an unsatisfactory briefing, a hot day, clouds of flies and then Churchill not in the best frame of mind met Gott, Inglis (2nd NZ Division) and Renton (7th Armoured Division). Gott had arranged a XIII Corps conference, expecting his meeting with the Prime Minister to be little more than social but, to his surprise, Churchill asked Gott to drive with him back to Berg el Arab.

Churchill was fully aware of Gott and his record to date because Anthony Eden, his foreign secretary and a long-term admirer of Strafer Gott, had lobbied vociferously on Strafer's behalf. General Sir Alan Brooke was aware of Eden's championing of Gott and had told the Prime Minister that it was not surprising that Eden would support a fellow Green Jacket.[7]

The XIII Corps conference was swiftly postponed. The politician and the soldier were introduced and then set off together. In the course of that journey, during which Strafer spoke frankly, the conversation was sufficient to allow the Prime Minister to make up his mind on who he wanted to command the 8th Army.

Brooke believed that Montgomery was best suited to be General Officer Commanding-in-Chief the 8th Army. He held Gott in high regard; he saw him as an army commander – but not the 8th Army's commander. Despite Brooke's opposition, Churchill decided that he would appoint Gott.

The case for Gott's appointment was that he was now by far the most experienced of the desert generals; he had the confidence of all his subordinates, apart from Pienaar. He was charismatic, calm and innovative. Auchinleck had named Gott as his successor assuming that he, Auchinleck, would remain C-in-C Middle East.

The case against his appointment was that he was exhausted and, by his own admission, desperately in need of leave to unwind from two years of almost non-stop action. His well-noted humanity and compassion, admirable traits though they were, would not necessarily be suitable for the brutal battles ahead in which tens of thousands of soldiers would die. His success as a corps commander had been limited – especially so during the previous month, when XIII Corps had achieved little and been consistently outfought. The coordination of his infantry and armour had been dire.

Churchill went on and had lunch with the Desert Air Force and the arrangements knocked breakfast into a cocked hat. It was an elegant meal, served in attractive surroundings and without any flies for company. The Royal Air Force had shown a great deal more style than the Army and so underscored the inadequate start to the Prime Minister's day – and the inadequacy of those responsible for it.

Churchill signalled to the Cabinet in London advising of his intentions to change key personalities in the Middle East. The following day, 6 August, his decisions were endorsed and Gott was told of his selection. His reaction is not recorded but it would be reasonable to assume that he was flattered, daunted, nervous, excited and secretly rather pleased with himself.

He had every right to be.

Brooke accepted Gott's appointment with some misgivings but then he and Churchill set about their wholesale cleaning of HQ Middle East. Auchinleck, Lieutenant General TW Corbett, the Chief of Staff, Dorman-Smith, and Ramsden (XXX Corps) were all sacked. The shopping list looked like this:

> Lieutenant General Alexander to replace Auchinleck
> Lieutenant General Montgomery to succeed Alexander in Operation Torch
> Lieutenant General Gott to command 8th Army
> Lieutenant General Corbett to be relieved – sacked
> Lieutenant General Ramsden to be relieved – sacked
> Major General Dorman Smith to be relieved – sacked

The response in XIII Corps to the selection of 'the boss' to be the Army Commander was ecstatic. The downside was that they would have a new commander who would be stepping into a very large pair of boots – not least because he would not be a desert soldier.

Strafer had planned a week's leave in Cairo but now he realised that much of his leave would be taken up in meetings with Alexander, Brooke and even perhaps his two new corps commanders, who had still to be selected. The XIII Corps conference, postponed from 5 August, was rearranged for the morning of 7 August and Auchinleck attended. There was a significantly different flavour at this conference, during which Strafer laid out his defensive plan. He covered in detail the manner that the first defensive zone would 'thin out' in the face of an enemy advance, the occupation in strength of Alam el Halfa and the position of the units under command. He went on to discuss the vital artillery fire plan, to be coordinated by his commander, Royal Artillery (CRA), Brigadier Stanford. He was confident and assured, his manner was infectious and the atmosphere in the tent was positive.

Senior British officers, colonel and above, wear a band of red flannel around their service dress cap and so the generic term for senior officers is 'red hats'. Strafer, having explained his plan, invited discussion from the participants. Major Paul Hobbs, his GSO 2, was sitting at the back of the tent and explained:

That last morning he spent with us presiding at an exercise – eighteen red hats around him with me at the back taking notes – all this in a big wigwam – all his ideas of how the battle should be fought so plainly.

The conference went on rather longer than was expected. By now it was clear that Strafer would not be free until after lunch and, on that basis, he could only get to Cairo if he travelled by air. In his usual courteous manner he asked that suitable arrangements be made. He had decided to have some lunch with Inglis and if possible fly from Berg el Arab to Cairo on the routine Bombay flight that moved mail and casualties. It was a hop of 150 miles or less but probably more comfortable than a long road journey in the heat of the day. Air conditioning was not on offer in 1942.

At around 1300 hrs an unidentified person had said words to the effect: 'Hold the flight at Berg el Arab for General Gott.' A wireless operator duly sent the message naming Gott and identifying the flight. It was another example of the poor signals security that had blighted the campaign. In this case it was ineptitude on a heroic scale and it was to have dreadful consequences.

The Germans intercepted the message.

Strafer averred that he wanted to be in Cairo on a Sunday because he wanted to go to worship in the cathedral. He also had to visit the dentist. There would not be much time for sitting around the pool with a cold gin and tonic.

Just before he left he said how sorry he was that Hobbs was not accompanying him and continued by saying, 'Back on the 11th – a big lunch of prawns at Shepherd's and back with a hell of a liver in the evening.'[8] That was unlikely because Strafer was never 'liverish' with the people around him.

Strafer Gott left the headquarters of XIII Corps at about 1400 hrs, driven by Corporal Nutter, his driver, accompanied by several of his staff. Captain John Poston KRRC,[9] his ADC, had gone on ahead with his kit to Cairo by road, and planned to meet the General at the other end of his journey.

Chapter notes
1. Churchill to Auchinleck, 27 July 1942, PREM3/292/1, The National Archives.
2. Alanbrooke, Field Marshal Lord, *War Diaries 1939-1945*, edited by Danchev & Todman, p.289.
3. The modern spelling is Borg el Arab. It is now a flourishing modern airport.
4. Later, MRAF Lord Tedder GCB (1890-1967).
5. Later, Air Marshal Sir Arthur 'Mary' Coningham KCB KBE DSO MC DFC AFC (1895-1948).
6. Dorman O'Gowan, A4: *Liquidation in Cairo* p.6, 1/2/19 Dorman O'Gowan MSS, John Rylands Library, Manchester University.
7. Alanbrooke, Field Marshal Lord, *War Diaries 1939-1945*, edited by Danchev & Todman, p.291.
8. Hobbs, Major P RHA, letter to his mother, August 1942.
9. Poston became ADC to Montgomery and was killed later in the war.

Chapter 15

Assassination
7 August 1942, 1425 hrs

At about 1345 hrs on 7 August 1942, Oberfeldwebel Emil Clade of Jagdgeschwader 27 'Afrika' had just been briefed about his next mission, which seemed to him to be straightforward. He was to intercept and shoot down a British transport aircraft due to take off from Berg el Arab in about thirty minutes' time.

The Germans had intercepted the routine radio message, explaining that General Gott was returning to Cairo. The unknown sender of the message breached all the security protocols by naming Strafer and the flight. It was very easy for the enemy to determine the route the aircraft would likely take.

Clade's flight of four Me 109s was lined up on the desert strip behind him and as he waited for clearance he saw the Intelligence Officer run from what passed as the headquarters and waving to him. Clade's cockpit canopy was open and he looked down at his comrade, who shouted up, 'I'm adding two more to your flight.' Clade protested mildly, explaining that four Me 109s were ample for the mission. As he spoke he saw the two extra aircraft manoeuvring for take-off. The Intelligence Officer said emphatically, 'There is to be complete radio silence – is that clear?'

Emil Clade nodded acceptance of the order and moments later he and his five formidable companions took to the air. The Me 109s took formation on their leader and went to the hunt.

* * *

Sergeant 'Jimmy' James eased his Bombay Bristol off the strip at Berg el Arab, climbed up to 50 feet and levelled off. At this height he had a measure of concealment as his aircraft, clad in camouflage paint, when viewed from above blended with the desert floor. Jimmy remarked, 'I'd been in this campaign for six months and never flew above 50 feet.'[1]

The aircraft was heading east to Cairo, where the wounded could have hospital treatment, most of the others could enjoy a bath and a cold beer and General Gott could hope to spend a week's leave, relaxing, catching up on his sleep and preparing himself for the momentous task and awesome responsibility that lay ahead of him.

About ten minutes into the flight there was a loud noise and the starboard engine suddenly stopped. Sergeant James's immediate assumption was that there had been an engine failure and that his co-pilot had failed to monitor the engine. He swore at Lawless, who gestured, and Jimmy saw tracer rounds streaking past the aircraft. He said later that it had been 'magnificent shooting' by someone (probably Clade) to disable his starboard engine with a single unexpected burst.[2]

The starboard engine burst into flames and the loss of power constrained the already limited options. The Bombay could barely climb, manoeuvre, dive or shoot back. The flight of Me 109s made a further pass at the Bombay and their guns delivered concentrated ordnance into the thin aluminium fuselage of the partially crippled aircraft. The port engine was now hit and its propellers stopped.

Sergeant James could see that his wireless operator, Harold Daniels, who had had most of his arm shot away, and his co-pilot, Sergeant Lawless, were wounded. Daniels's condition was very serious. James told Lawless to get to the rear of the aircraft and bring forward the Medical Orderly. This Lawless managed to do and he and the medic returned to the cockpit despite the fire dividing the aircraft in two. The medic was told to get all the wounded from their stretchers onto the floor.

Sergeant James made a quick appreciation of his options and realised that there was only one left open to him. He had to get the plane down on the desert floor but first he had to find the right spot. James eased his aircraft up to 100 feet to give himself a better view of the country ahead. He saw that he was approaching an escarpment and on the far side there was a very long downward slope.

The attacks continued; pieces flew off the wings and the main fuel tank was breached. Aviation fuel was pouring across the surface of the aircraft, entering the cabin, and the cockpit filled with acrid smoke. The aircraft was now, effectively, a glider. It was on fire and the lives of all twenty-three on board rested on the skill and courage of one very young man.

Jimmy recounted that, at that time and instantaneously, he consciously changed from a naïve schoolboy who was having fun in a war that had not yet really touched him into a confident, aggressive man. He spoke of experiencing a curious sensation that ran from the back of his head all the way down through his body – he even described it as a 'greenish yellow'.

The German attacks were continuous but, despite the shot and shell shredding the fuselage, quite incredibly, only Daniels, the Wireless Operator and Lawless, the Co-pilot had been hit. The aircraft breasted the ridge of the escarpment and Sergeant James had now to pick a rock-free length of desert on which to land.

He was doing about 100 knots, in a crosswind; when he lowered the plane onto the desert floor and felt the forward fixed wheels engage on the downward slope. There now remained the hazard of scattered rocks, which if hit would complete the wrecking of the aircraft. Also, patches of soft sand, if encountered, would cause the plane to stand on its nose. It was still possible to steer the aircraft by use of the rudders and this Sergeant James did, although he likened the experience to driving a 10-ton truck over soft sand.

He scanned ahead for rocks and waited to lose sufficient speed for the tail wheel to drop onto the sand. At that point, and not before, he could apply the brakes.

The slope was steep enough and the aircraft heavy enough to maintain the impetus and the downhill helter-skelter seemed to last forever. Finally, the tail wheel engaged and James applied the brakes, only to discover that they did not function – they had been shot away.

The downhill rush continued, unchecked.

Talking to the author in 2012 about the incident, Jimmy said that the downhill journey was over 'a distance of miles'. The plane slowed down and he ordered his second pilot to warn all on board to be ready to jump out sometime likely to be quite soon. He told Lawless to get the rear door off its hinges in preparation for a swift evacuation.

The aircraft was slowing but the flames had spread to the cockpit and Sergeant James was being badly burned on his hands and face. He stuck to his task and was dismayed to see the Me 109s circling like vultures above him. The Bombay was clearly a write-off and would never fly again. He wondered why the Me 109s had not gone home.

At about 20mph Jimmy gave the order for the hatch in the cockpit floor to be opened as he realised that Daniels, with only one arm, could not jump out of the side door. The Medical Orderly did as he was bidden and Lawless signalled that everyone in the back was awaiting his order. As the aircraft finally lurched to a halt Jimmy stole a glance over his shoulder – he has an abiding memory of Lieutenant General Strafer Gott smiling through the smoke and giving him a positive and assertive thumbs up.

Above, Emil Clade gestured to his youngest pilot, a man called Sneider, who side-slipped, turned and made a low-level strafing run on the now stationary, burning Bombay. As Sneider pulled up the two late additions to Clade's flight detached themselves and, without orders, they each also made a strafing pass, drenching the crippled Bombay in devastating fire. Emil Clade was furious; clearly they had been given separate instructions. This was not the way he had fought the war in the air; until now there had always been a degree of chivalry.

Sergeant James gave the order to jump and as he did so he slipped out of his seat to help with the evacuation. Seconds later, the first strafe hit the Bombay. Machine-gun fire pulverised the instrument panel and his recently vacated seat. The noise, smoke and fire made for total confusion. James noticed that the heels of his desert boots were on fire, the cockpit was burning and the clear Perspex canopy was distorting in the heat. He made an attempt to get into the back of the plane to ensure that everyone was safely disembarked, suffering further burns in the process. In the meantime four people exited the aircraft by way of the hatch in the cockpit floor.

At that point another volley of machine-gun and cannon fire hit the fuel tanks as the second and third Me 109 went about their deadly business.

The Bombay became a fireball.

This latest attack had shot away the landing gear to such an extent that the aircraft slumped onto the desert floor like a tired drunk on a Saturday night. James was unaware of this as he dropped through the cockpit hatch. He expected to fall 6 feet but there was barely sufficient space for him to crawl from underneath his aircraft, which was only supported by a single tyre – and that was burning furiously. When that tyre collapsed the Bombay would subside even further and lingering under the plane was not to be recommended.

James crawled out into bright sunshine and as he did so the burning tyre burst, the Bombay subsided with a crash and he realised that for the second time in only a few moments he had escaped death.

Sergeant James was still the Captain of the aircraft and still 'in command'. He made his way around the wing, which was now flat on the ground, fully expecting to see a group of his passengers awaiting his orders.

There were only four.

They were Second Pilot James Lawless, the sorely wounded Wireless Operator, Harold Daniels, a sick and confused casualty, Driver Leonard Atkinson RASC and the Medical Orderly (unnamed).

James was stunned. He had got this aircraft down in one piece and had directed the evacuation … and so where was everybody? They could only be on the fiercely burning Bombay, of which the rear door was firmly closed. James was distraught; he ran to the rear of the aircraft but the intensity of the fire drove him back. He tried again but even if he had been able to get to the door it would not have been possible to hold the handle, which by now was blisteringly hot.

The Medical Orderly restrained Jimmy when he gathered himself for another foray. The four men stepped back from the inferno as the Bombay lost its form.

The paint bubbled and was consumed, the components of the structure either burned or melted.[3]

It was evident that all of the others were lost, perhaps some had succumbed to a merciful machine-gun bullet, but the painful probability was that Strafer Gott and his companions had been burned to death. It is a dreadful irony that Strafer should fall victim to three strafing attacks.

* * *

The fire continued to burn as Sergeant James looked for an explanation for this frightful and avoidable loss of life. The reason was really very simple. The flight would normally have had two seasoned ground crew. But the delay on the ground before the flight had caused one of these to be replaced by a novice. It was the function of the ground crew to take the door off its hinges in the event of a crisis.

In this case the door had merely been folded back and latched open – presumably by the new man. In most cases this would have been sufficient but on 7 August 1942, this aircraft had taken frightful punishment in the air and on the ground and had endured a lengthy and very bumpy landing over an extended period. During this protracted process the door had slammed shut and it or the frame – or both – were distorted. The door was immoveable.

That being the case the only other exit from the aircraft was the escape hatch in the cockpit but the passengers did not know of its existence. However, anyone leaving after Jimmy James would have been crushed when the undercarriage finally collapsed.

* * *

It was mid-afternoon when Emil Clade led his successful patrol back to their base. He was still seething at the apparent ill discipline of the two additional pilots but had maintained radio silence and had not yet vented his anger. As he taxied in he saw the Intelligence Officer racing across to meet him. Clade pulled back his canopy, switched off his engine and heard the officer on the ground below him shout, 'Congratulations – you have killed General Gott.'

The whole German squadron was then swept up in a tide of self-congratulation. Strafer Gott was a legitimate target and, as such, he had been killed. Clade had nothing to reproach himself for. It was mission accomplished.

The evidence that Lieutenant General William Gott was deliberately targeted and killed is irrefutable. Does that make him the victim of an assassination? James Holland has no doubts, saying, 'German intelligence had learned that Gott would be on the plane and they had subsequently assassinated him.'[4] The definition of assassination is a matter of semantics. The Oxford English

215

Dictionary defines assassination as '*the taking the life of any one by treacherous violence, esp. by a hired emissary, or one who has taken upon him to execute the deed.*'[5] (Author's italics.)

The key word here is *treacherous*. In this case there was no treachery but there was a premeditated plan to kill Strafer Gott. He died as a direct result of a legitimate act of war and on that basis might be termed 'killed in action'. The Germans knew of the death of Strafer Gott long before the British and it would be hours before the news would arrive to stun the British High Command.

Caddick-Adams asserts that the Germans knew that Churchill was in the Middle East and that he was the target, not Gott. In effect, Gott was killed by mistake.[6] There is absolutely no evidence to support this theory. Clade's testimony that on his return Gott was named as the intended target is compelling and conclusive.

* * *

At the crash site the survivors were in very bad order. Only the Medical Orderly was not wounded but he was shocked and very committed to caring for the other three. The Commander, Sergeant James, was badly hurt. His hands were seriously burned, as was his face. He discovered that he had also been shot in the back. He was, demonstrably, a hospital case.

Nevertheless and despite his incapacity, in a remarkable demonstration of devotion to duty, Jimmy James did not relinquish his responsibilities. He ordered the Medical Orderly to stay with the three other survivors while he went for help. He commented:

> I took a very long swallow of water and set off; it was stupid, I should
> have taken one of the water bottles. It's extraordinary but I never felt
> any pain. I was single-minded in getting help.

His decision to go for help was not disputed as they realised that in their condition their survival depended upon the arrival of medical assistance – and soon.

So Jimmy James, wounded and badly burned, with his clothes in tatters and no hat, and without a water bottle set off across the desert to find help. Not even in the wildest fiction does such a mission bear fruit and Jimmy should have perished out in that featureless wasteland. He was either demonstrating bravery of the highest order or crass foolishness, but then, often the two are identical. What is certain is that he knew he was still responsible for the other four. He trudged off in what he thought was the direction of the British line.

This was almost a 'Captain Oates moment', except that Jimmy did not intend to die.

There may well be a medical explanation but he insists that he felt no pain and he struggled on until, looking down he saw that one of his boots was covered in blood. This did prompt a reality check and he realised, belatedly, that he had a problem. He was alone in a vast sand sea. Nothing moved and the sun glared down remorselessly. He climbed yet another dune and then … he just ran out of steam, crumpled and fell. He was unconscious and would, indeed should, have died on that spot.

Not the least of the incredible coincidences, chances and strokes of good fortune in this story is that a single Bedouin, mounted on a camel, happened by. Not even the most inept novelist would dare to create such an outlandish circumstance. But, in this case, truth is stranger than fiction. Not all of the Bedouin were well disposed toward the Allies but this particular individual was – another extraordinary piece of good fortune in this sequence of events. Jimmy recalled:

The Bedouin somehow pushed me up on a camel and we set off. It was very uncomfortable and we went about 5 miles, I think.

Two REME[7] soldiers, road testing a vehicle, hove into sight and were waved down; they stopped and took charge of Jimmy. The Bedouin who had saved him from his third recent brush with death retreated into the sands of the desert and the mists of time, unnamed but not forgotten.

The truck drove Jimmy back to their base and there he explained that General Gott had been killed. This electrifying news was passed up the line and it was the first the British had heard of it – perhaps three or four hours after the German High Command. He explained:

A captain RASC[8] wanted me to go straight to hospital but I refused and said I had to guide them to my plane. It took ages and I estimate that we'd done about 15 miles. He said, 'I'm going to overrule you on the direction we should take.' Just then we rounded some rocks and in the distance was a column of black smoke going up into the sky; it was my plane.

The four surviving men were brought in. However, Driver Atkinson died soon afterwards. Jimmy was removed to hospital and lingered close to death. It took four long months but he eventually recovered and lived to fight another day.

Exemplary bravery in the face of the enemy merits the Victoria Cross (VC) – this is available to NCOs. Almost exclusively available to members of the Royal Air Force for performance in air were the Distinguished Flying Cross (DFC), awarded to officers, and its equivalent the Distinguished Flying Medal (DFM), awarded to Other Ranks.

If Sergeant James was to be decorated the only options were the VC or DFM. He was undoubtedly a candidate for the VC. However, the VC does carry with it a veritable cloud of publicity. A recipient and his deeds are at once in common ownership and subject to discussion. There have been occasions when a soldier might have merited a VC but such an award would draw unwelcome attention to the theatre, location or circumstance of the award. Any of these might be politically undesirable. It is much easier to make a lesser award and attract no publicity.[9]

Throughout 7 August 1942 the conduct of Sergeant Jimmy James fell into the category of 'Exceptional valour, courage and devotion to duty while flying in active operations against the enemy' – the criteria for the DFM. *The London Gazette*, published on 4 December 1942, carried the following citation:

Distinguished Flying Medal
James, Hugh Glanffrwd, 1425959 Sergeant No. 216 Squadron
This NCO was Pilot of Bombay L5814, which was shot down on 7 August 1942. When flying between Burg-El-Arab and Landing Ground 90, the Bombay was attacked by two Me 109s. Sergeant James was shot through the shoulder and leg. In spite of this he managed to make a good landing. At the end of the landing run the aircraft was again fired upon. This time it burst into flames. Only five of the crew and passengers escaped, including the Pilot. Three of those who escaped were seriously hurt, the fourth a medical orderly, attended to these three. Sergeant James, in spite of his wounded shoulder and leg, walked 2½ miles and then rode a camel and then got a lift to a medical unit. There he organised help to be brought to the other survivors and refused medical assistance himself, insisting on guiding the rescue party to the survivors. Only when they had been reached did he allow himself to be attended to. Sergeant James has been in this squadron some three or four months, during which he has been engaged on flights to the Western Desert and shown himself to be efficient in his work. This last effort of his has shown him to be not only efficient but one who in a crisis completely ignores his own personal safety and welfare and acts in a clear-headed and courageous manner.

Jimmy James was in hospital in a life-threatening condition when this edition of the *Gazette* was published. The citation tells the bare, but inaccurate, bones of the story and, as written, the DFM was, clearly, the correct decoration.[10] The two Me 109s were now firmly lodged in the public record. Predictably, no reference to either Strafer Gott or the other fatal casualties is made – arguably in the interests of security. Jimmy James's conduct is recorded in muted terms and the reference to his 'efficiency' seems to be out of place in a citation for gallantry.

The Bombay had come down near Wadi El Natrun, a depression south-east of the Libyan Desert, west of the Nile Delta. It is a feature 75 feet below sea level, about 25 miles long and, in places, up to 5 miles wide. It occupies a tectonic joint deepened by ancient river and wind erosion. Wadi Natrun contains more than ten small salt lakes, whose water contains trona (Arabic *natron*, a rare mineral). Today that mineral is extracted.

When Strafer was buried there it was hoped that the wadi would be forever be named 'Strafer Wadi'.[11] However, as the Allied forces withdrew from the desert after the final victory, the name did not stick. Of course, to the indigenous population Strafer Gott was just another dead soldier who had occupied their homeland to fight a war in which they had no part to play. There was no reason why they should mark his passing.

During the Second World War the British forces numbered 777 major generals and above to officer an army of 2.9 million. Strafer Gott has the unenviable record of being one of only five British generals killed by enemy action in the war. Barstow, Hopkinson, Rennie and Lumsden were the others.[12] Several general officers died in air or road accidents; Major General 'Jock' Campbell VC was one of the latter.

In the First World War, thirteen generals were killed by enemy action and several others committed suicide.

If, as this writer firmly believes, Strafer Gott's death falls into the category of 'assassination' then he is unique because in both world wars and since, no other British general has suffered a similar fate.

Chapter notes

1. Conversation James/Nash, 9 February 2012.
2. Conversation James/Nash, 9 February 2012.
3. Aluminium melts at 660°C (1,220°F) and the burning fuel certainly generated this sort of temperature.
4. Holland, J, *Together We Stand*, p.208.
5. Oxford English Dictionary, 2012.
6. Caddick-Adams, P, *Monty and Rommel: Parallel Lives*, p.283.
7. Royal Electrical and Mechanical Engineers.
8. Royal Army Service Corps.
9. Discussion, General Sir Peter de la Billière/Nash, 1989.
10. Sergeant HG James DFM AFC RAF was later commissioned and fought throughout the remainder of the war. After hostilities ceased he was granted a regular commission. He rose to the rank of squadron leader and commanded his own squadron of jet aircraft before he eventually retired.
11. Major General CH Gairdner, quoted by Vernon, Brigadier HRW, *Strafer Gott*, p.64.
12. Mead, R, *Churchill's Lions: A biographical guide to the British generals of World War II*, p.31.

Chapter 16

Aftermath

The news of the demise of Strafer Gott was like a bombshell. It affected people in many different ways. His friends, of whom there were very many, were grief-stricken and disbelieving. Headquarters XIII Corps was temporarily paralysed, with all the officers and soldiers in a state of shock. Strafer was assumed to be indestructible – could he really be dead? Surely it must be a mistake.

There were some who saw Strafer's death as convenient. His appointment to command the 8th Army had not been greeted with unalloyed joy in all circles and now the way was clear to put Bernard Montgomery in Strafer's place. Field Marshal Lord Alanbrooke recorded in his dairy:

> Just as I was starting for home for dinner I received the news that Gott had been killed this afternoon while flying back from Berg el Arab! A very hard blow coming on top of all the planning we had been doing. After dinner PM, Smuts and I had a conference as to how the matter should be settled. He was one of our linkpins [*sic*]. I do feel sorry for Mrs Gott. Had some difficulty. PM in favour of Wilson.[1] However, Smuts assisted me and a telegram has been sent to Cabinet ordering Montgomery out to take command of 8th Army. I hope we get Alexander and Montgomery out soon so that I may settle details of corps commanders and chiefs of staff with them.[2]

Alanbrooke's diary was originally published in 1957 and it had the authority of Holy Writ. The extract above was contemporaneous with the events. After the war and for the publication of his diary he added a postscript in 1959. He wrote with great confidence the following account of the death of Strafer Gott:

> Gott's death was a very serious blow, and a most unexpected one. He was flying back on the Berg el Arab-Heliopolis route, considered to be so safe that no escort had been necessary for Winston when we flew

out. It happened to be an individual German plane driven out of high altitude in combat, and dashing home at lower altitude. It came across the slow transport on its way and shot it down in flames. It seemed almost like the hand of God suddenly appearing to set matters right where we had gone wrong.

Looking back on those days with the knowledge of what occurred at Alamein and after it I am convinced that the whole course of the war might well have been altered if Gott had been in command of 8th Army. In his tired condition I do not think he would have had the energy and vitality to stage and fight this battle as Monty did.[3]

* * *

Meanwhile, on 8 August 1942, everyone looked to Brigadier Bobby Erskine for a lead. Erskine made it his first priority to recover Strafer's body and arrange his burial. He took with him some of his staff and they drove over the featureless desert to the coordinates they had been given. The aircraft was hardly recognisable as such. The fierce fire had distorted the frame and much of the fuselage had simply melted. It was a sombre and harrowing occasion as the bodies, all very badly burned, were recovered from the wreckage. It is presumed that it was only the metal tags – always worn around the neck on active service – that identified the victims.

The dead were buried at the site and Brigadier George Erskine supervised the operation. He was understandably vastly distressed at the death of his old friend. The graves were dug in the hot desert sand and then thirteen officers and men and a photographer assembled while a padre conducted the burial service. Simple white crosses were erected to mark the first resting place of the eighteen men who had perished.[4] Gott was placed in the middle of his comrades, with the wreckage of their aircraft as a grim backdrop.

The photograph shows the shattered aircraft as a witness to the sombre occasion. Strafer was later to be reinterred in the Commonwealth War Cemetery at El Alamein. Squadron Leader Jimmy James visited Strafer's grave very many years later and laid a wreath, a poignant postscript to a brief but quite unforgettable meeting of two very brave men, one hot afternoon seventy-one years ago.

* * *

The Alanbrooke version of Gott's death was the official line and a news blackout was imposed. The consequence of this was that variations of 'a tragic accident', and 'just bad luck' story were generally accepted. This manipulation of the truth was, at least initially, pragmatic. It could *just* be argued that the death of a senior commander and the circumstances in which it happened was a matter of national security. However, the shroud of secrecy was kept in place for more than sixty-three years.

Could this desire for secrecy have influenced the award of the DFM to Jimmy James and not the VC? This is no more than speculation on behalf of the author and 'for the avoidance of doubt', as lawyers are wont to say, it must be made absolutely clear that Jimmy James has never had any aspirations for a VC and the topic has never been discussed with him.

When Sergeant James was debriefed in hospital in 1942 he described the sequence of events accurately – he was still telling the same accurate story decades afterwards.

No one listened.

However, in 2002, Jimmy James tracked down his adversary, Emil Clade, by now an old man of ninety. They corresponded and then in March 2005 the two men met at Bonn Airport. There was no trace of hostility and the meeting was rather an emotional affair – like the reunion of two lifetime friends. Although sixty-three years had elapsed since the events of that fateful day – which they had witnessed from vastly different viewpoints – their recollections meshed precisely. Emil Clade made it clear to Jimmy that Sneider was one of his most junior pilots and that is why he had been detailed for the initial strafe. He regretted the second and third passes, which he did not order. Clade asked Jimmy how many on the plane were killed and hopefully he held up five fingers. Jimmy recalled the moment and said, 'I held up all my fingers, put them down and held up eight more. Clade whispered in German, "Eighteen!" and then he burst into tears.'

Emil Clade was distraught and Jimmy consoled him by saying that he had merely done his duty in attacking a legitimate target.[5] Later on that day, Clade's family arranged for the two old aviators to fly together in the sky over Germany – another emotional event in a very emotional day. The most significant product of this meeting was that both of the surviving participants agreed, without reservation, that Gott was assassinated. Clade confirmed unequivocally that a radio message had indeed been intercepted and that Gott was specifically targeted as a result.

Jimmy James tells of attending countless functions and being told with compelling authority, by officers of great seniority, the precise details of the death of Strafer Gott. His protestations were consistently brushed aside. It was not until Jimmy told the story to James Holland, who published it on the Internet in 2005 that the true story emerged. Since then it has appeared in some form in several books, such as that written by Bierman and Smith.

Jimmy recounted the saga to the author in February 2012 and it was clear at that meeting that it is only now that Squadron Leader HE James DFM AFC is content that the record is correct.

* * *

Alanbrooke was uncompromising in his judgment of both people and events. He had been at the very centre of world affairs at a critical time in human history and he did not prevaricate. For example, he did not pull his punches when discussing Auchinleck and his attitude when removed from command of the 8th Army. He believed that The Auk could have restored his reputation if he had accepted command in Iraq-Persia, where active operations were thought to be likely. He said, 'It would have been more soldierly to accept what he was offered in war instead of behaving like an offended film star.'[6]

Alanbrooke was a shrewd, discompassionate judge. He was actively involved in the great events of the Desert War and knew the main players well. He could recognise a commander's attributes but still consider them unsuitable for certain appointments. More than seventy years later, it would be a brave man to challenge his judgement.

Pamela Gott was overwhelmed with messages and Brigadier Dick Vernon gathered some and published them in his book *Strafer Gott*. There was, predictably, a common theme and it would be repetitious to quote from them all here. The impact that Strafer had had on peoples' lives was evident. Unexpectedly, Clementine Churchill wrote on 15 August, and said:

> I have just had a letter from my husband in Cairo.
> He says, 'I have just had a long drive with Gott, and I convinced myself of his high ability and charming simple personality. One knows at once when one can make friends. Imagine my grief, when, even while the Cabinet was sitting [to endorse the decisions taken by Churchill on his trip to the Western Desert] I had a telegraph [saying] that he had been killed.'
> I hope that you will not think me intrusive in writing to you. But I share my husband's thoughts and feelings and so I feel I must send you my respectful sympathy and my prayer that you may be sustained and comforted in your grief.

That is a charming and thoughtful letter and it must have been very much appreciated. On 29 August Churchill himself wrote to Pamela Gott in the most generous terms. There is more than a whiff of hypocrisy here as Churchill had reconsidered Strafer's appointment and saw that his death had resolved a difficulty. Brooke recalled that, after seeing how Montgomery had revitalised the 8th Army, Churchill commented on 'the part that the hand of God had taken in removing Gott at the critical moment'.[7]

A most disagreeable element surrounding Strafer's death was the opinion expressed by some that his demise had actually been in the national interest. Churchill and Brooke, in particular, were responsible for Gott's appointment to the 8th Army and their ill-concealed relief at his death reflects badly on them both. Sadly, they were not alone, but they were in a minority.

Anthony Eden, the Foreign Secretary and member of the 60th, wrote warmly, Generals Marshall and Eisenhower more formally. Herbert Lumsden was a strong character and in his letter he said, 'I personally loved serving under him, and with him, as I was always in accord with his plans and wishes.' Lumsden was one of the uncounted majority who grieved at Strafer's death.

General Lumsden, an acerbic forthright individual, was going to have a new master and it was not to be a happy relationship. The story goes that one morning Lumsden was striding into the desert with a shovel in his hand for his daily defecation. A staff officer called out, 'General, General Montgomery is on the wireless and wants to speak to you.' Lumsden is reported to have replied, 'Tell him I'll call him back – I can only deal with one shit at a time.'

That sort of anecdote would never ever have been attributed to Gott but his successor was at the centre of many unflattering tales.

The list of officers, of all ranks, who felt the need to write was very long. Many felt Strafer's loss as one would a member of the family. One correspondent was the Regimental Tailor of the 60th, Mr GF Welsh, who wrote from his establishment at 15 Duke Street, St James's. His letter was brief but no less touching for that. 'It was always a pleasure to wait upon him,' said Mr Welsh.

All the newspapers reported Strafer's death and the obituaries were unwaveringly generous and regretful at his demise. His generalship was inevitably at the centre of these obituaries but all made mention of his human qualities.

There is no doubt that in August 1942 the death of Strafer Gott touched thousands of people and he was widely mourned.

In 1945, a plaque was unveiled in Cairo Cathedral honouring both Strafer and Jock Campbell. On 26 April 1959, a service was held in the chapel of the RMA Sandhurst to dedicate a similar memorial. Pamela Gott was very insistent that those attending the service should all have known her husband and that this was not an occasion for mere spectators.

Field Marshal Bramall recounts that, much later, in 1984, the tribute to Strafer Gott, edited by Brigadier Dick Vernon (and a valuable source document for this book), was to be launched. On the day, Pamela Gott was unwell and she was in two minds as to whether she would attend or not. She said to the Field

Marshal that she had 'spoken to Strafer that morning and he had said, "Of course you've bloody well got to go."' It would seem that since Strafer's death Pamela had had the ability to communicate with him; there are some people who have this spiritual gift and Pamela was one. She died in 1985 when, after forty-three years of widowhood, she was reunited with her much-loved Strafer.

Chapter notes
1. Wilson, Field Marshal Lord Henry GCB CBE DSO (1881-1964). He was Commander-in-Chief 9th Army in Syria and Palestine in August 1942. A very capable and shrewd commander, he was one of Churchill's favourites.
2. Alanbrooke, Field Marshal Lord, *War Diaries 1939-1945*, edited by Danchev & Todman, p.295.
3. Ibid.
4. Eventually three of them were re-interred in the Commonwealth War Graves Commission cemetery at El Alamein. Driver Leonard Atkinson RASC is buried in Moascar Military Cemetery.
5. As reported by Squadron Leader HE James to the author, Emil Josef Clade (1916-2010) was credited with twenty-seven victories and was, himself, shot down six times.
6. Danchev & Todman (Ed), *War Diaries 1939-1945, Field Marshal Lord Alanbrooke*, p.674.
7. Ibid, p.296.

Chapter 17

Strafer Gott, the General

*Your greatness does not depend upon the size of your command
but the manner in which you exercise it.*

(Marshal of France Ferdinand Foch)

S trafer Gott, the General – on what basis does one assess him?
Indeed, is it necessary to accord him a specific place in the pantheon
of great British generals? What are the measurements by which he can
be compared with, say, Norrie, Ritchie, Wingate, Godwin-Austen, Wavell,
Auchinleck, Wellington, Allenby, Marlborough, Slim, Montgomery, Horrocks,
Alexander et al?

Is it by battles fought and won?

The number of enemy soldiers killed?

The square miles of ground he took and held?

No. Those are not the criteria, because they are simplistic and reduce
generalship to mere arithmetic. The merit of any single general is a matter of
perception – his reputation is established by the perception of his peers and his
adversaries. Desk-bound, civilian historians are not best placed to make a
judgment on the professional ability of a soldier making life and death decisions
amid the fog and stress of war. Not that that inhibits them. Similarly, nor are
the soldiers commanded by the general in a position to make an objective
judgment. It is human nature to want to like and respect 'the boss' in any society
and the Army is no exception.

Field Marshal Haig, for example, was revered, post-war, by those who
survived the trenches. Russell Braddon wrote about the siege of Kut[1] and of its
defender, Major General Sir Charles Townshend, who surrendered the town in
1916. On the publication of his book in 1967, the soldiers who had been
captured there, and were then shamefully abandoned by Townshend,
nevertheless vigorously defended 'Our Charlie' and refuted the clear evidence
adduced by Braddon. This was despite Townshend's disgraceful behaviour and

226

the suffering of the prisoners at the hands of the brutal Turks.[2] The fact is that 'Tommy Atkins' is loyal to a fault and may he never ever change.

Soldiers can make a balanced judgment on their platoon or company commander because they have a personal relationship with an officer who shares the same weapon pit and probably eats and sleeps alongside them. There is invariably no personal relationship and precious little contact between a soldier and his general. In an unforced way Strafer Gott did reach out to his private men – it was his natural style and, of course, the men he chatted to felt that they had established a bond with their leader, although that does not qualify them to evaluate his talent as a general. They can, however, gauge his merit as a man and in this respect their view is important.

Different times produce different parameters and it is all too easy to make the mistake of trying to compare an apple to an orange. There are some generals whose deeds are etched in the nation's history and among those are generals of the first rank, warts and all, and they include the likes of Marlborough and Wellington. These were two men 100 years apart, but with similar skills and whose crushing victories are still having an effect today.

The British Army has, over the last 350 years or so, produced general officers of every hue. There have been a minority who, by any yardstick, are perceived to be 'outstanding' and if they also have enviable personal qualities then they are much admired. In that bracket Field Marshal Bill Slim springs to mind. Montgomery was arguably an equally skilled strategist, yet he was also a most disagreeable man. He makes the 'outstanding' category – based on his results. This is despite his perceived vanity, arrogance and the negative effect he had on the nation's allies.

Generals are made by the circumstances of the day, few of which they can influence. It is blindingly obvious that the successful general must have survived and indeed thrived in the politicking of a peacetime army, even to get to the 'start line'.

In wartime, a general's ability to excel is dependent upon the political aims of his government, the support of his military superiors, the quality of his soldiers and the capacity of his logistic tail. Most important, however, is *the quality of his opposition* – and this is a key factor in the case of Strafer Gott.

A general has to seek success and commensurate glory by playing, to best advantage, the hand he has been dealt in terms of the theatre of operations and a multitude of other factors he cannot control – not the least of these is the weather, as Napoleon and von Paulus would testify.

Any general who has vision and can control large forces with skill, tenacity and efficiency, while spending the lives of his soldiers very frugally, deservedly becomes a legend. Such men are few and far between. Arguably, Wellington fails the last of these tests but who can deny his greatness? So too failing the frugality test by a very wide margin are Field Marshals Haig and French. Marshal Foch, brilliant man though he was, wasted the flower of French youth. Pétain did much to assist him.

A country has every right to expect competence from its generals and the vast majority of British generals have been 'good enough', with many of those being 'very good indeed', bordering on 'excellent'. However, it is not only poor generals that have filled military cemeteries around the world. Death is the product of war and its management is the greatest single responsibility any man can accept. Strafer Gott was acutely aware of this and his inherent humanity and compassion perhaps affected his decision making. He could not muster hate for his enemies and indeed 'hate' for anything or anyone was absolutely foreign to him.

Some of the great generals of the past made a profound study of the business of war but Strafer Gott emphatically did not. He was only an average student at the Staff College and he was not invited back to teach. This is a clear indication that he was not perceived to be a military theorist, nor did he have the skills to be a teacher or trainer. Strafer Gott was no Wellington, nor was he a Slim. He won no campaigns and did not conquer swathes of territory. The only meaningful comparison for Strafer Gott is with his peer group and, more specifically, with those who fought in the desert.

Gott became a desert soldier purely by chance – it was where he was serving when war broke out. Had he been in the Far East he would have been a jungle soldier. In 1940 and early 1941 Strafer Gott demonstrated that, when commanding at brigade level, he had the vision and tenacity mentioned above. He mastered the geography and the elements and he limited his human losses to the absolute minimum, yet he achieved success well beyond normal expectations. He learned 'on the job' and at first he was fortunate in that he was faced by an irresolute enemy, moreover one that performed very badly. However, he can hardly be blamed for taking advantage of that Italian weakness – it was his job to do so. He dominated his opponents and instilled in his soldiers abundant self-confidence that served them well later when they came across a more determined foe. The historian Richard Mead expressed his opinion of Gott's generalship by saying:

> His record in the desert was patchy. His leadership of the Support Group was exemplary. He was less good in command of 7th Armoured Division, where the dispersion of his forces in Crusader nearly allowed them to be picked off one by one. No one could doubt his courage, however, which had a material effect in bringing the Division through. His record at XIII Corps was indifferent. His advice on Tobruk was poor and his reactions at Mersa Matruh and El Alamein were slow.[3]

Mead's opinion is well balanced and he might well have highlighted the indifferent performance of XIII Corps during July 1942 in front of El Alamein. The destruction of 23rd Armoured Brigade during that period has to be laid at Gott's door, despite the fact that the brigade was simply not prepared for the intensity and type of action to which it was exposed. That action was probably the lowest point during Strafer's time in the Western Desert.

Gott established himself as the archetype of the desert warrior and there is ample evidence of his directing operations at the front of his troops. This was not the act of a self-publicist but of a natural and courageous leader. The product of his style of leadership was the unswerving loyalty of those he commanded. Someone once said, 'If you command wisely, you will be obeyed cheerfully.' Strafer Gott was the personification of that aphorism.

He enjoyed the confidence of his superiors and increasingly during the rest of his life he was seen as the confidant and advisor to many. Both his peers and seniors sought his counsel because his judgment and tactical savvy were widely admired. This is particularly unusual as Strafer Gott was not a student of the profession of arms. He wrote no papers, held no pronounced views on any aspect of his business. He merely applied his own brand of common sense compounded by a feel for the ground and an empathy with his soldiers.

He was highly successful at one-star level and, in truth, had less success to show when commanding a division – he was defeated at Sidi Rezegh, albeit by a superior force. Strafer's intuitive approach did not find universal favour with all historians, especially those from the Dominions. JAI Agar-Hamilton, the official South African war historian, was one critic who, writing soon after the war, claimed that Gott was out of his depth and then remarked:

> It has not been unknown for a commander to pass from disaster to disaster, but it is quite without precedent for any commander to pass from promotion to promotion as a reward for a succession of disasters.

That is actually far too all embracing. Rommel, for example, was defeated by Crusader, at Montgomery's defence of Alam Halfa, at Second Alamein and would have been defeated in Normandy had he not been wounded. No one would deny Rommel's ability or his well-earned rise to the top echelons of the German Army.

Bierman and Smith were equally dismissive of Strafer Gott and although they readily conceded that Strafer was admired for his personal qualities, they did offer the view that 'a cold appraisal of his soldiering in North Africa reveals no stunning display of tactics or Rommel-esque grip that bends scarred and exhausted men to the will of a born leader.'[4]

This opinion is, in part, quite valid. Rommel was a 'one-off' and there was no other commander on either side during the campaign that demonstrated similar skills. A failure to be Rommel-esque is not total damnation and it does not reflect mainstream contemporary opinion offered by the men who were in the North African desert alongside Strafer Gott.

After Michael Carver had challenged his earlier opinion Agar-Hamilton readdressed Gott's qualities. In his later book, *Crisis in the Desert,* he added:

> Gott's outstanding reputation recurs persistently in any analysis of the desert campaigns. He was one of the three commanders in Africa who became legends in their own lifetime [presumably Rommel and Montgomery were the other two] but his fame was not based on any train of victories, for success as a commander rarely came his way. Nor was his a superficial popularity, for his influence was potent among his seniors, and his reputation shows no sign of diminution with the passage of time.
>
> The foundation of his fame was probably his complete fearlessness, but courage alone could not have created or supported the vast extent of Gott's influence. Men felt that in him they could rely on a rocklike stability, a certainty of touch and judgment, which convinced them that their cause was sure, allayed their anxieties, and gave them courage for the future.[5]

Kippenberger labelled him 'defeatist' after the retreat to El Alamein. Perhaps at the time Gott's morale was low and his remarks reflected that – or was he just being realistic? There is no doubt that after a series of defeats he was exhausted and running out of ideas. His condition, mental and physical, would show in those circumstances.

Agar-Hamilton, Bierman and Smith all failed to mention the succession of decorations bestowed on Gott by a chain of command that was more than satisfied with his generalship. During the period January 1940 until October 1942, the attrition among desert generals was noteworthy. In no particular order, the following were casualties: Wavell, Cunningham, Auchinleck, Norrie, Ritchie, Lumsden, Gatehouse, Rees, Godwin-Austen, Beresford-Peirse, Dorman-Smith, Corbett, Hobart, O'Creagh, Ramsden, and Messervy. In addition, Pienaar was killed in action in December 1942. The majority of those named were sacked, having been found wanting, and the sole survivor with his reputation intact was Strafer Gott.

Was this just luck?

Field Marshal Lord Harding[6] did not think so. He served in the desert campaign and observed that Strafer:

epitomised in my judgment, all the fine traditions, the enterprise, resolution and skills of the famous Light Division. ... He combined firmness with charm and ... had the complete confidence of all under his command. ... No one knew the Western Desert better, or how to adapt his tactics to its peculiar conditions of terrain and climate, than Strafer Gott. His name as a desert warrior was legendary with all those like myself who 'had sand in their ears'.

Those who served with him or observed him in action, without exception, recognised his charismatic personality and extraordinary powers of leadership. He most certainly was able to 'bend men to his will' and his capacity as a 'born leader' is exhaustively recorded. One of those who had first-hand and regular contact with Gott was Michael Carver. His authoritative and valuable appraisal was in response to Agar-Hamilton in 1950, to whom he wrote, saying:

> Strafer's appeal lay not only in his appearance of complete serenity in troublesome times, not only in his unfailing good humour, his indefatigable energy, his intense and very real human sympathy, his readiness to propose a solution when others could not decide what to do, his integrity, his charitable ability to forgive; but also, to me at any rate, because one knew that his confidence was not based on blindness to the unpleasant realities of the situation.
>
> One felt that there was never any doubt but that he had considered all the unpleasant consequences that might arise from any action, and had decided what was most likely to achieve the best results in the circumstances.
>
> He knew the risks involved and he faced them cheerfully and courageously, even when orders he had to execute were the reverse of what he himself had advised. The fact that through all those difficult times he rose from command of the Support Group to being chosen as Army Commander was a tribute to his personality and judgment, which no wisdom after the event should be allowed to cloud. It was not the easy progress of a commander who had won success when all the dice were loaded in his favour.[7]

Carver's interjection clearly altered Agar-Hamilton's position because, as mentioned above, in his next book[8] he reiterated Carver's words and added more in the same tone. It was a generous re-appraisal.

On his death Strafer was eulogised in all the national newspapers and magazines. Accordingly, there exists a plethora of tributes to Gott, most of which were faithfully reproduced in Brigadier Dick Vernon's book *Strafer Gott*. They are all, clearly, an expression of sincere regard but inevitably they are somewhat repetitious. Among these tributes Strafer was described as 'The Greatest Rifleman' and what is more, he was compared favourably with Sir John Moore.

For The Rifles this is serious stuff bordering blasphemy because Moore is thought to be close to sainthood in Rifle circles. Dorman-Smith addressed the issue when he said:

> You cannot fairly compare Moore and Strafer. Moore was an independent commander – Strafer never was. Historical opportunity favoured Moore as it never favoured Strafer. That is not to denigrate Strafer, I am being objective, Strafer needs no comparisons.
>
> In some ways, he might more aptly be compared to 'Stonewall' Jackson. Strafer's handling of the difficult situation on the Egyptian frontier in 1941 when Rommel had driven past Tobruk and Strafer was alone in the Western Desert, has something of the epic action of Jackson's brigade standing 'like a stone wall' at the crisis of 1st Bull Run. The very fact that Strafer was there seemed to calm GHQ in Cairo.[9]

If Strafer Gott made one mistake during his time in North Africa, it was probably out of a sense of duty. He had made clear his position on 'duty' and an officer's wider responsibility to the Army as far back as 1933 to Major Buller (see page 63). When he was selected to replace Auchinleck as General Officer Commanding-in-Chief of the 8th Army he willingly accepted the responsibility.

General Brooke admired Gott and, on 5 August 1942, he drove to HQ XIII Corps to meet him. An entry in Brooke's diary that was amended by him in 1959 reads:

> It was not until we were sitting at tea together that he began to open his heart to me. He said, 'I think that what is required out here is some new blood. I have tried most of my ideas on the Boche. We want someone with new ideas and plenty of confidence in them.' I knew Gott well enough to know that he would never talk about having 'tried most of my ideas' unless he was tired and had temporarily lost some of his drive. This confirmed my opinion that he was probably not the man to lead the 8th Army in an offensive to turn the tide of war.[10]

However, Alanbrooke did aver:

> Let it not be imagined from these remarks of mine that I had not got a high opinion of Gott. On the contrary; I held him in the highest esteem and capable of great things.

Brooke saw Gott as *an* army commander but not *the* 8th Army Commander at that juncture of the war. That Gott should be so transparently honest with the professional head of the Army at such a personally critical time is vastly to his credit. Nevertheless, Churchill had his way and the following day, Strafer's appointment to command the 8th Army was announced. Twenty-four hours later, he was dead.

Field Marshal Lord Carver was able to give an objective opinion of Gott, the soldier, because he was on the ground and alongside Gott from first to last. Carver took the view:

> Tragic though it was for all who were his friends or admirers, it was probably providential that he did not get command of 8th Army instead of Monty. He was a very tired man at Alamein. For so long he had borne the burden not only of command in the field, but more of being the figure to whom all, high and low, turned to for advice, sympathy, help and encouragement in difficulty. He continued to give it, but it exhausted him; and the prospect of the heavy responsibility before him must have been a heavy addition to the weight he carried, particularly as the only way to carry it out appeared to be a reversion to 1914-18 warfare with its heavy casualties, which he detested.
>
> He hated to see men killed and was determined to avoid the vast casualties for minor tactical gains, which that type of battle involved. We discussed this a few days before his death – it may have been the very day. He was determined to see if he could not organise a vast left hook through Siwa rather than face a dogfight on the Alamein line. That feeling may be behind some of his differences with Pienaar and the New Zealanders, who always seemed to be happier the closer the plan resembled that of a 1914-18 battle. He had not the ruthless determination, one might almost say the callousness, which enabled Monty to face the colossal casualties in the first week of Alamein with equanimity, comforted perhaps that they were not as bad as those at Ypres and Passchendaele. Strafer imagined all too keenly what casualties meant in terms of human suffering.

Strafer enjoyed the approbation of Field Marshals Wavell, Auchinleck, Alanbrooke, Carver, Harding, Wilson and Bramall, a group singularly well qualified to identify a first-rate general. Their corporate opinion of his generalship should be sufficient. The generals who also held him in high regard are far too numerous to name – Strafer's only critics are academics.

The opinion of Field Marshal Carver, above, was written relatively soon after Strafer's death and seems to sum him up as a general. Notwithstanding the opinions of Agar-Hamilton and Mead, the consensus on Gott is that he was a dashing and courageous leader with a distinct flair for desert operations. In these he performed more effectively than any other general officer during the period 1940-42 and only Godwin-Austen was remotely his equal in the desert, although the latter fell by the wayside in early 1942.

Strafer had not had the time to emerge from the general malaise affecting British operations in the Western Desert and, considering that he was frequently on the losing side, it is remarkable how unsullied by failure he was. Overall, Gott's performance has to be seen against two years of almost constant British defeat interspersed with only one or two successes.

The factors affecting a general's success and reputation were mentioned earlier in this chapter and the quality of the General's adversaries was identified as being critical. Strafer Gott had the grave misfortune to be confronted by Erwin Rommel. Gott was good, he was very good indeed, but Rommel was much better and *it was Rommel who has placed restraints on Gott's place in history*. Alan Moorehead was one of many who wrote epitaphs of Strafer Gott and he said:

> His body rested on his chosen battlefield, the sand. He was the last of the old desert rats to go. He was a great man for England.

Strafer was not one of those generals that alter history but he was, without doubt, one of the most admired ever to wear a general's badges. Although he did not have the chance either to exploit his potential for high command or contribute to his country's final victory over fascism, he nevertheless left behind an indelible memory.

He was the epitome of courage, humanity and leadership and these are the three essential characteristics of a great general.

Chapter notes
1. Braddon, R, *The Siege*.
2. Nash, NS, *Chitrál Charlie*, p.272-6.
3. Mead, R, *Churchill's Lions: A biographical guide to the British generals of World War II*, p.180.
4. Bierman, J and Smith, C, *Alamein: War Without Hate*, p.215.
5. Agar-Hamilton, JAI and Turner, LCF, *Crisis in the Desert*, p.107.
6. Field Marshal Lord Harding of Petherton GCB CBE DSO** MC (1896-1989). He went on to be CIGS 1952-55.
7. Vernon, Brigadier HRW, *Strafer Gott*, p.19.
8. Agar-Hamilton, JAI and Turner, LCF, *Crisis in the Desert*, p.107.
9. Major General E Dorman-Smith June 1946, quoted by Brigadier HRW Vernon, *Strafer Gott*, p.78.
10. Danchev & Todman (Ed), *War Diaries 1939-1945, Field Marshal Lord Alanbrooke*, p.292.

Chapter 18

Strafer Gott, the Man

Strafer Gott.

This is the penultimate and shortest chapter in this book because the opinions of any number of witnesses as to Gott's human qualities have liberally adorned the preceding pages. The evidence is all to hand and not a scintilla of it is to Gott's discredit; quite the contrary. He was, indubitably, an unconscious social paragon and a person universally admired.

It is interesting to note that even those who may have voiced reservations about his generalship admire him as a man. Winston Churchill remarked, 'One mark of a great man is the power of making lasting impressions upon the people he meets.'[1]

Gott had this 'power'.

Many men who rise to a position of eminence in any aspect of public life win approbation. Generals, by the nature of their calling, are usually accorded a degree of admiration commensurate with their success. Some generals excite an emotion warmer than admiration but Strafer Gott is an extreme case, because he gave rise to an emotion akin to love.

Many officers and soldiers who knew him personally felt as one might for a much-loved brother, uncle or father. His qualities of compassion, equanimity, good humour and generosity were a very powerful combination and when in concert with an engaging and open personality, made him an easy man to get to know.

The sense of grief that his death generated was testament to the value that he had added to the lives of so many and nowhere more so than in the ranks of the 60th in which his standing was incomparably high. The flood of letters to Pamela Gott was graphic and tangible evidence of the impact of his death.

235

Strafer was a quiet and undemonstrative Christian; it was this faith that he drew upon in the times of greatest danger and stress and, one presumes, produced the mien of a man entirely at ease with himself. Field Marshal Carver, as remarked on earlier, was a singularly demanding man, somewhat austere and not given to flights of public emotion; nevertheless, he wrote of Strafer:

> Perhaps he was too great a man to be a really great soldier. There was nothing small or mean about him. He had all the Christian virtues in abundant measure. I have never met another soldier whom I would rank as his equal.

Strafer is buried in the Commonwealth Cemetery at El Alamein alongside many of his men. The cemetery is beautifully maintained and is located on the west face of an escarpment. It overlooks the arid, but now increasingly developed, desert in which Strafer established his reputation and won the hearts of so many. On his headstone are the following words from the hymn *O Valiant Hearts*:

> *Tranquil you lie your knightly virtue proved,*
> *your memory hallowed in the land you loved.*

These entirely apposite words, written by JS Arkwright in 1917, were selected by Pam Gott and inscribed in Strafer's Portland headstone; so far, they have resisted the corrosive effects of wind and weather.

The sentiment, however, is imperishable.

Based on all the available evidence, there is no doubt that Lieutenant General Strafer Gott CB CBE DSO* MC was the very best of men and it is to be hoped that this biography will preserve his memory for future generations.

Chapter note
1. Greenhill book of Military Quotations, p.227.

Chapter 19

What If?

S ince 1942 many people have wondered '*what if* Strafer had not been killed?'
The most charismatic young general in the Army, he was already marked out for the highest command; the world was at his feet. How would his life have developed and what service would he have given to his country had he not died when he did?

There is a range of '*what if*' views that cover the whole spectrum – of course; there is no correct answer. Some, albeit a minority, did not subscribe to the idea that Strafer was cut off in his prime and his loss was a national calamity.

For example, Field Marshal Lord Montgomery, who was probably one of the most uncharitable of men, was also a talented, forceful commander. He rarely, if ever, offered a warm view of his contemporaries or seniors. On the eve of the Second Battle of El Alamein he wrote scathingly of the Army he had inherited and of those commanders who had preceded him. He damned Auchinleck for just about everything, saying that 'gross mismanagement, faulty command and bad staff work' were the direct product of Auchinleck's period in command. He also took a negative view of Gott, saying:

> Gott was to have commanded Eighth Army. I am convinced that this
> appointment was not sound and might have led to disaster. Gott was
> one of the old regime and had been in Egypt all the war, his tactical
> ideas were influenced by past events, his plan in XIII Corps for fighting
> Rommel if he attacked in August was very bad and if it had been put
> into effect I consider the Eighth Army would have been defeated.[1]

Although Montgomery had never served with Gott it would have been wildly out of character if he had said anything else. However, his view was shared by a junior and inexperienced officer, one Captain Tom Witherby the wireless officer of 23rd Armoured Brigade, which 'had been ordered into suicidal battle on 22 July 1942'. Given the circumstances of that action, and as a survivor of the 23rd Armoured Brigade debacle, it is little wonder that in retrospect he was quite certain that, had Strafer Gott lived:

> we would have been defeated at Alam Halfa and would have probably lost the war. … The Army that General Montgomery took over on 13 August could not possibly have stopped Rommel's German-Italian attack. Montgomery was a giant. Gott was a brave man, but he was tired and simply did not have the intellectual stature for the command. I do really feel that the circumstances in which Montgomery appeared at this critical time was one of the rare examples of direct intervention by the almighty!

General Sir Harold Pyman expressed a more authoritative opinion.[2] He served under Gott as his GSO 1 in 7th Armoured Division. In his memoirs Pyman addressed the *what if* question. Specifically, had Gott taken up his appointment as GOC-in-C 8th Army, would he have beaten the Germans and Italians more quickly and more efficiently than Montgomery? His response to that was unequivocal:

> No. Montgomery was the best field commander I ever knew during the whole of my military career. He was the complete soldier, with a capacity to outfight his enemy, which put him in a class of his own. Gott, great man though he was, had some shortcomings. I was never certain that he understood the correct use of artillery fire, or that he had that decisive grasp of timing that is essential to any commander, let alone an army one.[3]

A lot less definite in his opinion was Alexander Clifford, a meticulous observer, who conjectured *what if* Strafer had been in command at Gazala in May/June 1942 and concluded that we 'might easily have won'. He added, 'And if he had been in command of the Armoured Corps straight away it might just have made the essential difference.' Clifford was not a soldier but he was a journalist and it was his professional duty to report on events objectively. He went on to aver:

> I have come across a school of thought, which includes 8th Army veterans, who were intense admirers of Gott, that claim he would not have done so well in command of a large army fighting in almost static conditions. It is argued that Gott was essentially a marauding, swift-moving, individual leader who was at his best in the patrol conditions of the early desert warfare; and that he would not have understood as Monty did, that Alamein was something entirely different from all preceding desert battles.[4]

Clifford sits uncomfortably just on the negative side of the fence but Major General Dorman-Smith did not and he took a much more positive position. He was happy to speculate, as far back as 1946, when he wrote:

> I believe he would have done very well as Commander of 8th Army, particularly had Auchinleck remained as C-in-C Middle East for the two men understood and respected each other. I believe too, that had he been in command of the 8th Army in May and June 1942, we would not have lost the battle of Gazala/Tobruk.[5]

Brigadier (later, General) Bobby Erskine had absolutely no doubts and he said of the XIII Corps conference, held just before Strafer took his ill-fated flight:

> The conference he held before he left and the orders he gave was the basis of the battle we fought on 31 August. We defeated two German divisions with a very small force, and that was Strafer's last piece of work, although it was carried out by others. Strafer's reputation was never higher than it is today. His care in not wasting life was wonderful and that was what gave everyone such confidence in him.[6]

Erskine indicates here that, from his favoured viewpoint as Brigadier, General Staff, Strafer Gott was well equipped to fight and win the battle of Alamein and by implication go on to greater glory thereafter. His view is perhaps coloured by his affection for an old and valued friend.

Auchinleck had come to depend on Strafer and had faced up to the fact that there would be a need for a new GOC-in-C for the 8th Army after himself. He wrote to the CIGS on 25 July 1942, saying:

> I believe Gott might command 8th Army well and so far as I can see he shows no signs of weariness and is learning to handle big formations every day. He impresses me most favourably in every way.[7]

This is very positive and offsets the remark he made when he was sacked and replaced by Gott. Being vastly discommoded at his removal from command, he said then that he did not think that 'Gott was all that bright'.[8]

Strafer Gott was anything but 'ruthless' and the final defeat of Rommel in the Western Desert would call for just that quality in the British Commander. Strafer's concern over the loss of life among his soldiers is well documented and Field Marshal Bramall highlights this characteristic that made Gott, on the one hand a compassionate human being, but on the other, a general not best suited to the attritional battles that lay ahead.

Field Marshal Lord Bramall was not in that Western Desert but subsequently got to know well those that were and who had served with and under Gott; and has long been an admirer. In a letter to the author he speculated by saying:

> Certainly Gott was on his own admission very tired after three years of intense campaigning and badly needed a break. If this had happened he would certainly have played a further useful and no doubt significant part in the final defeat of Nazi Germany. While if he had commanded at Alamein with all the new equipment coming into service and the tide so significantly turning in our favour numerically and logistically, he might just have been as successful as Montgomery was in winning the battle, perhaps with even fewer casualties than the 13,000 that the victory was to cost.
>
> On the other hand, what the 8th Army probably needed more than anything else before the Battle of Alamein was a completely fresh and ruthless commander, who in order to restore confidence and morale, which had sunk so very low after the defeat at El Adem and the loss of Tobruk, could optimistically put behind him any thoughts of defeat and failure as none of the in situ generals could find it so easy to do.[9]

The Field Marshal recognises the two sides of the *what if* coin and, just like everyone else, he simply does not know the definitive answer. Nevertheless, his realistic summary of the options endorses the view of Field Marshal Lord Carver (Chapter 17) that the prospective casualties to be anticipated at Second Alamein were more than Strafer could stomach. He was not the man 'to manage death' on that, almost industrial, scale.

The weight of opinion is that Montgomery was better suited to command the 8th Army but Strafer Gott would still have had a great deal to offer if he had not died in that furnace on 7 August.

In a perfect world – and, of course, the world is anything but perfect – *what if* his offer to take command of Tobruk in June 1942 had been accepted? He would probably have been captured there but lived to fight another day.

What if Strafer Gott had not been the victim of one of Churchill's whims and had not been selected to command the 8th Army in the first place? It was a poor decision to select him and in hindsight it may have been an equally poor decision for him to accept the appointment. *What if* he had declined?

In that perfect world of *'what if'*, suppose if, on 7 August, the British Radio Operator had not said, in clear, 'hold the plane for General Gott' and the Germans had not intercepted the transmission?

What if, on 7 August 1942, he had travelled to Cairo by road, enjoyed a few days of rest and returned to command XIII Corps under Montgomery? How the two men would have related to each other is key to further speculation. Strafer would have been repelled by the anticipated 'butcher's bill' at Alamein and he would have found Montgomery's curious, egocentric personality difficult to deal with. But then he had had to put up with Pienaar and so he was experienced in dealing with difficult people, albeit a notional subordinate.

Montgomery and Gott came from opposite ends of the military and human spectrums and although 'opposites attract', a harmonious relationship between them is, at best, only a possibility. *What if* they had clashed? Strafer might well have been sacked, been moved sideways and later commanded, at corps level, later in the war.

What if Strafer had thrived under Montgomery? The probability is that he would have commanded a corps in Italy and possibly an army in the battle for Normandy in 1944. During that campaign Montgomery was almost sacked by Eisenhower.

What if Montgomery *had* been sacked?

In those circumstances and, given that a high-calibre alternative like Strafer was available, *what if* Strafer had succeeded Montgomery? Was Strafer ruthless enough to pursue the enemy to final defeat? Did he have the intellectual ability to manage the 21st Army Group?

Let us presume (and when you speculate there are no rules) that the answer to each of those questions is 'yes'. At war's end he could have expected to move to the top of the Army and would have been a field marshal, eventually CIGS, and then, perhaps, governor of one of Britain's remaining colonies. Field Marshal Lord Gott of Alam Halfa might then have died in his bed, in the mid-1980s, revered by the entire nation. This biography would have been written by one of his admirers about thirty years ago – it would probably have run to two volumes and sold thousands.

All of the above is pure speculation and has absolutely no justification whatsoever. The reader is invited to apply his or her own imagination to the 70-year-old conundrum, 'what if?'

Chapter notes
1. Hamilton, N, *The Full Monty*, p.547-9.
2. General Sir Harold Pyman GCB KCB DSO (1908-71). He completed a distinguished military career as Commander-in-Chief Allied Forces North Europe 1961-64.
3. Pyman, General Sir H, *Call to Arms*.
4. Ibid, p.80.
5. Vernon, Brigadier HRW, *Strafer Gott*, p.78.
6. Ibid, p.62.
7. Auchinleck to Brooke, 6/2/14, Alanbrooke MSS, Liddell Hart Centre for Military Archives.
8. Bierman & Smith, *The Battle of Alamein*, p.216.
9. Letter to the author, 5 July 2012.

Bibliography

Articles

Auchinleck, FM Lord, 'Despatch on Operations in the Middle East from 5 July 1941 to 31 October 1941', *The London Gazette* supplement No. 37,695, p.4,215-30.

Books

Barnett, C, *The Desert Generals*, 2nd edition, Cassell, London, 1983.

Barr, N, *Pendulum of War, the Three Battles of Alamein*, Jonathan Cape, London, 2004.

Bidwell, S & Graham, D, *Firepower: British Army Weapons and Theories of War. 1904-1945*, Allen & Unwin, St Leonard's, Australia, 1985.

Bierman, J & Smith, Colin:
    Alamein: War Without Hate, Penguin, USA, 2012.
    The Battle of Alamein, Viking Penguin, USA, 2002.

Bryant, Sir A, *The Turn of the Tide*, Collins, London, 1957.

Caddick-Adams, P, *Monty and Rommel: Parallel Lives*, Arrow, Random House London, 2011.

Carver, FM Lord RMP:
    Britain's Army in the Twentieth Century, Pan Books, London, 1998.
    Dilemmas in the Desert, BT Batsford Ltd., Anova Book Group, London, 1986.
    Short History of Seventh Armoured Division, October 1938-May 1943, private publication.

Chandos, Lord, *Memoirs*, The Bodley Head, London, 1962.

Chickering, R, *Imperial Germany and the Great War, 1914-1918*, Pen & Sword, Barnsley, 2004.

Churchill, WS, *The Second World War*, Vols. III & IV, Houghton Miflin, Boston, 1950.

Clifford, A, *Three Against Rommel: The Campaigns of Wavell, Auchinleck and Alexander*, GG Harrap, London, 1943.

Connell, J, *Auchinleck*, Cassell, London, 1959.

Corrigan, G, *Mud, Blood and Poppycock*, Cassell, London, 2003.

Danchev & Todman (Ed), *War Diaries 1939-1945, FM Lord Alanbrooke*, Weidenfeld & Nicolson, London, 2001.

Dixon, N, *On the Psychology of Military Incompetence*, Cape, London, 1976.

Erskine, Gen Sir G, *Recollections of Strafer Gott*, unpublished manuscript, RGJ Museum archives, Winchester.

Ford, K:
    Gazala 1942: Rommel's Greatest Victory, Osprey, Oxford, 2005.
    Operation Crusader, Osprey, Oxford, 2010.

Gott, WHE, *Memoir of a POW 1917-1918*, unpublished manuscript, RGJ Museum archives, Winchester.

Gregg, V, *Rifleman:A Front Line Life,* Bloomsbury Publishing, London, 2011.

Hamilton, N:
    Monty: Master of the Battlefield 1942-1944, Hamish Hamilton Ltd, Great Britain, 1983.
    The Full Monty, Penguin Press, London, 2001.
    The Making of a General, 1887-1942, Hamish Hamilton, Great Britain, 1981.

Hare, Maj Gen Sir Steuart, *Annuls of the King's Royal Rifle Corps*, Vol. V: *The Great War*, John Murray, London, 1932.

Harding, *FM Lord of Petherton*, Weidenfeld & Nicolson, London, 1978.
    Memoirs of a Field Marshal, Hutchinson, London, 1989.

Holland, J, *Together We Stand*, HarperCollins, Hammersmith, London, 2005.

Horne, CF, *Source Records of the Great War* Vol. II, National Alumni, 1923.

Hughes, D, Ryan, D and Rothwell, S, *British Tank and Armoured Brigades, 79th Armoured Division and Armoured Car Regiments*, GF Natziger Collection, Boston, USA, 2002.

'Jon', *The Two Types*, Ernest Benn, London, 1960.

Keegan, Sir J (Ed), *Churchill's Generals*, Weidenfeld & Nicolson, London, 1991.

Kippenberger, Brig HK, *Infantry Brigadier*, Oxford University Press, 1946.

Liddell Hart B:
> *Colonel Lawrence: The Man Behind the Legend*, Dodd, Mead & Co., New York, 1934.
> (Ed) *Rommel Papers*, Collins, London, 1953.

Mason, D, *Who's Who in World War II*, Weidenfeld & Nicolson, London, 1978.

Mason, Capt WW, *The Second Libyan Campaign and After (November 1941-June 1942)*, the official history of New Zealand in the Second World War, 1954.

Maule, H, *Spearhead General: The Epic Story of General Sir Frank Messervy and his men in Eritrea, North Africa and Burma*, Odhams Press, London, 1961.

McKay, S, *The Secret Life of Bletchley Park*, Arum, London, 2010.

Mead, R, *Churchill's Lions: A Biographical Guide to the British Generals of World War II*, Spellmount, Tonbridge, 2007.

Mills, G & Nixon, R, *The Annuls of the King's Royal Rifle Corps,* Vol. VI, Leo Cooper, London, 1971.

Mitchell, Maj TJ, & Smith, Miss GM, *Official History of the War, Casualties and Medical Statistics*, Imperial War Museum (reprinted), London, 1997.

Montgomery, FM Lord B, *Memoirs*, The Book Club, London, 1958.

Morehead, AM, *African Trilogy*, Hamilton & Harper, London, 1945.

Murphy, WE, Fairbrother MC, *The Relief of Tobruk*, The official history of New Zealand in the Second World War, 1961.

Pitt, B, *The Crucible of War: Western Desert 1941*, Papermac, Basingstoke, 1986.

Playfair, Maj Gen ISO with Stitt, Cmdr GMS RN, Toomer, AVM SE, *The Mediterranean and Middle East* Vol. I, HMSO, London, 1954.

Playfair, Maj Gen ISO with Flyn, Capt FC RN, Toomer, AVM SE, Molony, Brig CJC, *The Mediterranean and Middle East* Vol. II, HMSO, London, 1956.

Playfair, Maj Gen ISO with Flyn, Capt FC RN, Molony, Brig CJC, Gleave, Capt GP, *The Mediterranean and Middle East Vol. III, Sept 41-Sept 1942*, HMSO 1960.

Parkinson, R, *The Fox of the North: The Life of Kutzov, General of War and Peace*, David McKay, New York, 1976.

Pegler, M, *Out of Nowhere: A History of Military Sniping*, Osprey, Oxford, 2004.

Pitt, B, *The Crucible of War*, Cassell, London, 1980.

Pyman, Gen Sir H, *Call to Arms*, Leo Cooper, London, 1971.

Smart, N, *Biographical Dictionary of British Generals of the Second World War*, Oxford English Dictionary, Oxford University Press, 2012.

Stewart, A, *8th Army's Greatest Victories*, Leo Cooper, London. 1999.

Tuker, Lieut Gen Sir Francis:
> *The Pattern of War*, Butler and Tanner, Frome, 1958.
> *Approach to Battle*, Cassell, London, 1963.

Vernon, Brig HRW, *Strafer Gott*, Culverlands, Winchester, 1983.

Weal, J, *Jagdgeschwader 27 'Afrika'*, Osprey, Oxford, 2003.

Television
Dimbleby, J, *Churchill's Desert War*, BBC2, 5 November 2012.

Index

246

247

249